© Kenneth Willardt

About the Author

GUY GARCIA is an award-winning journalist, novelist, and multimedia entrepreneur. A former staff writer for *Time*, he has also published articles in the *New York Times*, the *Los Angeles Times*, *Rolling Stone*, *Men's Journal*, *Harper's Bazaar*, *Spin*, *The Face*, *Interview*, and *People*. A three-time judge for the National Magazine Awards, Garcia has also written two novels, *Skin Deep* and *Obsidian Sky*, as well as the nonfiction book *The New Mainstream*. Born in Los Angeles, he lives in Manhattan.

Also by Guy Garcia

Fiction

Obsidian Sky
Skin Deep

Nonfiction

The New Mainstream

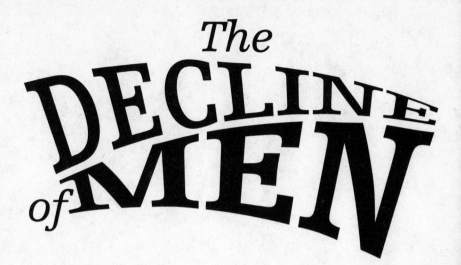

The DECLINE of MEN

HOW THE AMERICAN MALE IS GETTING AXED, GIVING UP, AND FLIPPING OFF HIS FUTURE

Guy Garcia

HARPER  PERENNIAL

NEW YORK • LONDON • TORONTO • SYDNEY • NEW DELHI • AUCKLAND

HARPER ● PERENNIAL

A hardcover edition of this book was published in 2008 by Harper-Collins Publishers.

THE DECLINE OF MEN. Copyright © 2008 by Guy Garcia. All rights reserved. Printed in the United States of America. No part of this book may be used or reproduced in any manner whatsoever without written permission except in the case of brief quotations embodied in critical articles and reviews. For information address HarperCollins Publishers, 10 East 53rd Street, New York, NY 10022.

HarperCollins books may be purchased for educational, business, or sales promotional use. For information please write: Special Markets Department, HarperCollins Publishers, 10 East 53rd Street, New York, NY 10022.

FIRST HARPER PERENNIAL EDITION PUBLISHED 2009.

Designed by Emily Cavett Taff

Library of Congress Cataloging-in-Publication Data has been applied for.

ISBN 978-0-06-135315-4

09 10 11 12 13 WBC/RRD 10 9 8 7 6 5 4 3 2 1

For Dad

Down is the new up.

—Radiohead

Contents

Introduction   xi

1   Samson Shorn   1

2   Eve's Rib   29

3   There's Something Terribly Wrong with Me   60

4   Mechanical Bulls   92

5   Punked   127

6   Fight Club   154

7   Boys Will Be Boys   190

8   X-Men   225

9   Samson Unbound   253

Acknowledgments   285

Introduction

One moonstruck night in the middle of Nevada's Black Rock Desert, standing in front of a hand-hewn sign that said "TRUTH," I gazed at a sixty-foot-tall man with half a head. I had come to this isolated expanse of white sand to partake in the Burning Man festival, a weeklong self-proclaimed "special Olympics" of art, music, and unbridled human expression that culminates each year with the ritual burning of a totemic male effigy. As more than forty thousand "burners" cavorted around me, I couldn't ignore the looming metaphor in our midst. In a few days, the wood-and-neon idol would be incinerated as planned, and the throng would cheer as his charred carcass crashed to the ground in a burst of flame and sparks. The immolation would symbolically clear the way for a new cycle of creation, planting the seeds of regeneration and rebirth. But for now, at this pivotal moment during the first decade of the twenty-first century, the man was still in progress, half-built, undone.

Meanwhile, outside Black Rock City, in the so-called real world, time-honored notions of the American male were also being torched. Within months, the longest and deepest recession in the post–World War II era and the implosion of the financial and automotive industries would send millions of men's jobs up in smoke. As male workers took the brunt of the economic meltdown, the Bureau of Labor Statistics reported that women held 49.1 percent of all jobs and were poised to become the majority of the U.S. workforce for the first time in American history.

But while the dollars lost in the downturn are tremendous, the social costs have yet to be tallied. A pillar of male identity is the ability to work, and when men lose their jobs, their entire sense of self-esteem is threatened. Psychologists and family therapists have reported a sharp rise in men seeking help for emotional stress related to job loss. Dr. Louann Brizendine, a psychiatrist at the University of California, San Francisco, and author of *The Female Brain*, has noticed a 20-percent increase in male patients at her clinic since the recession took hold. Common symptoms include anxiety, sleeplessness, and depression. This body blow to the male psyche is just the latest sign that men are losing their grip, opting out, coming apart, and falling behind. They are losing their sense of place in society and their direction as individuals. Trapped between unattainable ideals and a downsized reality, they risk morphing into muscle-bound weaklings who seek solace in the *Fight Club* rituals of hyper-violence and aggression or the narcissistic escape of their latest YouTube close-up.

The sorry state of the American male is a looming emergency with economic, sociological, and cultural ramifications for both men and women and generations to come. Yet most men are maintaining a business-as-usual stance, even as the status quo dissolves under their feet. The media, smelling profits in denial, has done its part to keep men in a state of blissful insouciance. After all, men—at least in male-oriented ads and glossy magazine spreads—have never had it so good. They are wealthier and healthier than ever before, stay younger longer, and have an endless array of choices in the things they buy and the places they can go. At work and at play, at the office or in the bedroom, men call the shots and always get what they want. They are focused, confident, powerful, and decisive. Armed with wi-fi laptops, GPS navigators, and rock-hard abs, these twenty-first century Marlboro men excel at their jobs and still have plenty of time and energy left over to be terrific husbands, lovers, friends, and fathers. They are role models and leaders on the international stage and on their hometown turf. There is even a body spray for men that turns women into fawning nymphomaniacs. For men, the world is their oyster—and they have a six pack of premium, low-carb beer in the fridge to help them wash it down.

But behind this glossy media fantasy lurks a dark and disturbing reality: men are in trouble. At home and at work, in the boardroom and in the classroom, they are flailing and failing to live up to their full potential. Like an invisible epidemic with catastrophic implications, the decline of men cuts across all ages, races, and social-economic groups. It affects affluent white men in the heartland and young Mexican immigrants in the Southwest. It cripples computer nerds and football jocks, family guys and boomer retirees. It is not just eroding the ability of men to earn a living and become contributing members of society, but is also undermining the very definition of what it means to be a man.

Corporate America, once the natural habitat of the American male, has become an intimidating minefield of layoffs, foreign competitors, multicultural consumers, and better-qualified female colleagues. The ability of women consumers to make or break a brand is being felt in industries ranging from publishing to health care, banking, and the Internet. Women are increasingly seen as the decisionmakers in housing, food, and Internet shopping, and as their buying power continues to grow, they are setting the marketing agenda. In advertising and the mass media, men are demonized, denigrated, and dismissed, routinely portrayed as clueless cavemen, lackluster lovers, or deadbeat dads. It's no coincidence that reality shows like *Ice Road Truckers* and *Deadliest Catch*, which glorify men who do dangerous, physically demanding jobs, have struck a nostalgic chord in the zeitgeist.

Meanwhile, new figures based on the U.S. Census show that young women in New York and several other major cities already earn more money than their male counterparts. The trend has surfaced in Los Angeles, Chicago, Boston, Minneapolis, and Dallas. At the same time, overall wages for men, including those with college degrees, have steadily declined. Most disturbing of all, perhaps, is the drift of able-bodied, employable men of all ages who are dropping out of the workforce altogether. Yet even as more women step up as the main breadwinners in their families, men have lagged when it comes to filling the domestic gap. According to data from the American Time Use Survey, women in two-earner families generally take on most of the domestic duties. When women lose their jobs, their share of household and family-centered work increases. But when men become unemployed, the amount of time they spend on domestic chores stays the same, while they use the extra time to sleep, watch TV, and look for a job.

In myriad ways, both large and small, it seems like the world that men built is falling apart or turning against them. Some observers hold men accountable for the bust-and-boom mentality that created the recession in the first place. According to a study published in the *Proceedings of the National Academy of Sciences* by John M. Coates, a research fellow in neuroscience and finance at the University of Cambridge, and his colleague, Joseph Herbert, the testosterone-fueled ups of the boom magnified Wall Street traders' aggressive, risk-taking behaviors while the ensuing bear market flooded their system with cortisol, which is now making them—irrationally—fearful and risk-averse. "Testosterone doesn't create bubbles, but it exaggerates them," Dr. Coates told the *New York Times*. "It's possible that bubbles are a male phenomenon."

But men aren't just getting poorer; they're also getting dumber. In 2005, 53 percent of working women in New York were college grads, while only 38 percent of men the same age could make that claim. Over the past twenty-five years the number of women enrolled in undergraduate colleges has grown more than twice as fast that of as their male counterparts. By 2006, women outnumbered men on college campuses by more than 2 million, and the gap is growing. Women now earn more than half of all business bachelor degrees, up from one third in 1980. Women also now earn a majority of the bachelor degrees awarded in the biological and social sciences, as well as in history, education, and psychology. Educators agree that men as a group are losing their drive to earn a college degree. "Women have been making educational progress, and men are stuck," Tom Mortenson, senior scholar for the Pell Institute for the Study of Opportunity in Higher Education, told the Associated Press. "They haven't just fallen behind women. They have fallen behind changes in the job market." Those changes tend to favor women, whose innate networking and social skills give them an edge in the service industry, now the largest and fastest-growing sector of the U.S. economy.

Meanwhile, the number of American couples who marry has been declining for decades. Married couples, who accounted for 84 percent of households in 1930, were down to only 56 percent by 1990. But the evolution of the American family unit has reached a tipping point: in October 2006, married couples in the United States became a numerical minority for the first time. Demographers give several reasons for the trend, including the fact that couples are waiting longer to get married and that it is more socially acceptable for men and women to remain single. But as women advance and men continue their downward slide, it's also true that more and more women are simply unable to find a man that they think is worth marrying.

It gets worse. According to the U.S. Census, a growing number of men without college degrees are reaching middle age without getting married at all. About 18 percent of men age 40 to 44 without four years of college are still single, up from 6 percent a quarter century ago. Over the same period, the number of non-college-educated single men between 35 and 39 has risen from 8 percent to 22 percent. Experts agree that at least part of the reason is that men without college degrees have more difficulty finding women who will marry them. This trend of fewer male college graduates and the resulting decline in the number of married men is creating a vast pool of undereducated, lower-income bachelors for whom the economic, social, and emotional benefits of a stable family environment are permanently out of reach. Even grimmer are the prospects for a generation of young men who will grow up without the example, support, and guidance of a loving father. Women have a stake in this, too. Not just because they often end up doing the jobs of both sexes, but because these flailing fellows are their sons, their daughters' boyfriends, and, increasingly, their own ex-husbands.

Is the growing gap in the life expectancy between men and women—and a plethora of other male health problems—a sign of something deeper? Could it be that Maureen Dowd is right in predicting that "the male chromosome could go the way of the dial up connection"? There is, in fact, a creeping sense that men are in some way an endangered species. From young boys who are slacking off and dropping out of school in record numbers, to grown guys who fritter away their time on video games and Internet porn, males are adrift and out of touch with their inner dude. As Madison Avenue struggles to figure out what makes men tick, the male consumer lurches between metrosexual vanity and exaggerated machismo, groping for a sense of self that has fragged into a fun-house mirror of distorted reflections. Do the ballyhooed Hollywood "bromance" and celebrity-endorsed "man crush" signify an evolutionary leap forward, or are they just snarky new labels for male friendship? The bewildering blur of masculine identities reached a crescendo of sorts with the surgically-assisted phenomenon of the "first pregnant man," a transgender father who greeted the gaping world with a beard and a basketball belly. Thomas Beatie, opined *Details* magazine, "forced us to glimpse what male motherhood is like—both beautiful and terrifying."

The roots of the dilemma go back at least as far as Creation, when Adam banished the sacred feminine and severed his own connection to Mother Nature. Since then the gleaming sword of technology that men forged has cut both ways; the same tools that gave males limitless power have eroded their physical relevance. Man-made machines and male-waged wars gave women freedom and economic independence, while men stayed frozen in a patriarchal past. Science gave humankind "the pill," but more than half a century after the sexual revolution it's starting to look like women got the better part of the bargain. But to blame the no-longer "second" sex for the current male malaise is missing the point entirely. After all, what could possibly be less manly than seeking a scapegoat for our troubles? The first step is for men is to take responsibility—not just for what's gone wrong, but also for what might go right.

It is painfully obvious that the standard, rigid definitions of masculinity are outdated and dysfunctional. Men can no longer hammer women—or the world, or each other—into submission without ramifications. That game is over. Instead, men need to resurrect the male virtues that are much older than the gender wars: compassion, generosity, loyalty, modesty, humility, farsightedness, curiosity, and patience. Does the election of Barack Obama and his tendency toward negotiation over aggression, communication over silence, and compassion over ruthless ambition point the way to a more humane and sustainable form of masculinity? So far, the answer is yes. In his Inaugural Address, the president spoke about a "sapping of confidence across our land" and the need to regain the can-do spirit of Americans as "the risk-takers, the doers, the makers of things." These are tasks that men have always done well; it's why they matter and are necessary. The United States can lead the world again, but it won't happen if the male half of the population forgets what has always made them—and America—great.

There is growing evidence, meanwhile, that the decline of men may be an international phenomenon. In the U.K, where the perpetual adolescence of "laddism" has long been a feature of the social landscape and David Beckham first emerged as a metrosexual role model, *Daily Mail* columnist and British *GQ* editor Amanda Platell bemoans the proliferation of men who "shimmy about with their exfoliated, rehydrated skin carrying their Prada manbags and waxing their backs." In Japan, males are morphing into *soushoku danshi,* or "grass-eating boys." These postmodern "herbivores" shun sex with women and eschew spending money and other traditional male pastimes, preferring to take long walks or stay at home, where they play video games with their pals and grow radishes in their living rooms. A consulting subsidiary of Japan's largest ad agency estimates that 60 percent of men in their early twenties and at least 42 percent of men between the ages of 23 and 34 identify themselves as grass-eaters. Ominously, social psychologists trace the roots of the herbivore epidemic to increased female competition in the workforce during the 1980s and lowered expectations for men brought on in the 1990s by Japan's economic slump. In the United States, the former has been true for a while, and the latter has already begun.

Is there a form of masculine makeover that goes deeper than pimping one's ride? Can men stop being defensive without going on the offensive? Is "The Buried Life," a new MTV reality series about a quartet of young men who roam the country to do good deeds, a signal that male selfishness and cynicism have become passé? Part of the answer may lie not just in our animal selves, but also in other animals. There is surprisingly much to be learned, scientists say, from the behaviors of elephants, walruses, and other über-macho mammals, not to mention matriarchal cultures where the sexes have lived in harmony for thousands of years. It may be that something important was discarded along with the outlawed rituals of male-only social clubs, something that has nothing to do with misogyny and everything to do with the natural solidarity and resilience of the male spirit. As history—both ancient and more recent—shows us, men have reinvented themselves before. It just may be high time for guys to rise from the ashes, suck in their gut, and do it again.

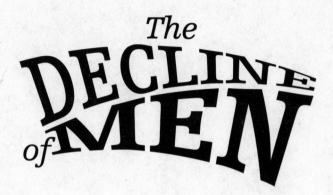

CHAPTER 1

Samson Shorn

The mood in the sumptuous ballroom at Cipriani Wall Street was exultant. An all-female jazz band had played during the reception, and the crowd of several hundred of New York's movers and shakers at the "Women Who Make a Difference Gala," hosted by the National Council for Research on Women, were tucking into their grilled lamb chops and sipping wine, all paid for by the evening's sponsor, Goldman Sachs. Then it was time for Dina Dublon, a member of the board of directors at PepsiCo, to introduce one of the evening's honorees: Steve Reinemund, PepsiCo's chairman. His successor, an Indian-born woman named Indra Nooyi, had just delivered a glowing video testimonial, carried on giant screens throughout the room, and now it was time for Reinemund to get his award. In her introduction, Dublon noted that Reinemund, one of the most powerful and respected men in American business, was the first man to ever receive this award, adding that he was "part of our No Man Left Behind policy." Reinemund graciously went along with the joke, saying that he was very glad not to be left behind. The mostly female audience laughed appreciatively.

The sad fact, however, is that men—as individuals, as a group, as a gender—*are* being left behind. Around the table, the suddenly pensive diners traded stories about men they knew who had lost their jobs or their marriages, or both, and were now basically idle, taking up golf or the piano, writing that novel, doing nothing. The women spoke about brothers, sons, nephews, and husbands. "It's weird how everyone has a story like this," remarked a female executive from a Fortune 100 company. "There's definitely something going on."

What's going on is a seismic shift in the current status and future of American men that reaches from before the moment of conception until after their death. No one can say exactly when it began, but the change was well under way by the time noted genetics expert Jenny Graves was asked by a reporter from the Australian Broadcasting Corporation if men were heading for extinction.

"The future of the Y chromosome is certainly at risk," said Graves, a professor of comparative genomics at the Australian National University. "We've been looking at the Y chromosome in lots of different animals, so we were able to tell where it came from and where it's going. . . . The Y chromosome of course is what makes men men—if you've got a Y you're male. But the Y chromosome's actually derived from the X. It's just a pale shadow of its once glorious past as an X chromosome."

Some 300,000 years ago, when the Y chromosome was equal in length to the X chromosome, it had 1,400 genes on it. Today the Y contains a paltry 45.

The shrinking Y chrome has prompted Graves and other scientists to grimly suggest that the Y chromosome—the genetic code for the male gender—may be gone altogether in around 10 million years. Never mind that in 2003 a forty-person team of scientists led by David Page of the Whitehead Institute at the Massachusetts Institute of Technology reported that the Y chromosome actually has an elaborate backup system with as many as seventy-eight genes, and that it seems to have the ability to morph and grow and quite possibly survive. For researchers like Jenny Graves the demise of the male gene apparently can't come soon enough. When asked to pinpoint how long it would take the Y chromosome to disappear, she replied: "Now, of course, it could be tomorrow. In fact, there could be . . . right now there could be a tribe of humans somewhere that have already lost their Y."

Are Y guys about to become X men? Males may indeed be genetically hardwired to fail, but not for the reason that Professor Graves suggests.

The truth is that men may be doomed, not because of their genes, but because of their brains. Or, to be more precise, the innate biology of males may be increasingly at odds with the modern world that they inhabit. In fact, the very qualities that have helped men succeed for so many years may actually be a contributing factor to their current difficulties.

A growing body of scientific evidence attests that men are chemically predestined to share not only certain gender-specific physical traits but also a host of social, emotional, and behavioral attributes that are so different from those of women as to render them almost a separate species.

The classic male virtues—physical strength, aggression, self-sufficiency, resolve—that were so useful in agrarian and industrial societies, are increasingly out of date in a postmodern world where networking, cooperation, and communication are key. In other words, are men—or at least the traditional ideal of masculinity that has till now defined the American male—in danger of becoming obsolete? Are men at the beginning of a long, downhill slide to oblivion? And is it possible that the slippery slope begins to tilt against them even before they are born, and continues to skew the arc of their entire lives, through an undereducated childhood, an underemployed adulthood, and on to an unnecessarily premature death? As the ground beneath them rumbles and shifts, are men changing too little or too much? And how did they get into this mess in the first place?

THE CHICKEN OR THE EGG?

At the moment of conception, twenty-three chromosomes in the female's egg are joined by the same number of chromosomes present in the male's sperm. Forty-four of the chromosomes join up to form the blueprint for an individual's physical characteristics—height, body type, eye and hair color, and so on. But the last two genes are different—they control gender. The mother's egg contains a female, or X, chromosome. If the father's contribution to the egg is another X, the baby will be female (XX). If the father contributes a Y chromosome, the baby will be male (XY). It is the Y chromosome that triggers the release of androgens that begin to shape the body and brain of the fetus into something we will recognize as a boy. Researchers now think that those hormones do much more than cause the development of physical attributes that we all recognize as male. Recent studies have shown that the same hormones that determine gender also have a decisive effect on the development and structure of the brain itself, which in turn shapes the different ways that men and women respond to each other and the world around them.

This new picture of how gender influences brain function and sensory development has profound implications for anyone trying to understand why men and women think and behave the way they do. So how are the brains of men and women different, and why should we care? The second part of that question continues to be a topic of heated social and ethical debate. The first part, while far from conclusive, has become considerably clearer thanks to advances in psychology and neuroscience that suggest our gender plays a bigger role in the way we behave, perceive, and feel than previously suspected.

Most people are aware that the brain is divided into two different parts, or lobes. The left side of the brain is the central processing station for verbal ability, numerical problems, and orderly, logical thought. The right side of the brain is the main engine for abstract ideas, visual perception, and emotions. Conventional wisdom has characterized the left side of the brain as more dispassionate and intellectual—the "male" side of the brain—and the right side as the more emotional and creative "female" lobe. Yet new research paints a considerably more complex picture.

Biologically speaking, all human beings begin as females.

All human embryos begin with a "female" brain. Then, about six weeks after conception, the Y chromosome triggers a flood of male hormones that transform the body and brain in ways that scientists are still trying to sort out. For example, a 1977 study by the Danish scientist Berte Pakkenberg found that men's brains have around 4 billion more brain cells than a woman's, yet females score on average about 3 percent higher in general intelligence tests than males. Females also have more gray matter in their frontal cortex, which gives them an advantage when it comes to processing several types of information or analyzing different kinds of situations at the same time. The corpus callosum, a bundle of fibrous nerve cells that straddles the brain's left and right hemispheres, is thicker and more bulbous in women than in men. Beginning in early childhood, girls as a group are more coordinated than boys and are better at tasks that require fast and nuanced physical movement. Girls also tend to be more articulate and have better communication skills than boys. One reason may be that women process information over a greater area of their brains, allowing them to consider different variables in a more complex way than the opposite sex.

Boys, whose left brains generally grow faster than those of girls, excel at mathematical reasoning, crossword puzzles, and the arrangement of three-dimensional puzzles. Their tendency to process information on one side of their brains enhances their ability to compartmentalize feelings and thoughts and focus on a problem. In their interactions with other people and the physical world, males are, literally, more single-minded than females. Men are also, due to higher levels of testosterone, more likely to exhibit aggressive behavior, even when such behavior is frowned upon or contrary to their own self-interest. Testosterone has been linked to aggressive behavior in both sexes, but it is the much higher amounts of the hormone in males that seems to account for many of the traits historically associated with men.

"The biggest behavioral difference between men and women is the natural, innate aggression of men, which explains to a large degree their historical domination of the species," assert Anne Moir and David Jessel in their book *Brain Sex: The Real Difference Between Men and Women.* "Men didn't learn aggression as one of the tactics of the sex war. We do not teach our boy children to be aggressive—indeed, we try vainly to unteach it. Even researchers most hostile to the acknowledgement of sex differences agree that this is a male feature, and one that cannot be explained by social conditioning."

To be sure, much of the evidence of what some call "brain gender" is grounded in conventional wisdom: boys are rambunctious and competitive, girls are sensitive and demure. It's been noted that little boys will gravitate toward trucks and cars without encouragement, and, much to the mortification of their gun-control-favoring parents, will figure out how to make a weapon from Play-Doh or Legos.

But it's equally obvious that not all men and women fit into traditional sexual stereotypes and that the very definitions of "male" and "female" behavior are increasingly overlapping and blurred. Are young men who date confident, older females acting like women, or just enlightened guys? Were the women who humiliated and abused prisoners at Abu Ghraib acting like men, or just being bad soldiers? Is sexual biology destiny, or are we shaped by our environment and social pressures to behave and conform to the cultural consensus of what it means to be a "woman" or a "man" at any given time? Are gender-bashing feminists out of touch with human nature, or is it the men-are-from-Mars, women-are-from-Venus camp that is in denial of the human ability to morph and evolve beyond our primitive impluses?

The scientific threads of the debate, like the brain itself, are more subtle and tangled than they might at first seem. Male and female brains differ not just in architecture but also in the ways they process information and stimuli.

Because a woman's brain is better integrated than a man's, she is more likely to consider all the implications of a decision or action, as opposed to focusing on an immediate or obvious goal.

Men and women also react differently to stress. When confronted by pressure or a crisis, an area in the brain called the amygdala triggers the release of adrenaline and cortisol, which helps us to remember and thus avoid danger. In women, estrogen causes the amygdala to release an extra dose of cortisol, which causes a larger field of neurons to be stimulated for a longer period of time. Another hormone, oxytocin, induces a woman to cultivate and protect alliances and relationships with other people who can help her protect herself and her loved ones; as a result, women are prone to experience stress more intensely than men and to remember it longer.

"Why would we evolve with different methods of coping with stress?" Marianne Legato asks in her book *Why Men Never Remember and Women Never Forget*. "From an evolutionary perspective, we have had different jobs. Viewed in that light, men's poor memory for the emotions they had during events loaded with danger makes sense. Let's say that the survival of our tribe depends on the hunting ability of men. A good emotional memory is hardly advantageous to them: if they remember exactly how cold it was on the last mammoth hunt, how tired they were during the chase, how frightened they were, and how much it hurt when they caught a tusk in the thigh, how enthusiastic are they going to be the next time?"

Indeed. But it's doubtful they get much consideration for that when their spouse is lambasting them for forgetting to take out the trash.

Those who maintain that men and women are made instead of born got a powerful boost from research showing that experience not only had a profound effect on human behavior but actually changed the brain itself. By studying the way memory affects synapses in the brains of sea slugs and other creatures, Dr. Eric R. Kandel, a professor at Columbia University College of Physicians and Surgeons, revolutionized our understanding of how memory and learning affected the brain. Kandel, who was awarded the 2000 Nobel Prize in Physiology or Medicine for his work, showed that the process of remembering could alter the physical structure of the brain by strengthening and enlarging synapses that connect individual neurons. This revolutionary insight added a new wrinkle to the nature-or-nuture debate: if experience can change our brains, and if our brains in turn determine our perceptions, thoughts, and behaviors, then the potential for human beings to transform themselves is suddenly limitless.

For those who see the blurring and merging of the sexes as a positive and inevitable progression, the implication is obvious: under the right circumstances, men's brains could, in theory at least, become physically more like a woman's—and vice versa. For Legato and others, Kandel's findings have opened the door to an unprecedented bio-merging of the sexes. "If practicing piano changes our brains so that we get better at those skills, might we not be able to change our brains as well by "practicing" the competencies of the other sex?" she asks. "We no longer have to wonder at the vast chasm that separates us: Let us instead take advantage of the brain's natural plasticity and use it to become more alike."

It's a process that may already be under way. A study of more than 1,500 Massachusetts men, reported in the *Journal of Clinical Endocrinology and Metabolism* in 2007, found a population-wide decline in men's testosterone levels over the past twenty years.

Testosterone levels have dropped 1.2 percent per year, or about 17 percent overall between 1987 and 2004.

In commentary accompanying the report, Shalender Bhasin, a physician at Boston Medical Center, observed that it would be unwise to dismiss the findings "as mere statistical aberrations because of the potential threat these trends—if confirmed—pose to the survival of the human race and other living residents of our planet."

Is it any wonder then that many men feel skittish and out of sorts in an increasingly ambisexual world, their very sense of manhood imploding? There's a TV commercial in which a dressed-for-success Neanderthal glimpses his own image in a museum exhibit; similarly, men find themselves snared in a kind of testosteronic time warp, damned if they do and damned if they don't, caught between the desire to conform to a gentler, kinder masculinity and a competing urge to swing from the trees and bring home a fresh kill for dinner. At the very least, it's got to be disconcerting for a fellow to hear that if he just tries a little harder, he can, neurologically speaking, become a woman, too.

"In sport and war, the big fear of men is to be feminized," Dowd opines in *Are Men Necessary?* "In the workplace, the big fear of women is to be diabolized. So when a man kids a woman about being castrating, it is never more than half a joke. It's discouraging. Can men and women ever meet in a place that's not about sex? It's enough to make a girl reach for a sharp object."

Ouch!

Such is the sorry state of the modern man: with saber-toothed tigers and woolly mammoths in short supply, they wander the hostile savannahs of the twenty-first century, under attack in the lab and at the office, hounded by gene-counting scientists and assailed by blunt words and well-honed arguments. Are men wimps or bullies—or both? Is it possible for them to be failing regardless of by who—or how—manhood is defined?

To be sure, there is something seriously amiss with men. And the signs of the slide are nowhere more obvious—or urgent—than in the classroom.

DUMBING DOWN

One hundred miles north of New York City, in the leafy exurbs of the Catskill Mountains region, the future of American education is coming into view. It is not a manly sight. In 2006, the ratio of female to male valedictorians in Orange, Sullivan, and Ulster county high schools was nearly two to one. In nearby Pine Bush High School, a Theory of Knowledge honors class that focuses on critical-thinking skills had nine girls and two boys. The class was taught by the father of one of three Pine Bush girls who were admitted to MIT for the following year. No Pine Bush boys made the cut.

"At Sullivan Country Community College, where 63 percent of the students are girls, an honors history class has nine girls and two boys," reported Steve Israel in the local *Times Herald-Record*. "The inferior performance of boys is so common that girls in elementary schools have a saying to describe it: "Girls rule, boys drool."

Sullivan County, population 76,000, is a typical snapshot of present-day America: 87.7 percent white, 11 percent Hispanic, and

9 percent black. The median household income is $37,489, just slightly below the national average of $44,139. Women make up 49.2 percent of residents. It is also a microcosm of an educational malaise that is quickly snowballing into a national emergency.

In small towns and big cities, in the East, West, South, and Midwest, from grammar school to college, male students are failing, flailing, and falling behind.

Three decades ago, boys and girls read and wrote at roughly the same level. Today an eleventh-grade boy writes and reads at the level of an eighth-grade girl. In 2007, for the first time in the sixty-five-year history of the National Science Awards, the forty finalists were equally divided between boys and girls. Forty years ago, three-quarters of all college graduates were men. Women now make up more than half of all college students and are gaining. Equally telling is the fact that women now earn a majority of diplomas in fields men used to dominate. Female college students now outnumber men in biology and business, and have reached numerical parity in law, medicine, and optometry, up from 22 percent just a generation ago. In 2006, women were already earning the majority of bachelor's degrees in the biological and social sciences, education, psychology, math, and agriculture. Even as the female-to-male population ratio in the U.S. has remained stable at about 51–49 percent, respectively, the number of women enrolled in undergraduate classes has grown at double the rate for men.

"The gender gap among college students is widening," announced the Associated Press. "The story is largely one of progress for women, stagnation for men." This is worrisome not because girls have managed in recent decades to close the educational gender gap but because it suggests a widespread lack of motivation among boys to excel.

Boys are also much more likely to drop out of high school than girls. In 2004, 12 percent of males between the ages of 16 and 24 were high school dropouts, compared with 9 percent for girls. Boy dropouts outnumbered girls by 57 to 43 percent. The news is even more dire for immigrants and men of color. The high school dropout rate for foreign-born students in 2004 was about 25 percent, as compared with 17 percent for children born in the United States to foreign-born parents. Foreign-born students make up 11 percent of the total population of students ages 16 to 24, yet they make up 28 percent of the dropout population, according to Child Trends Databank. In 2004, 7 percent of non-Hispanic whites ages 16 to 24 were not enrolled in school and had not completed high school, compared with 12 percent of blacks and 24 percent of Hispanics.

The implications for men of color were particularly grim when high school dropout rates are correlated with unemployment and incarceration. "Only half of black men age 16 to 24 who are out of school are employed at any given time," Harry Holzer, a professor of public policy at Georgetown University, wrote in the *Washington Post.* "Thirty to 50 percent of these men will not finish high school. About one third will spend time in prison before their 35th birthday. Among high school drop outs, the majority will be incarcerated. While young black women have been achieving high levels of education and higher incomes, black men are doing worse and worse."

Holzer thinks that the disparity is only exacerbated by the changing nature of the American economy. "The U.S. economy has morphed into something new," he wrote. "The good blue-collar jobs that men with high school diplomas or less could expect to get a generation ago—in manufacturing and other sectors—have either disappeared or pay much less than before. The education and skills required for higher paying jobs has clearly risen."

The male education crisis is hardly confined to boys and young men of color. In a 2006 *Newsweek* cover story titled "The Trouble with Boys," Peg Tyre noted that "By almost every benchmark, boys across the nation and in every demographic group are falling behind." Some experts controversially blame the feminist movement for pressuring legislators to pass federal legislation like Title IX, widely hailed as a groundbreaking step forward for women, which was passed in 1972 and required schools to create a female-friendly environment where girls could compete with boys. Some critics contend that a mistake was made in the 1990s, when educators failed to pull back the throttle even as girls were pulling even or ahead of their male counterparts.

The tipping point seems to have come sometime between 1992, when a report by the American Association of University Women titled "How Schools Shortchange Girls" claimed that girls were not receiving the same quality or quantity of education as boys, and 2000, when Diane Ravitch, former director of the U.S. Department of Education Office of Educational Research and Improvement debunked the AAUW report as "just completely wrong." The report, said Ravitch, "might have been the right story twenty years earlier, but coming out when it did was like calling a wedding a funeral. There were all these special programs put in place for girls, and no one paid any attention to boys."

"The representation of American girls as apprehensive and academically diminished is not true to the facts," asserts C. H. Sommers in her 2000 book *The War Against Boys: How Misguided Feminism Is Harming Our Young Men.* "Girls, allegedly so timorous and lacking in confidence, now outnumber boys in student government, in honor societies, on school newspapers and even in debating clubs. Only in sports are the boys still ahead, and women's groups are targeting the sports gap with a vengeance. . . . Girls read more books. They outperform males on tests of artistic and musical ability. More girls than boys study abroad."

In her 1998 article for the Women's Freedom Network, titled "The Myth That Schools Shortchange Girls: Social Science in the Service of Deception," Judith Kleinfield, a professor of psychology at the University of Alaska, noted: "The overrepresentation of males in special education classes and in virtually every other category of emotional, behavioral, or neurological impairment is undisputed."

Parents and educators, desperate to even the playing field without discriminating against girls, are taking a second look at all-male schools and rethinking the way that children are lumped together in middle schools during the critical ages of eleven through thirteen, a time when many boys show the first signs of going off track. In cities as disparate as New York, Philadelphia, Baltimore, and Milwaukee, educators are experimenting with schools that run from sixth to twelfth grade, and others that run from kindergarten to eighth grade.

Others blame the residue of outdated male stereotypes that hold boys back from achieving their full potential, thereby stacking the odds against boys and depriving them of male encouragement and masculine role models. There is also newfound recognition that boys might not be as tough as they seem.

In his influential book *Real Boys: Rescuing Our Sons from the Myths of Boyhood*, William Pollack writes about the "Boy Code," a defensive mask that young men use to deflect scrutiny and keep their emotions hidden from others, and even themselves.

"The Boy Code puts boys and men in a gender straightjacket that constrains not only them but everyone else," Pollack writes, "reducing us all as human beings, and eventually making us strangers to ourselves and to each other—or, at least, not as strongly connected to one another as we long to be."

Concerned parents and sympathetic teachers also point to the innate learning advantages that girls have over boys as a result of their advanced cognitive and social development.

Girls are better suited to classroom environments that reward self-control, cooperation, and verbal participation— the exact behaviors that many boys find difficult or impossible.

Not everyone is convinced. Among those who deride the very notion that anything is seriously wrong are Caryl Rivers and Rosalind Chait Barnett. "The boy crisis we're hearing about is largely a manufactured one, the product of both a backlash against the women's movement and the media's penchant for continuously churning out news about the latest dire threat to the nation," they declared in an article for the *Washington Post* titled "The Myth of 'The Boy Crisis.'" Rivers, a journalism professor at Boston University, and Barnett, a senior researcher at Brandeis University, described scientific evidence that girls categorically outstrip boys in communication and verbal abilities and learn in fundamentally different ways as inconclusive and potentially misleading. They caution that quick-fix solutions like single-sex schools and "boy-friendly" learning environments are divisive and misguided. They contend that the problem, to the extent that it even exists, is largely confined to lower-income and minority children. "The alarming statistics on which the notion of a crisis is based are rarely broken out by race or class," they write. "When they are, the whole picture changes. It becomes clear that if there is a crisis, it's among inner-city and rural boys. White suburban boys aren't significantly touched by it."

Tell that to the teachers and parents of Sullivan County.

Even if Rivers and Barnett are right and the top 15 percent are doing just fine, that hardly bodes well for the future of American men. Worse yet is the possibility that the roots of the problem go much deeper than curricula and classroom composition. Is it possible that what we are seeing are the symptoms of an erosion in male identity that is more pervasive—and debilitating—than even most whistle-blowers would admit? What if American men are not so much failing as simply retreating to what they see as safer ground in a culture where the very definition of manhood is up for grabs?

In his column in the *Times Herald-Record*, Lance Mannion pointed the finger back at the people who presumably have the biggest motive to do whatever it takes to make boys succeed: their fathers. "The biggest enemies to a serious look at the problem aren't feminists but loud-mouthed Right Wingers who take advantage of the issue to attack Feminism in particular, and Liberalism in general," he opined. "Whatever problems boys are having in school aren't the result of 'feminizing' them or 'feminizing' the culture in a way that penalizes masculinity. Just the opposite. They're mostly the result of hypermasculinization, of a weird warping of our concepts of manliness and masculinity that makes being smart, being academically ambitious, being studious, being conscientious, being successful at school nerdy, geeky—*girly*. Real men are intellectually incurious, disdainful of good grades and the work necessary to earn them, and generally anti-everything that would help them succeed in school. Real men are brutish, loutish, ignorant, ill-mannered slobs. As far as I can tell, if there is a War on Boys, it is being waged on them by their own parents, particularly their fathers. And the weapon of choice is sports."

Is football really destroying the American male? Or are men just clinging to one of the last domains that allow them to be proudly, unabashedly male?

"Sport is the modern replacement for hunting," write Barbara and Allan Pease in their book *Why Men Don't Listen and Women Can't Read Maps*. "Most sporting activities began after the year 1800; prior to that, most of the world's population still hunted animals for food and recreation. The Industrial Revolution of the late 1700s and advanced farming techniques introduced around the same time meant that it was no longer necessary to chase and catch food. Thousands of years of men being programmed to hunt suddenly came to a stop. They had nowhere to go."

It's true, as the Peases point out, that most sports mimic or re-create many of the physical attributes of hunting—running, jumping, chasing, and hitting targets—and burn up extra energy. The Peases postulate that without sports as an outlet for pent-up aggression, there would be even higher levels of violence, crime, and road rage.

In fact, a study by Daniel Kruger, a social psychologist at the University of Michigan, found that men with hypermasculine features were perceived by fellow students to be more likely to get into fights or cheat on their spouses. For the study, the results of which were published in the academic journal *Personal Relationships*, 854 male and female undergraduates were shown composite photos of men's faces. Asked which of the men in the photos they would select to date their daughters or accompany their girlfriends out of town, both sexes chose men with more feminine features—small chin, larger lips and eyes—over the faces with more masculine features associated with high levels of testosterone—an exaggerated brow, a strong jaw, and thinner lips.

So, is Justin Timberlake more trustworthy than, say, Sylvester Stallone? And, by extension, are baseball players less likely to get into a brawl than hockey players? In other words, are some forms of recreation more conducive to positive interaction than others? The Peases think so. To avoid antisocial forms of aggressive behavior, they offer the flowing advice: "Before enrolling in a sports club, examine the objectives, values, role models, and leaders of the club. If they're in it 'for the game' and the game is all-important then these people are still slaves to their biology—so join a fishing club."

Okay, but didn't cavemen fish, too?

"There are many clubs like yoga or martial arts that still teach the principles for effective living, such as health, relaxation and sound life values," the Peases continue. "Avoid any clubs that emphasize the financial gains members might make."

There was a time, not so long ago, when women clamored to be

allowed into all-male clubs precisely because of the business connections and financial gains that came along with being members.
Now men are being advised to avoid men-only clubs because social-
izing to make money is bad manners.

And, statistically, now it's females who have become the con-
summate networkers.

WORKING STIFFS

One of the pillars of male identity is the ability and willingness to
work—to earn money and social status, to help support a wife and
family. Sociologists and identity theorists agree that for men, work
and career are enmeshed with their sense of personal identity and
self-esteem. For most men, their performance at work—as bosses or
employees—is inextricably connected to their identities as spouses,
fathers, and citizens. If men are failing at their jobs, it's harder for
them to perceive themselves as good husbands and fathers. In fact,
psychologists know that a disruption in any one of these key areas
will affect the others.

**When a man fails to fulfill his roles as an employee, spouse,
or father, or if those roles conflict, his entire sense of
well-being and worth is undermined.**

Ronald Mincy, a professor of social policy at Columbia University, has spent more than a decade tracking what he considers a very
ominous number. "We've seen no growth in the average hourly
earnings of men in 25 years—and that is the biggest, most glaring
statistic because as the earnings of men go, so go the fortunes in a
lot of ways of men," he observes. "The basic position of men in the
labor market hasn't changed much."

Mincy believes that the stagnation of men's wages is both a reflection of enormous change and the catalyst for a whole range of social ills, not the least of which is a major disruption in the economic underpinnings of male pride and self-confidence. "When you look at it broadly, you do have this odd phenomenon where you have more substantial increase in the growth of earnings for women but you have essentially flat earnings for men," he notes. "And that is related to a lot of other significant challenges that we're facing as a society, including things like delays in marriage, a higher divorce rate, increases in economic participation rates of women, and increases of fatherlessness, whether this comes from marriages or not. Because if you're a man, you can't play house if you're not making enough money at your job."

Since the postwar heyday of the 1950s and '60s, the working-man has been on a long steady slide. Men are working harder and longer for less pay than ever in jobs that are unfulfilling or disappearing or both. They are more likely to work over fifty hours a week than they were a quarter century ago. Jobs that offer full benefits—medical, dental, and life insurance, disability, and vacation pay—are dwindling, particularly for men without college diplomas. After declining for most of the twentieth century, the number of hours that American men spend on the job began to increase in the 1970s and has continued to climb. A study by economists Peter Kuhn, from the University of California at Santa Barbara, and Fernando Lozano, from Pomona College, found that the share of employed men between the ages of 25 and 64 who work more than fifty hours on their main job rose from 14.7 to 18.5 percent between 1980 and 2001. The trend, according to the study, is "especially pronounced among high-educated, high-wage, salaried and older men."

Men in the lower social rungs have suffered even more. As manufacturing jobs have been eliminated or outsourced, males without college degrees have lost traction on the path to upward mobility. Thirty percent of black men will spend time in prison before their thirty-fifth birthday. For those men, getting work and keeping it becomes even more difficult with a prison record. In many cases, ex-inmates resort to pickup jobs with no benefits, and many will be back behind bars in three to five years.

Illegal immigrants, most of whom emigrate to the United States from Mexico and Central America, face different hardships, including exploitation and physical abuse by "coyotes" who help them cross the border, below-minimum-wage pay, and the constant threat of deportation and arrest. The estimated 7.2 million undocumented workers in the United States make up about 5 percent of the country's workforce. According to estimates by the Pew Hispanic Center and the U.S. Census Bureau, undocumented workers fill a quarter of all agricultural jobs, 17 percent of the office- and house-cleaning positions, 14 percent of construction jobs, and 12 percent of those in food preparation. Most of those workers are men who live crowded together in substandard housing with scant prospects of moving up to better-paying jobs with security and health benefits.

But the cloud hanging over male workers in the United States extends to all socioeconomic groups as government projections for high-growth sectors over the next decade tilt against industries that have traditionally favored men. The long-term shift from a goods-producing economy to a service economy will continue, with the biggest gains anticipated in education and health, professional and business services, and leisure and hospitality.

By contrast, employment in goods-producing industries that favor men has been stagnant since the 1980s and will actually decline by 0.4 percent over the same period. Among the biggest job losers: manufacturing, agriculture, forestry and fishing, and mining.

Occupations Projected to Grow Fastest, 2004–2014 (in descending order):

1. Home health aides
2. Network systems and data communications analysts

3. Medical assistants
4. Physician assistants
5. Computer software engineers (applications)
6. Physical therapist assistants
7. Dental hygienists
8. Computer software engineers (systems software)
9. Dental assistants
10. Personal and home-care aides
11. Network and computer systems administrators
12. Database administrators
13. Physical therapists
14. Forensic science technicians
15. Veterinary technologists and technicians
16. Diagnostic medical sonographers
17. Physical-therapist aides
18. Occupational therapist assistants
19. Medical scientists (except epidemiologists)
20. Occupational therapists

Occupations with the Largest Numerical Increases in Employment, 2004–2014 (in descending order):

1. Retail salespersons
2. Registered nurses
3. Postsecondary teachers
4. Customer service representatives
5. Janitors and cleaners (except maids and housekeepers)
6. Waiters and waitresses
7. Combined food preparation and serving workers (including fast food)
8. Home health aides
9. Nursing aides, orderlies, and attendants
10. General and operations managers

With the possible exception of construction and software engineering, all of the projected high-growth industries are either gender-neutral or favor females. The biggest losers—manufacturing, agriculture, and mining—are traditionally male professions. But most disturbing of all is the trend of able-bodied unemployed men of all ages who are giving up and dropping out of the workforce altogether.

Most of those men, which number about 4 million, are former blue-collar workers who have been displaced by the Information Age economy. But a growing number are college-educated professionals in their thirties and forties who have been out of work for years and have no intention of rejoining the workforce. I have spoken to guys who feel that the professional landscape has tilted against married heterosexual men with families. They see themselves at a disadvantage against ambitious single men and gay men, who don't think twice about staying extra-late to finish an important project or work through the weekend to prove their dedication to the firm. Men with spouses and families vying for their time and attention are simply finding it difficult to compete.

The Internet boom—which spawned a whole generation of young men who felt entitled to instant riches—certainly didn't help. When the first dot-com wave crested and then suddenly receded, hundreds of thousands of "new media" workers, who had left more traditional careers to chase Internet gold, found themselves washed up on the shores of Social Security. Some eventually got offers in related industries, others weathered the storm by accepting demotions or lower pay. But many new media workers found it difficult to find employment that matched the glamour and allure of the days when it seemed anybody could—and would—become wealthy overnight. By the time the dot-com economy heated up again, many of those workers had given up on finding a job they considered worth their time. For men who not so long before were millionaires on paper, or still dreamed of announcing their own IPO one day, the prospect of working for someone else is anything but motivational.

The uppermost tier of this group represents a new kind of leisure class, comfortably adrift in a culture that no longer considers unemployment a stigma. In many cases, the woman in the family becomes the chief wage earner, causing domestic tension as men adjust to the new reality of being the financially dependent spouse. Tellingly, about 8 percent of unemployed men between 30 and 54 live in households that reported incomes of at least $100,000 in 2004.

More often, though, this growing pool of idle male workers scrape by on disability and debt, postponing the day of reckoning. In the worst cases, they have lost their families and self-esteem along with their jobs, sliding into isolation and mental depression without medical insurance or the social mechanisms to help them reach old age.

"What happens to a lot of guys who become unmoored from family life, they become unmoored from everything," Kathryn Edin, a sociologist at the University of Pennsylvania told the *New York Times*. "They are just living without attachments and by the time they are 40 or 50 years old, the things that kept these men from falling away—family and community life—are gone."

LIFELINES

Men are notoriously self-destructive. They smoke more than women. They drink more than women. They are prone to risky behavior, don't like to admit they are feeling pain, and avoid visits to the doctor. It's been known for a long time that women outlive men by an average of five years, and until recently few people wondered why. But medical advocates and scientists are beginning to ask questions that would have been unthinkable just a few years ago: Are men getting sicker than they should? Are men dying younger than they need to? Are we even looking at the right symptoms? And what, if anything, can be done about it?

In recent years, women's health has become a national priority.

Pink ribbons symbolize the fight against breast cancer. Pins shaped like red dresses are meant to signal awareness of female heart disease. In government agencies at the local, state, and national level, offices of women's health have sprung up to offer information and free screenings. In 1990, the National Institutes of Health established an Office of Research on Women's Health. In 1993, the U.S. Food and Drug Administration emphasized the importance of including men and women in clinical trials evaluating new medications and the following year established its own Office of Women's Health. One of the largest government studies on the role of hormones and diet in aging was focused entirely on females.

Up until recently it was presumed that women's health issues warranted special attention because they had been historically neglected. Men, it logically followed, were already taken care of because the health system was designed and managed by and for men. But a growing body of evidence suggests that the health-care industry has failed to acknowledge or adjust to men's changing needs. As a result, doctors and health-care experts are mobilizing at the state and national levels to address what they see as a looming health crisis for men. The Men's Health Network, a nonprofit educational foundation based in Washington, D.C., has called for the establishment of a federal office of men's health similar to the office of women's health that already exists in the U.S. Health and Human Services Department. And five states—Maryland, Georgia, New Hampshire, Louisiana, and Oklahoma—have either created or plan to establish offices or commissions on men's health.

"We've got men dying at higher rates of just about every disease, and we don't know why," notes Dr. Demetrius J. Porche, associate dean at Louisiana State University's Health Sciences School of Nursing. "The biggest thing is looking at the disparity that continues to exist—the age that men die is still much earlier than women."

American men have an average life expectancy of 75.2 years—for black men it is 69.8 years—as compared to 80.4 years overall for women. Men die at a younger age than women of nearly every leading cause of death, including lung cancer, influenza, pneumonia, chronic liver disease, diabetes, and AIDS.

Dr. Porche believes that men's health has suffered as a result of certain social assumptions, including the mistaken belief that men as a group have already been adequately studied and diagnosed. "Men have always been the bulk of the research subjects, so everybody thought, well, we're always testing men, so we must already know everything about them," he explains. "And, yes, men have been used in research, but they have not usually been the *subjects* of research. Because we never looked at them and said, 'What's different about you, as opposed to women?'"

Dr. Porche did just that in 2007 by founding the *American Journal of Men's Health*, which he created as a global forum and a catalyst for a discussion of men's health issues. He hopes to redefine men's health within the modern context of changing gender roles and demographics in the American male population.

"We keep throwing out lifestyle as an explanation for the differences in longevity, saying that men come in later for care and have unhealthy behaviors, but I'm not sure we really know the reason," says Dr. Porche. "We want a more complex picture of what constitutes a healthy man. In a couple of years we hope to have a body of knowledge about where men's health is. What I want to do is show that there are more aspects to men's health beyond the prostate, the testicular, and the penis. There are more issues to deal with—depression, all these other issues that traditionally men's health has never looked at."

Among the articles in the journal's debut issue are "College Men's Knowledge, Attitudes, and Beliefs about Testicular Cancer," "Male Preventive Health Behaviors: Perceptions from Men, Women, and Clinical Staff Along the U.S–Mexico Border," "Mental Health

Symptoms Among Male Victims of Partner Violence," and "Hot Flashes in Prostate Cancer: State of the Science." Dr. Porche hopes that the *Men's Health* journal will help other physicians understand that the kinds of health issues that today's men face may be rooted in sociological and economic causes.

Men often avoid the doctor's office until a problem becomes so serious that they can no longer be productive in society through their work.

"It's not just about men," says Dr. Porche. "We can't say it's just a male issue. I know that some people involved in women's health see no need for men's health. And I start laughing and say, what about their sons and their husbands and their brothers and uncles that they have in their family? We want to increase the longevity of both men and women—and we also want to increase the quality of life for both men and women," Dr. Porche says. "Gender roles are in flux, and then there are cultural variations, age, race and ethnicity, gay men, young men, Latinos, Asians, and African-Americans. Let's say that the Latino family has been very matriarchal—will it continue to be matriarchal? That's something we need to look at. We want to raise awareness about men's health—it's not about taking sides. It's about realizing that men's and women's health are interconnected and affect each other. We're all in this together—everybody has a stake in men's health."

Government funding for research on the diseases that afflict men the most has lagged. Breast cancer research funding in 2005, for example, exceeded prostate cancer funding by more than 40 percent in 2005 ($394 million for prostate cancer versus $710 million for breast cancer). And while it's true that more women die of breast cancer than men die of prostate cancer, the projected number of men to be diagnosed with prostate cancer in 2007 (218,890), was higher than the corresponding rates of projected breast cancer diagnosis for women (178,480). Nevertheless, health experts say that there is wider support for development of breast cancer drugs and more attention paid to the quality-of-life effects of breast cancer as well as more clinical trials on breast cancer drugs than on those for treating prostate cancer.

Men, for better or worse, now even have their own version of menopause. Daniel Federman and Geoffrey Walford, of the Harvard University Medical School, reported in *Newsweek* magazine that as men age the slow decline in their testosterone levels can cause a host of potentially serious disorders, including loss of muscle mass and bone strength, increased body fat, decreased energy, erectile dysfunction, irritability, and depression. Male menopause—"manopause"?—is tricky to diagnose and treat, since testosterone levels fluctuate hourly and affect individual men differently. Additional research is needed, the authors argue, to understand the extent and seriousness of the syndrome and find alternative treatments to male hormone injections, which have been tied to prostate cancer.

The health advantages of women over men reach back to the very first stages of life. Even though more male than female fetuses are conceived, males are more prone to stillbirth and miscarriage than females. Mortality rates are also higher for premature baby boys than for preemie girls. Girls are less likely than boys to be autistic or color-blind, and boys have higher rates of hearing loss and are believed to have a weaker immune system. Consequently, even though more boy babies than girl babies are born, by the time Americans have reached their thirties, the women have numerically caught up and overtaken the men.

"It's not that we 'could be' the weaker sex—we are the weaker sex," Dr. Robert Tan, a geriatrics specialist in Houston who is on the advisory board of the Men's Health Network, told the *New York Times*. "Even when men and women have the same disease, we often find that men are more likely to die."

Part of the reason, experts speculate, could be that men are notoriously bad at taking care of themselves. Besides being more likely to drink and smoke, males are less likely to wear seat belts or use sunscreen. Men are more likely than women to be injured in an accident and are 77 percent more likely to die in a car crash. They are three times more likely to be a victim of murder, four times more likely to commit suicide, and, as teenagers, eleven times more likely to drown.

But, if evolutionary psychologists are right, then isn't the male proclivity to take risks and ignore danger embedded in the very structure and chemistry of his brain? Are men—not entirely unlike the fast vehicles that they love to possess and drive faster than the speed limit—designed by Mother Nature with a certain degree of planned obsolescence, the better to make room in the genetic showroom for the updated new model?

Are men genetically programmed to self-destruct? Are the seeds of the masculine demise preordained—not just in our brains but deep in our own biological blueprints, a ticking time bomb of inherent weakness and susceptibility just waiting for the right physiological and historical moment to detonate? In that harsh light, the question is not why women at the beginning of the twenty-first century have managed to wrest the social, cultural, and economic advantage away from the once dominant sex, but how men have managed to hold out and hang on for so long.

CHAPTER 2

Eve's Rib

On an unseasonably warm November evening, I attended a panel discussion at the Columbia University Graduate School of Journalism in New York City that promised to explain: "What Women Want—Media, Myth, and Reality." Seated on the dais were Sheryl Hilliard Tucker, an executive editor at Time Inc.; Rita Henley-Jensen, editor in chief of *Women's News;* Geralyn Lucas, a director of public affairs at the Lifetime Network; Lynn Povich, a former *Newsweek* senior editor and co-chair of the International Women's Media Foundation; and Trip Gabriel, editor of the *New York Times* Style section.

As a mostly female audience of about two hundred listened, the panelists eloquently and forcefully argued that women, while gaining ground in the news media, still had a long way to go. There was a discussion about how some of the best reporting from the war in Iraq was being done by women. (Without a doubt.) Did men and women write about war differently? (Harder to say.) During the Q&A session that followed, a question began to formulate in my mind. As I waited in line for my chance to address the panel, a woman complained that her daughter enjoyed playing with Barbie dolls. The panelists sympathized, assuring the woman that her daughter would eventually outgrow her doll phase.

"At least Barbie is better than the Bratz," offered Lucas, referring to the pouty-lipped, tan-skinned dolls that have used their sassy street appeal to take a major bite out of Barbie's market share. Lucas informed the audience that her own young daughter played with boys' toys as well as Barbies, adding that "a few of her guy friends are dressing up in high heels when they come over."

There was a murmur of acknowledgment from the crowd. I looked around the room. A few young women, most of them students at the journalism school, I guessed, were hunched over notebooks, writing. Others merely nodded.

Another audience member rose to bemoan the mindlessness of TV morning-show programming.

"Change the channel," Trip Gabriel of the *New York Times* suggested.

"But it's the same thing on every network," the woman protested.

"So don't watch," Gabriel replied. "Are you really missing that much?"

Finally it was my turn at the mike. I identified myself as a Columbia Journalism School alumnus and former *Time* magazine staff writer. Then I recounted a story: When I was at *Time* during the eighties and early nineties, the president of Time Inc. was a man and the men's titles—*Time, Fortune, Sports Illustrated*—were the most prestigious and profitable magazines. Today, less than fifteen years later, everything was different: the president of Time Inc., Ann Moore, was a woman, and the most profitable magazine at the company was *People*, a publication dedicated to the kinds of celebrity gossip and human-interest stories that appealed to female readers. What, I asked the panelists, was their explanation for the shift? And what were the implications for journalism, the publishing industry, and the rest of American society?

There was a lull as the panelists looked at each other with consternation. At last, Sheryl Hilliard Tucker spoke.

"The male readership for magazines is dropping off," she said. "Men are doing other things."

I waited for someone to tell me what men were doing instead, but no one seemed to know.

While reading rates are down for younger people in general, the slide is steepest among males.

A study by the Associated Press and the market research firm Ipsos found that the typical American read only four books in 2006. But when broken down by gender, it turns out that women read twice as many books as men. The researchers found that women read more than men in all categories except for history and biography. The British novelist Ian McEwan made a similar discovery when the respondents to a free giveaway of his books in a London park were overwhelmingly female. "When women stop reading," he told *The Guardian*, "the novel will be dead."

The theories for the gender-skewed reading disparity range from the fact that women are inherently better communicators than men, to the fact that girls can sit still longer than boys. Some scientists speculate that women's brains are wired to be more intrinsically empathic, allowing them to better relate to books with detailed characters and emotional themes.

Reached by phone at her office, Tucker elaborated on Time Inc.'s response to the puzzling case of the disappearing male reader. At least part of the answer, she said, is that men have migrated from print to other media. "We've always looked at men starting with the magazines," Tucker told me. "What's happening now is that we have to start looking in different places in different ways for different audiences to find that place when it comes to men and young men. It may be that the best way to reach millennials [i.e., anyone who was twenty or younger in 2000] is through podcasts, but if we're doing it through *SI* instead of ESPN, then that's good. You can't connect to men these days with just one platform."

According to Tucker, even ideas about what a men's magazine is supposed to look like are going out the window. When the Time Inc. editorial team was redesigning *Money* magazine, one of the prototypes was closer in color scheme and layout to what usually works well in women's magazines. She says the new design "tested well on men" and it got the green light even though "it might have been construed as not manly or serious."

The goal was not to feminize *Money*, Tucker contends, but to give men a friendlier way to access complex information. "When we did the redesign of *Money* a lot of people thought we were abandoning men," she admits. "The fact that it might be a little close to the look that traditional women's magazines often turn to—the boxes and colors, etc.—wasn't because we were trying to get women; it was because this is how men wanted very complicated, not easy-to-swallow information. We found that the only color that didn't connect with men was purple. Men said, if you can find a way to give us information in a way that makes us feel more comfortable and empowered, we'll take it. And for *Money*, that has proven to be a very successful approach."

With male-oriented media facing an increasingly uncertain future, even publications that have traditionally catered to men are reaching out to women.

In early 2007, the *Wall Street Journal* launched a series of ads aimed at increasing its appeal to business-minded females, who already made up about a third of the paper's subscribers. The campaign was built around a series of profiles of notable men and women who have had a positive impact on others, including food guru Alice Waters, Vietnam War Memorial designer Maya Lin, and pop singer Sheryl Crow. For Crow's profile, a guitar wire traces her career arc, starting with "Studies Music—Graduates with Degree in Music Education" and ending with "Faces Music: Beats Breast Cancer Thanks to Early Diagnosis." The accompanying website explained to prospective subscribers: "Life is a journey. Each has unexpected twists and turns. Let these journeys inspire you. Every journey needs a Journal." The same edition featured a "Home & Family" section with articles on fall fashion trends and another with a headline that asks: "Is More Money Worth Less Time With Kids?"

As female audiences become more affluent and desirable, the case for gender diversity has taken on a bottom-line imperative. As a result, some see women as better qualified and positioned than men to lead the industry into the multicultural markets of the future. A report by Northwestern University's Media Management Center, titled "Women in Media 2006: Finding the Leader in You," noted a correlation between newspapers that had women in senior decision-making positions and those that were doing well financially. "Newspapers that enjoy growth from innovation and development are more likely to have a diverse set of leaders at the top," Michael P. Smith, the center's executive director, wrote in the report. "We can tie women in leadership to profitability."

SWITCHING CHANNELS

Print is not the only medium where men are being eclipsed. Katie Couric's history-making, if wobbly, debut as the first solo female anchor of a major network evening-news program notwithstanding, women are transforming the nature of TV news just as men seem to be tuning out. According to a national survey by the Radio and Television News Directors Association, the number of female TV anchors reached an all-time high of 57 percent in 2005. Women also accounted for 58 percent of all TV reporters, 55 percent of executive producers, 66 percent of news producers, and 56 percent of news writers.

"Outside of a few traditionally male bastions—the sports guy, the weathercast, the boss—men are disappearing from TV," Paul Farhi wrote in the *Washington Post*.

Experts attribute at least part of the trend to lower salaries and shrinking job opportunities in the TV news business. The erosion of male TV professionals is making its way upstream to journalism schools, where male enrollment has been shrinking for years.

"Young men are just not interested," Craig Allen, a broadcasting professor at Arizona State University's Walter Conkite School of Journalism, told Farhi. "There's been almost an evacuation of men from this field."

More provocative is the charge that with so many women on the air and behind the scenes, TV news programming is being skewed toward a female sensibility. Andrew Tyndall, a New York–based blogger who tracks the amount of time devoted to various topics by the major news networks on a daily basis, has documented a shift in the kinds of news stories that have been broadcast by CBS and other news organizations over a thirty-year period. Comparing CBS news broadcasts in November 1968 and November 1998, Tyndall found a sharp increase in the number of women who both reported and were interviewed for stories. In his blog, *The Tyndall Report*, he also cited a drop in stories devoted to politics, government, and war, and a corresponding increase in women-friendly topics like abortion, child care, and gender discrimination in the workplace. Network news is no longer aimed at a predominantly male audience.

Tyndall found a similar effect when he analyzed the TV anchorship of Elizabeth Vargas, who had a two-month stint in 2006 as the sole anchor of ABC's *World News Tonight* when her coanchor, Bob

Woodruff, was injured covering the war in Iraq. During March and April, after Woodruff's injury and before Charles Gibson took over as the new full-time evening news anchor, Tyndall's tally showed that *World News Tonight* devoted more time to stories on contraception, abortion, autism, prenatal development, childbirth, postpartum depression, and child pornography than CBS and NBC combined. Tyndall found that after Vargas, who was expecting a child, left the show in late May, and Gibson took over, the number of family-centric news stories diminished.

For others, the real issue was about a cultural bias against working women, particularly if they're pregnant. Writing in the online zine *Slate*, Dahlia Lithwick, observed: "Everyone is turning Elizabeth Vargas' pregnancy into a referendum on pregnant women in the workplace, and particularly in the media, because it's happening on a big screen in front of us, but also in our homes and our book groups. Vargas isn't just carrying the extra weight of her unborn baby here; she's carrying the weight of a whole nation of people who still see gender in absolute and defining terms. Maybe the reason we can't quite stomach a hugely pregnant news anchor is that we can't even manage to talk coherently about all the ways in which they somehow freak us out."

In *The Huffington Post*, political pundit Arianna Huffington fumed at "Farhi's fear mongering that our very news is in danger of being co-opted by 'family' stories. . . .

"Just listing the litany of stories that were supposedly inspired by Elizabeth Vargas' girlishness isn't enough to prove that she dragged the ABC news department kicking and screaming into the dark recesses of her womb," wrote Huffington. "The real irony of this story is that if you strip away the conjecture and dark mutterings, you're left with statistics: newsroom balances have shifted from male to female, up from the days of Ron Burgundy and Veronica Corningstone and also from the early 90s when parity was reached."

Almost lost in the brouhaha over Vargas's departure was the

bigger question of whether or not TV news was becoming any more or less "feminized" than the rest of society. Is the media the problem or merely the messenger, reflecting a cultural trend that extends into every aspect of American life? Could this, for example, help to explain the journalistic feeding frenzy over the depressing demise of Anna Nicole Smith?

A onetime *Playboy* Playmate of the Year, bit actress, and reality TV star, Smith fueled her fame with psychological exhibitionism, eagerly flashing the torrid details of her personal predicaments for the unblinking media eye. She became tabloid fodder by marrying an eighty-nine-year-old billionaire and then taking the fight for his estate all the way to the Supreme Court. And the apparent suicide of her twenty-year-old son, in the same hospital room where days before she had given birth to a daughter, was genuinely sad. But Smith's real talent was in sensing that the American hunger for sordid human-interest stories that could be tied to a self-help tip-of-the-day was insatiable. Her tragic rise from third-rate celebrity to national news staple was more about the pervasive cult of celebrity than Smith's overexposed life and mysterious death, which predictably made the cover of *People*, but also dominated mainstream newspaper, radio, and TV coverage for days on end. What exactly had killed Smith and who was the real father of her now motherless infant? *Americans needed to know.*

But why? What's at the source of this burning desire to learn everything we can about people we don't even know? Is it boredom, idle curiosity, or something deeper?

In his book *Grooming, Gossip and the Evolution of Language* the British psychologist and University of Liverpool professor Robin Dunbar uses biology, sociology, and anthropology to show how grooming is the social glue that binds all primates and allows them to function as a group. Just like present-day monkeys and apes, our ancestors used grooming to exchange personal information, build trust, and establish alliances that would come in handy in fighting wars and protecting and raising offspring. As the tribes of Homo sapiens grew in size and complexity, however, physical grooming became impractical, even as the evolutionary imperative for social bonding only increased. Thus language, Dunbar argues, developed, not simply as a tool to help males hunt more effectively, as many anthropologists had formerly contended, but rather as a way for humans to expand their social and emotional networks over ever-larger groups, and eventually across time and space. Hence, gossip, and the trafficking of information about other people, is a genetic imperative that dates back to the earliest days of our species.

As evidence, Dunbar points to the popularity of biographies and news stories that focus on the emotions and motivations of other people. After measuring the ratio of space devoted to information-driven articles "about politics and economics" versus "human interest" stories in the upscale London *Times* and the mass-market tabloid *The Sun*, Dunbar found the percentage of column inches devoted to human-interest stories to be 43 percent for the *Times*, and 78 percent, or 1,063 column inches of text, for *The Sun*. The amount of space devoted to "gossip" at both papers was roughly equal—850 and 833 inches, respectively.

"Our much vaunted capacity for language seems to be mainly used for exchanging information on social matters; we seem to be obsessed with gossiping about one another," Dunbar writes. "Even the design of our minds seems to reinforce this." In other words, it follows that women, who on the prehistoric savannah depended on building social networks and alliances with other males and females to ensure the well-being and protection of their children, would develop brains that are particularly well-suited for communication and empathic connection.

For Dunbar, this explains why women gravitate to books and

TV shows that concentrate on romance, relationships, and emotions. And perhaps, by extension, why they read more. "One of the more peculiar features of modern urban life is the extent to which we are locked into the tiny world of our own homes," he observed. "Separated from relatives and with limited opportunities to create circles of friends, the modern city dweller is forced increasingly to draw on the ready-made imaginative family of the soap opera for a social life and sense of community. It is conspicuous that the largest audience for these programmes is found among housebound women, trapped at home by young children."

But what happens when women are no longer trapped at home—by children or anything else? What happens if they use their inherent networking and communication skills, not to create alliances with other tribe members to protect their children from predators, but to build careers and become the principal breadwinner? And what if some men, by choice or bad luck, refuse or are unable to adapt? What if those men become ostracized, marginalized, and unemployed, and the image of men as knuckle-dragging losers who refuse to grow up—this growing sense that males are out of time and out of touch—becomes part of the zeitgeist? In other words, what if the Geico caveman made the evolutionary leap from insurance ad to TV sitcom not because he was so strange but because he was so familiar?

Rob Bragin, a TV producer-writer based in Los Angeles, agrees that the images of clueless cavemen on TV and in the movies reflects a shift in gender roles outside the studio, but wonder if both sexes are in on the joke. Did the same men who related to ABC's *Cavemen* also pay good money to watch the hyperaggressive man-killers of *Charlie's Angels*? It just might be that when the sexes switch places on TV and in films, it connects with the collective unconscious by turning this reality into harmless amusement.

"I think the idea for a strong woman is not just appealing to women," Bragin says. "I think for guys it's become a cool thing to see women who can kick ass. Now, are guys into it because they think that it's become a universal ideal, that women kick ass and men have been relegated to this position of watching a woman kick ass? I don't know."

The stock "dumb blonde" character perfected by Marilyn Monroe, and living on in the personas of Paris Hilton and Jessica Simpson, now has a male counterpart. Bragin sees a similar dynamic in the portrayal of hopelessly incompetent male authority figures in shows like *The Office*. "It is a rampant stereotype of men, comparable to Stepin Fetchit, of portraying dads as not just bad, but as stupid and inept," he says. "I suspect it's because they're comedies and that's what's funny, you need a buffoon for the pratfall. Look at *The Office*. It's a great show. But you could never put a woman at the head of that show and make fun of a woman boss. The boss, who's played by Steve Carell, just wants to be loved, but he's a complete and total idiot and buffoon. There was an episode about one of the characters getting flashed. And he thought it was funny, but the women didn't find it funny at all. And the whole episode was about him trying to reach out to the women and be sensitive, to the point where one of the women calls him a misogynist and he says, 'Yes, I am, thank you.' And she says, 'Well, that's sexist.' And, because he doesn't know the meaning of the word, he says, 'No, I really *am* a misogynist.' It clearly makes him a buffoon. I don't think there's anything wrong with it. But that's where the culture is right now. Men have been portrayed as bad guys for so long, so guys tolerate it because it's like now you're getting your just desserts."

RUDE AWAKENING

Over a breakfast of blueberries, bacon, and coffee in the Time Warner Center in New York City, I raise the subject of male decline with Richard D. Parsons, the chairman and CEO of Time Warner,

Inc., the world's largest media company and the parent corporation of Time Inc., as well as CNN, HBO, AOL, Warner Brothers, and many other iconic brands. I asked him if Time Warner executives were aware that they were losing males, not just as employees but also as customers for their products. And if so, what were they doing about it?

"I think people notice it, people are thinking about it, and it's inevitable," Parsons replied. "It's happening now." The only question, for Parsons, is "the rate of speed at which it happens. Now, what's inevitable? Not that we will live in a female-dominated society much in the same way that for the past forty thousand years it has been male-dominated. But parity is inevitable."

Then, Parsons, a tall man with a firm handshake who has the rare ability to be simultaneously imposing and disarming, told me about an "epiphany" he had during an African safari he had recently taken to celebrate his fiftieth birthday. "We came upon this pride of lions," he recalled. "Two big males, about nine female lions, and a few cubs. And every time we would roll up, the females were engaged in some sort of activity—looking after the cubs, cleaning them up, or they were hunting, preparing the food, or eating. The cubs were always playing, that's what they do, and the males were always sleeping. Always! You know, you want a picture of a lion sitting up there roaring, and so I asked the guide, 'What's up with these guys? They're asleep all the time!' And he said: 'You've got to understand, this is nature and everybody's got a role, and they have theirs. And their role is: one, to procreate, and, two, when the bad guys show up, they get up and go to war and protect the pride.' And it was a very simple thing, don't ask me why, it just sort of hit me like a bolt: in nature, you don't think about it, you just do what nature dictates, everybody's got a role. And that's their role. And if you risk-weight things, yeah, the females are always busy, and they seem to be working harder, and doing stuff, but it's all low-risk stuff. The guys don't do much, but when they do something it's all high-risk stuff. If you weigh it all at the end, it about balances out; it's the balance of nature."

And so, how, in Parsons' view, did modern humans, men and women, get out of balance? His answer, not surprisingly, given his role as a leader of consumer-brand behemoths, echoes the free-market forces that decide which brands sell and prosper while others wither away. If men were a brand, their value would be dropping, because society is simply not buying what they're selling. In a sense, men, who once controlled the means of production, have become products themselves. And now, in a cruel twist from the system they helped to build, they have outlived their shelf life.

"Almost from the beginning of man's time on this earth, his role has been as the protector-provider," observed Parsons, who untangled the Time Warner–AOL merger and fought off a shareholder assault led by Carl Icahn during his tenure at the helm. "And then the rest of the time he sits in front of the TV and watches football and—whatever—drinks beer. That protector-provider role was based on certain, largely physical attributes, though I'm sure there are also some mental and emotional attributes, just less visibly apparent. We were bigger, stronger, faster, and that made all the difference in terms of our role. The women's role was to bear children and be provided for, so to speak. But today the world is, if not changing, changed—I think it's changed. Brains weren't as important as brawn, if you go back to forty thousand years ago. Over those forty thousand years there has been an evolution in terms of which functions are the most important. Brawn has been relegated to deep second place and brains have been elevated to way, way first place; and women are, at least, equally as smart as men. I think women do certain things better, and they definitely multitask better. And the combination of being at least equally smart and having better multitasking skills is trumping sheer brawn."

The issue, in Parsons' view, is not that females are smart and successful, but that the social and economic gains that have propelled women forward have also put them on a collision course with men.

Almost overnight, men and women in the workforce are chasing the same economic prey, and when living creatures compete for sustenance, the fur is bound to fly.

"Guys and gals didn't used to compete as directly with each other as they do today," Parsons said, putting down his napkin and leaning back in his chair. "It's like leopards and lions. Lions don't eat leopards and leopards don't eat lions, but they'll kill each other in the open field if they get a shot, because they compete for food. Fewer leopards, more gazelles—good for us lions. Women used to have a more defined role. Women's role was, let's just say for this conversation, in the home, with all that entails. And the guys' was outside. You go get it, I'll fix it, and I'll look after the kids and make sure the kids grow up well. Now women and men are like leopards and lions, they're competing for the same prey. You want to be a journalist; you have to best a bunch of women who are equally accredited and maybe equally talented. So that's introduced an element of greater competition into the relationship."

PURSE POWER

And almost everywhere one looks these days, the leopards are leaving the lions in the dust. Evidence of women's economic ascendance reaches across every industry and is reshaping the social landscape, with major implications for how all Americans spend, work, play, and vote. While men still cling to the uppermost rungs in the worlds of business, politics, and sports, their grip is loosening as women continue their steady climb toward the top. Women are the decision makers in 85 percent of all consumer purchases, including

95 percent of home products and 89 percent of vacations. They command $7 billion in consumer and business spending and have $14 trillion in assets, a number projected to grow to $22 trillion during the coming decade. According to the Bureau of Labor Statistics, American women's earnings as a percentage of men's earnings on a weekly basis steadily increased from 63 percent (or $585) to 81 percent (or $722) in 2005.

Experts estimate that if current trends continue, women will earn more than men by 2028.

Women already buy 50 percent of all cars and trucks and shop for 90 percent of home furnishings. They are also a growing force at traditionally male-oriented "big box" retailers like Best Buy, and have enlarged their share of the market for computers and home electronics.

Marketers have begun to recognize women's purchasing power and are taking advantage of their thoughtful, efficient, and organized approach to shopping. "Crave parties," all-female gatherings that combine shopping, bonding, and professional networking, are now held in thirteen cities. For a small fee, women arrive at a single destination and are treated to stores, restaurants, and personal services like massages and manicures. Originally targeting younger women, crave parties have caught on with women in their forties and fifties. The group's motto: "Everything you crave, under one roof."

Economic empowerment is not just changing how women shop; it's also changing where they live. Armed with swelling savings accounts and a newfound confidence to trust their instincts, women are buying houses and condos in record numbers. Realtors across the country report a sharp increase in the number of single and married women who are buying their own homes with their own money—and encouraging their girlfriends to do the same. Women also seem to be better at evaluating a good deal and acting on it, while their male counterparts hesitate, banking on the steal that never comes.

The National Realtors Association reports that single women represent one out of every five home buyers and that women between the ages of 35 and 44 purchased 1.76 million homes between July 2005 and June 2006. Single women make up 22 percent of all home-buyer households, up 14 percent from a decade ago, while single men make up just 9 percent of such households, a figure that has remained flat. Single women are more likely to have children and need the extra space and security of a house. And although married couples still make up the majority (61 percent) of home buyers, women are key influencers in the buying decision. A study by Harvard University's Joint Center for Housing Studies found that unmarried female buyers bought more than $550 billion worth of real estate between 2000 and 2003.

In an article for *Realty Times* titled "The Buying Power of Women," Wanda McPhaden hailed the arrival of the female homeowner as a real estate phenomenon. "I'm encouraged that women, led by their younger cohorts, are finally getting over that emotional bump in the road to profitable real estate investment and financial independence—needing a male opinion," wrote McPhaden, a principal at BCA Real Estate Investments, headquartered in Ridgefield, Connecticut, and New York City.

Home builders are beginning to follow. Shane Homes, a developer based in Calgary, Alberta, is one of several firms in Canada and the United States that have begun to rethink the layout and functionality of the typical dwelling with an eye toward women's tastes and needs. When women were asked for their input, the list of amendments and custom touches ranged from larger sinks and windows that overlooked areas where children played to laundry rooms that were partitioned away from messy entrance foyers. And when a boyfriend or handyman isn't in the picture, women are increasingly willing to tackle a fixer-upper themselves. In June of 2006, women bought 47 percent of all painting supplies, up from 42 percent three years earlier. They also bought half of all bathtubs, up from 35 percent in 2003. Women are also behind the push for larger, more luxurious bathrooms and his-and-her showers. Sales agents at Kohler, for example, are struggling to meet the demand for bathtubs that comfortably seat two.

Women with the means are turning their bathrooms into an oasis of comfort and serenity, complete with designer fixtures, flat-screen TVs, plush carpeting, imported marble, and Buddhist sculptures.

Empowered by Oprah and accessorized by Martha, women can tend their own gardens, repair their own roofs, and vacation where and with whom they please. An iVillage poll found that 92 percent of all women would like to go on vacation with a girlfriend and 65 percent would vacation alone. According to "Women Travelers: A New Growth Market," a report by the Pacific Asia Travel Association, female travelers are increasing worldwide and make 70 percent of all travel decisions. In 1996, 44 percent of all business travelers were women; today there are more than seventy-five travel agencies that cater specifically to women. Women are traveling solo and in single-sex tour groups. They are traveling to major cities in Europe, Africa, Asia, and South America, but they are also signing up for eco-adventure trips with hiking, rafting, diving, sailing, and spelunking activities. Travel experts predict that the trend will continue and that female travelers will represent the most significant travel trend of our generation.

"We are entering a brave new world where there are no pat answers, no magic bullets or easy templates for how to reach women—if indeed there ever were," writes Fara Warner in *The Power of the Purse: How Smart Businesses Are Adapting to the World's Most Important Consumers—Women*. "We are on the verge of a major transformation in the way corporations view women consumers and how they then adapt to women's needs and wants in the future."

And while men have only begun to feel the financial and professional impact of that transformation, the outlines of what's to come are already visible. As women continue to consolidate their position in the workforce and the new consumer economy, men will find it harder to keep the job they have and find a new one when they need it. Already, there are signs that middle-aged men who lose their jobs due to corporate downsizing are finding it difficult if not impossible to regain their former status or income level.

Sheryl Hilliard Tucker is among those who see a dawn of harsh new realities for mid-level male professionals. "I think what's happening is that the rules of the game are changing and not everybody is prepared to deal with some of the new realities of how quickly you become not relevant in your field," she says. "I remember when the tech field started they had to figure out how not to push everybody into management because [older people] could no longer compete with young people when it came to the tech edge. The destructive behaviors of when high achievers are idle are scary—this is when they have affairs, this is when they sabotage their team by doing crazy stuff." Tucker notes that the surge in dysfunctional men is even evident in Italy, where widows would rather live alone than suffer the foibles of the opposite sex. "It's such an issue in Italy that it's affected the birthrate," she says. "Women don't want to get married again after their husbands die because they feel that they've already done that—they don't want to have to take care of them and they don't want to spend the rest of their lives catering to men."

For many men over thirty, the business environment that males once ruled has become a treacherous labyrinth of dead ends and close calls. "All the rules are changing," Hilliard says. "Some traditional people can't deal with this landscape that just doesn't seem to be familiar or predictable."

Female buying power is also changing how companies develop and market their products and signals a shifting balance in industries as diverse as media, fast food, and real estate. Like Hispanics, gay men, and other so-called minorities that are redefining the mainstream consumer marketplace, women are learning that when money talks, corporations listen. Increasingly aware of their collective economic clout, they expect the products and brands that they buy to reflect their values and to speak to their emotional as well as their material needs. As shopping patterns morph along with evolving gender roles, women are driving a lot more than the grocery cart.

In the fast-moving currents of this new mainstream economy, companies—and the men who work in them—must adapt, or find themselves stranded on the shoals of outdated assumptions and business models.

Women consumers, it turns out, don't just have different tastes but actually relate to money differently than men do. In the financial sector, companies like Citibank and MassMutual have either changed the way they were doing business or launched entirely new divisions to serve the tastes and needs of their female customers. Despite the huge rise in their collective wealth, for example, women's knowledge of financial strategies and services has not kept pace. Citicorp's answer was to create Women and Company, a custom banking membership program that was created with the mission to "address the unique needs of women as they seek more command over their personal finances. The goal? To help you feel that your money is working for you—not the other way around."

By surveying more than 1,200 women nationally, Women and

Company learned that women differed from men not just in how they spent money but also in the ways that they saved it. Women put a premium on financial and physical security for their children. They are also concerned about how to financially compensate for the fact that they collectively leave work for an average of eleven years to raise a family. And because women live longer than men, they often need additional assistance and counseling in estate-tax and life-insurance issues, as well as in planning for retirement without a spouse. Younger women, it turns out, are determined not to follow in the footsteps of their mothers and grandmothers, who in many cases found themselves suddenly widowed or divorced with no clue about their financial situation or how to improve it. Merrill Lynch and American Express are among the many financial institutions that have recently acted to reach female clients with customized services, and conferences with titles like "Strong Women, Powerful Financial Strategy."

The learning curve goes both ways. MassMutual recently introduced "Pearls of Wisdom," a video-based financial seminar for women, and began a seminar for its sales agents to sensitize them to women's concerns and needs. "When it comes to financial advisors, women will share the most intimate details of their lives," Susan W. Sweetser, a vice president in the women's marketing department at MassMutual told the *New York Times*. "Women don't just buy based on information; they buy based on emotions, coupled with the facts."

And, increasingly, their emotions tell them that men can't be counted upon for financial security. As a result, women are hedging their bets and learning how not to be so dependent on men. Sarah* is a fifty-year-old writer who lives in Detroit. When her husband

---

* Here and below, names followed by an asterisk have been changed for reasons of privacy.

gave up an important job at the Internal Revenue Service, she supported him while he started his own business. But when Sarah, after eight years of being a homemaker and mother of two, voiced her own aspirations to be a writer, he scoffed. "That was not acceptable to me," she says. After the couple divorced, Sarah was left to raise her children with scant support from her ex. "I was financially in such a bad situation," she recalls. "In fact, we ended up with food stamps at one point and there was no way I ever would have done something like that for myself—it was too humiliating—but when you have two kids that aren't getting enough to eat, you do what you need to do. For many years I lived without health insurance."

Her former husband, meanwhile, had failed in his business venture and become an alcoholic. "Rob was completely absent," she says. "When a man gets hit with something, he can walk away. There were plenty of times I was exhausted and wanted to walk away, but you just don't. It's not an option. Women emotionally are a lot stronger than men."

Sarah recently landed a plum job with a good salary, and her career as a writer is thriving. "I don't need a man in my life for finances," she says. "Many of us women are very strong, and we're strong in our careers, we make a good paycheck, we keep our own households, we raise kids by ourselves, we're strong, vibrant women." Wherever Sarah looks, she sees women pulling ahead of men who are unable to keep up—financially, emotionally, professionally. "My boss and my boss's boss are both women," she notes. "At my former job, the president and vice president of the college were women. The mayor of the town I worked in was a woman. The governor of Michigan is a woman. All the major colleges and universities in Michigan are run by women. Everywhere you look women are in positions of power."

Sarah would still like to find a man with whom to share her life, but the trend she sees around her doesn't make her optimistic. "Women are becoming increasingly independent, especially as we get older, around my age—we just don't need men anymore," she says. "We want them on occasion, we're not ready to throw them out entirely, but we don't need them the way that we used to. It's by invitation only, rather than 'Take care of me, support me, make my decisions for me.' That's gone."

"So men have to redefine themselves, too, and learn how to become better partners. I'm not sure they know how—there's a lot of confusing messages out there."

THE HAND THAT ROCKS THE MARKET

In Marilyn Monroe's iconic 1953 version of the song "Diamonds Are a Girl's Best Friend," she sings:

> *The French are glad to die for love*
> *They delight in fighting duels.*
> *But I prefer a man who lives*
> *And gives expensive jewels.*

More than half a century after Monroe immortalized those words in the movie *Gentlemen Prefer Blondes*, diamonds are still a girl's best friend, but the man who "gives expensive jewels" is fading out of the picture. One of the most beguiling examples of how businesses and social norms are being upended by female buying power is the tale of the right-handed rock, and how the $29 billion diamond industry learned to love being ambidextrous. In 2003, responding to a growing pool of women who loved diamonds and could afford to buy them but were still single, the DeBeers diamond company launched a campaign that encouraged a gal to own a diamond even if there wasn't a special guy in her life.

In a series of ads that appeared in *Vogue* and *Vanity Fair*, De-Beers announced: "The left hand rocks the cradle. The right hand rules the world." The ads depicted athletic, self-assured women unabashedly sporting sparklers on their right hand. In deference to single women who still hoped to meet Mr. Right or had willingly postponed marriage, the text on one ad declared: "Your left hand declares your commitment. Your right hand is a declaration of independence. Your left hand lives for love. Your right hand lives for the moment. Your left hand wants to be held. Your right hand wants to be held high. Women of the world, raise your right hand!"

The message flew in the face not just of social convention but of DeBeer's own ad strategy, which up until then had hewn to the romantic ideal of a man using diamonds to express his affection for the woman in his life. DeBeers made a calculated bet that women were perfectly willing to wear a diamond as a symbol of independence from men without closing the door on love and commitment, and it paid off beautifully: within two years, annual sales of right-hand rings had reached $4 million.

Monroe's man—"who lives and gives expensive jewels"—is not only rare, he is practically extinct. Women are not only, in the words of Annie Lennox, "doing it for themselves"—they are also doing it with their sisters, or, if necessary, alone, in their own house, with their own hard-earned money. In business, media, politics, and just about every other realm of contemporary life, women are the force to be reckoned with, seemingly locked in an upward trajectory that men can only watch, mouths agape, their feet hopelessly stuck in some outdated mirage of gender dominance. At the dawn of the twenty-first century, men are not just the weaker sex, they are also fast on their way to becoming poorer, dumber, sicker, lonelier. More marginal, more unnecessary, less loved.

The only thing that could possibly make things worse for men is if they made the mistake of blaming women for their predicament.

The causes of the current male malaise are myriad, but one thing is clear: the solution certainly doesn't lie in shifting responsibility to the opposite sex. It would not just be wrong and false; it would be, well, unmanly. But if men, relatively speaking, have stopped learning, reading, working, and traveling, then where did they go, and what are they doing? Have guys given up the battle? Or are they in denial that they're losing the war? If the world has changed, how—if at all—have men changed with it? Have the lions lost their pride? The irony is that, despite the fact that the gender crusades have never been fiercer, and the gap between men and women never wider, finding the answers to these questions is every bit as important to women as it is to men.

LADIES WHO LAUNCH

When Janet McKinley, a micro-loan philanthropist for Grameen Bank, ran across the Vietnam Women's Union in 1995, she instantly realized that she had come to the right place. She and her husband ended up giving the Union a five-year grant of one million dollars because they understood how, in the right hands, a small amount of money could change the lives of thousands. The investment—often parceled out in amounts of as little as twenty dollars per borrower—was well spent. Within a few years the women had used the cash to start businesses and become leaders in their villages. Some of the women pooled their money to buy a water buffalo, which they would then rent to the men in their village. Others aggregated their captial to build entire factories, which created jobs and secondary businesses that served the entire community.

Founded by Nobel laureate Muhammad Yunus, a professor of economics at Bangladesh's Chittagong University, the Grameen Bank has disbursed more than $5.3 billion to nearly 7 million borrowers who would otherwise have no way of getting a loan. Ninety-six percent of the recipient groups are run by women, most of them living in cultures where previously only men were considered the appropriate beneficiaries of credit. For women in developing countries, less is always more—more than anyone thought possible, more than men are willing or able to do. "There was a woman who started out with a mud hut," McKinley told *The New Yorker*. "When we came back she had a three-room house with a cement floor, and the pigs were in the hut she had stayed in before." Meanwhile, many of the men in the village had dropped out, given up, gone missing.

A similar pattern is emerging in the United States, where businesswomen like Grace Welch, a mother of two who sells round baby-changing pads out of her home in San Francisco, and Camille Young, the founder of BaGua Juice, a health-drink company based in New Jersey, are contributing to a surge in female-owned businesses. The number of woman-owned small firms jumped from 5.4 million in 1997 to 7.7 million in 2006. According to the Center for Women's Business Research, the number of female-owned firms with employees expanded by 28 percent between 1997 and 2004, or three times faster than the average national rate for similar companies. The number of female-owned companies of any size grew twice as fast as all other firms.

Women entrepreneurs are also making gains in industries that were once dominated by men. Between 1980 and 1990, women's share of sole proprietorships in agriculture, forestry, and fishing rose from 10 percent to more than 17 percent. Over the same period, female ownership of companies in transportation, communications, and utilities increased from 6.3 to 14.6 percent. And while women still own only 2 percent of the nation's 19,000 new car and truck dealerships, female enrollment in the National Automobile Dealers Association's Dealer Candidate Academy has jumped from zero to more than 20 percent since the Academy opened in 1979. Seventy-five percent of all Academy graduates become either dealership owners or general managers of dealerships.

Minority women are also gaining ground, outpacing both the overall growth of businesses and those started by minority men. Between 1997 and 2004, the number of woman-owned start-ups grew by 63.9 percent for Hispanics, 69.3 percent for Asians and Native Americans, and 32.5 percent for African-Americans. Women of color, while still lagging behind whites in income and managerial positions, are following in the footsteps of white women, and for many of the same reasons. Black and Hispanic women as a group are more educated than their male counterparts and more likely to be the single head of a household with children. Women are known to be productive employees and effective bosses, and are more likely to support the rise of fellow females, while men tend to regard members of their own gender and ethnic background as competitive threats.

Women are starting to crack the glass ceiling, too.

When Sumner M. Redstone ousted Tom Freston as the chief of Viacom, one of the first calls Redstone and Philippe P. Dauman (Freston's replacement) made was to Judy McGrath, the chairwoman of MTV Networks, a division of Viacom. Their fear was that McGrath, who had spent most of her twenty-five-year career as Freston's protégée, would follow her boss out the door. Instead, McGrath stayed and consolidated her position as one of the most influential women in media.

McGrath is not alone. PepsiCo, Xerox, eBay, ADM, and Kraft Foods were just a few of the major U.S. companies that announced the elevation of female top executives in 2006. In its "50 Most Powerful Women in Business" issue the same year, *Fortune* magazine noted that for the first time the top seven positions on its list were held by female CEOs. Topping the list was

Indra Nooyi, the new CEO of PepsiCo. Indian-born Nooyi, who as CFO and president under Chairman Steve Reinemund helped Pepsi overtake the Coca-Cola Company in market value, is the first woman to hold the position at the company, which is valued at $108 billion. Following Nooyi on the list were Anne Mulcahy, chariman and CEO of Xerox; Meg Whitman, CEO and president of eBay; Pat Woertz, CEO and president of Archer Daniels Midland; and Irene Rosenfeld, CEO of Kraft Foods. Concluded *Fortune*: "There's no question that the power of women in the corporate sphere is rising."

"The most successful people in the world spend 85 percent of their time building and maintaining relationships," says Julia Hubbel, lecturer, corporate trainer, and author of *The Art of Principled Networking*. Based on her research on highly successful leaders and networkers, she teaches "the discrete skills that people need to become 'hubs' in their own right: the ability to make social connections in virtually any social situation, create mutually beneficial relationships, connect clients for business opportunities and more." Are men missing the boat by competing instead of connecting? What will it take for them to keep up with the zeal of their female counterparts? Do they even want to?

THE FIRST GENTLEMAN

At 2:08 p.m. on January 4, 2007, Nancy Pelosi, a Democratic senator from California, transformed American politics by being sworn in as the first female Speaker of the House in U.S. history. She had already broken the gender barrier in politics by becoming the first woman to become House Leader for her party five years earlier. "This is an historic moment," Pelosi said in her first remarks after accepting the Speaker's gavel from Republican John A. Boehmer. "It's an historic moment for the Congress. It's an historic moment for the women of America. It is a moment for which we have waited for over two hundred years."

Less than a month later, Hillary Clinton, the junior senator from New York and the wife of former two-term president Bill Clinton, announced that she was joining the race for the 2008 presidential elections. "I'm in it to win!" proclaimed Mrs. Clinton, the only former First Lady ever elected to the U.S. Senate, or any other national office, for that matter. Mrs. Clinton is not the first woman to run for president in this country, however. In 1972, Shirley Chisholm, the first black woman to serve in Congress, competed for her party's nomination in the Democratic presidential primaries. Chisholm received 151.25 delegate votes before losing the nomination to George McGovern. Twelve years later, Geraldine Ferraro became the first women ever to run on a major party's presidential ticket when Walter F. Mondale tapped her to be his running mate. The crushing defeat of the Mondale-Ferraro ticket was interpreted by some as a sign that the United States was not ready for a woman in high office.

But what about now?

Can a woman be elected president of the United States today? The question is no longer rhetorical.

Mrs. Clinton is not the first woman to run for the nation's top political office, but she is the first one to be taken seriously. Early polls showed her leading in a head-to-head contest with John McCain (50–47 percent) but behind when matched against Rudolph Giuliani (48–50 percent). In a Fox News/Opinion Dynamics poll in February 2007, Clinton led the field when voters were asked who they would "definitely vote for." But she also led in the category of those respondents who said she was the candidate they would "never vote for."

The pressing question at the time: Were those progressives who said the time had come for a woman to lead the nation delusional?

Or were the naysayers ignorant of the inevitable? And was the prospect of a notoriously randy former U.S. president becoming the First
Gentleman in a second Clinton White House a plus or a minus?

Female voters have outnumbered men in every presidential election since 1980.

In 2000, 7.8 million more women than men voted. In 2004,
with 67.3 million women voting, that gap had grown to 8.8 million.
Women are more likely to register to vote than men. They are late
deciders and make up a greater number of undecided and swing voters than men, making up an estimated 60 percent of undecided
likely voters. In 2004, women outvoted men in every ethnic and
racial group—African-American, Latino, Asian/Pacific Islander,
and white. The gender gap will also prove pivotal in 2008. In the
two previous elections, women voted for John Kerry and Al Gore
over George W. Bush by about 10 percentage points. In the 2000
election, 43 percent of women versus 53 percent of men supported
Bush, and 54 percent of women versus 42 percent of men supported
Gore. Four years later, 51 percent of women as compared to 41 percent of men supported Kerry, and 50 percent of men and 39 percent
of women voted for Bush.

When a *USA Today*–Gallop poll asked, "If your party nomi-
nated a generally well-qualified person for president who happened
to be a woman, would you vote for that person?" in 1988, 88 percent answered yes and 11 percent responded no. But at least one
study has found that even women who support feminist causes can
harbor antifemale attitudes that influence their behavior. And a
2007 Gallop poll that asked men and women to match characteristics to the most appropriate of the three leading Democratic
candidates—Clinton, Edwards, or Obama—found that while 66 percent of female respondents thought Clinton to be the "most

qualified to be president," only 44 percent believed she "Has the best chance of beating the Republican nominee in the 2008 presidential election," slightly *less* than the 45 percent of men who agreed when answering the same question.

At the start of the 2008 presidential race, Mrs. Clinton was in many ways the embodiment of American voters' highest hopes and greatest fears, a paradox wrapped in contradictions. Her biggest strengths were also her most damaging weaknesses. Her resourcefulness and ambition made her well equipped for competing with male politicians, but some women still hadn't forgiven her for standing by the Philanderer-in-Chief. Her moderate, pragmatic style of liberalism appealed to the center, but her refusal to apologize for her early votes on authorizing the Iraq war made her vulnerable to charges that she was an opportunist without core principles.

Even the way she dressed rubbed some women the wrong way. Italian designer Donatella Versace made international headlines when she criticized Hillary's habit of wearing conservative, gender-neutral pantsuits. "I can understand [trousers] are comfortable, but she's a woman and she is allowed to show that," Versace told the Germen weekly *Die Zeit*. "She should treat femininity as an opportunity and not try to emulate masculinity in politics."

Even before Barack Obama's unexpected surge put the presumptive Democratic front-runner on the political defensive, Versace's sartorial critique foreshadowed the vague sense that Mrs. Clinton, for all her trailblazing and chutzpah, was somehow out of sync with the modern gal. It may have been a sign that regardless of Mrs. Clinton's dress code or her stance on Iraq, she was already an anachronism, a vestige of the days when women downplayed their sexuality and could succeed only with the support of a man. In fact, Mrs. Clinton's stunning loss to Obama in the South Carolina primary and the string of humbling defeats that followed were at least partly attributable to the heavy-handed campaign antics of her husband. Mrs. Clinton arguably made the double mistake of seeming too dependent on her mate while simultaneously trying too hard to be like him. Meanwhile, Obama was scoring points with both sexes for doing the opposite.

"Hillary was so busy trying to prove that she was one of the boys," wrote Maureen Dowd in the *New York Times*, "getting on the Armed Services Committee, voting to let W. go to war in Iraq, strong-arming supporters and donors, and trying to out-Macho Obama—that she only belatedly realized that many Democratic and independent voters, especially women, were eager to move from hard-power locker-room tactics to a soft-power sewing circle approach."

Did Mrs. Clinton go too far in redefining the image of female politicians, or not far enough? Was her candidacy derailed by a headline-hogging spouse who couldn't tell the difference between auditioning for First Man and running for a third term? What is certain is that neither Hillary Clinton nor Barack Obama nor John McCain—nor any presidential candidate who follows them—will ever even have a shot at the White House without the clout of the female vote.

CHAPTER 3

There's Something Terribly Wrong with Me

(And It Happens to Be You)

In a ubiquitous ad for the Gap, a youngish couple cavort together on a soundstage. As the woman sings, "Anything you can do, I can do better," she pulls off the man's khaki trousers, leaving him in his boxers. The ad ends with the woman jumping into the man's arms, wearing his pants.

They both seem happy about this.

Was there ever any doubt about who wore the pants in the American family? With breathtaking brevity, the commercial sums up the history of the feminist movement—from emancipation, to equality, to beating men at their own game, and, finally, in a psychosexual coup de grâce, taking men's pants, the symbol of their masculine authority, and putting them on themselves. The only false note comes at the end, when the two stare into the camera with big satisfied grins. We can believe that the woman is happy she got his pants, although exactly why she wanted them isn't clear. As for the man, well, maybe he's smiling because he no longer has to worry about "wearing the pants" in the relationship; it's *her* problem now.

It used to be that women took the man and dropped the pants. These days, it seems more and more women are electing to take the pants and drop the man.

Single women now outnumber married women for the first time in American history.

In 2005, married women became a minority, with 51 percent of American women saying that they lived without a spouse, up from 35 percent in 1950 and 49 percent in 2000. In a trend that has far-reaching cultural, political, and economic implications, this statistic coincides with the news that married couples became a minority of all U.S. households the same year.

The surge of single Americans is like an approaching demographic wave that finally crashed onto the beach, and experts are still searching through the flotsam for explanations. The married mainstream is being eroded at both ends of the age spectrum: young women are marrying later or not at all, or electing to cohabit with partners out of wedlock. At the other end, widows are living longer, and many divorced women are choosing not to remarry. In the middle, marriages are breaking down for myriad reasons at an alarming rate.

William Frey, a demographer at the Brookings Institution, sees the numbers as the culmination of post-1960s social trends that have given women greater flexibility and choice in determining how and with whom they live. "For better or worse, women are less dependent on men or the institution of marriage," Frey told the *New York Times*. "Younger women understand this better, and are preparing to live longer parts of their lives alone or with nonmarried partners. For many older boomer and senior women, the institution of marriage did not hold the promise they might have hoped for, growing up in an 'Ozzie and Harriet' era."

Or even in the Ozzy Osbourne era, for that matter. While about 53 percent of men are married or living with a spouse, compared with 49 percent of women, and men tend to remarry sooner than women after divorce, they are also delaying marriage longer than in previous generations. The decline in marriage is particularly steep among the young—between 1950 and 2000 the percentage of women between ages 15 and 24 who were married dropped from 42 percent to 16 percent, and from 82 to 58 percent for 24-to-34-year-olds. Some demographers have dismissed this as merely the result of young people delaying marriage, but a casual survey of young women suggests that something much more funda-mental is going on. While books like *The Feminine Mistake* argue that women should pursue professional careers at all costs because they can't afford to be dependent on men for financial security, many young female professionals already take a career-centric life-style for granted.

"Women are in a *Sex and the City* phenomenon; it's like, 'I don't need a man,'" explains a single thirty-two-year-old woman living in Manhattan. "Women my age are more married to their jobs than they are to a man. They'd rather find a career first, then fall in love. It's this whole mind-set of 'It's okay if I'm single, it's okay if I'm in the office till ten p.m. every night. I have my job, I have my Black-Berry, I don't need a guy.' I think it's everywhere. Most of those cool A-list celebrities are these sexy single girls. And the married celeb-rities, they're not as prominent as the single women."

Young women's take-it-or-leave-it attitude toward marriage is shaping how men view relationships and calculate their own chances of getting married. While most men still aspire to meet the perfect mate, they are coming to grips with the possibility that it may never happen.

Thomas* is a good-looking, affable, thirty-four-year-old instruc-tional software designer in the Washington, D.C., area. Like a lot of men his age, he graduated from college, traveled the world, and eventually settled in a major metropolitan area with an interesting, well-paying job. And, again like a lot of men his age, he is still sin-gle. While he doesn't worry about spending the rest of his life alone, he's well aware that the incentives to get married—for men and women alike—have decreased and continue to drop. The high odds of ending up divorced are a consideration, but he also figures that he can afford to be choosy.

"There are plenty of women that want to get married, but I only want to if it feels really right and makes sense," he says. "It seems that many people think that marriage is their ticket to happiness, but that is not always the case—over half of marriages now end in divorce. As the saying goes, you've got to love yourself before you can love someone else."

Thomas, who shares an apartment with another single man in Washington's trendy Georgetown neighborhood, is one of the "young cosmopolitans" who are driving the Information Age economies of other up-and-coming towns like Austin, Atlanta, and Portland. Like his fellow members of the Creative Class, Thomas is multicultural by choice and affinity, rather than by reason of ethnicity or race. He speaks fluent Spanish and travels frequently to Latin America, where he plans someday to open an eco-travel lodge. Meanwhile, he is enjoying his life as a young man in a happening town. His friends are important to him, and he regularly joins his male pals on multiday road trips to the beach or indie music festivals like Lolla-palooza in Chicago, and Bonnaroo in Tennessee.

Exercising and looking good is important to Thomas, but he thinks hypermasculine bodybuilders are "ridiculous." At the same time he dismisses the "steak-eating, hungry, insensitive, big-truck-driving" image of men in advertising and media as "a bunch of BS." Still, like a lot of guys his age, he shares a passion for technology, good times, alcoholic beverages, and women.

Once in a while, on weekends usually, he visits the bars and clubs of Washington's Dupont Circle, always alert to the possibil-ity of hooking up with an attractive coed or one of the many ambi-tious, smart women who grease the gears of democracy. Images of ambitious, superconfident women don't put him off—nor does the prospect of meeting one—"because a lot of it is a front," he says. "I think they are going for the shock value."

Still, he knows that women are gaining on men. And he feels the contradictory pressure to be sensitive and kind, but also to be tough and successful. He's cognizant of the way women try to improve men, how they regard males as "fixer-uppers," even when guys don't want to be fixed. A lot of men he knows are feeling the same thing. Are they pushing back?

"No, they're more running away than fighting," Thomas says, "like in that Bud Light commercial with the underground 'beer bunker' where guys do nothing all day but watch ball games and drink beer. Women are playing a bigger role, but I think it's a good thing. Change is difficult, though, and some guys will have growing pains and an identity crisis."

But guys aren't supposed to have identity crises. How can they when there are so many people telling them how to be a man? Never mind that those messages are often confusing, contradictory, or demeaning. Anyway, guys know that it's those other men who are insecure. Not them, not yet, anyway, not when they can still dodge all that gender-blender flack, hunker down in the bunker, and knock back another Bud.

HOME ALONE

The long-term predicament of men like Thomas is wryly captured by a recent *New Yorker* cartoon that shows a middle-aged couple standing outside an apartment door. The woman, who is holding the keys, is dressed for business, with a prim, short hairdo and a ladies' suit. She is speaking to her companion, who is bearish and rather slovenly. The caption reads: "I don't want to be alone when I'm old, either, so when we're old let's get back in touch."

The jarring notion of a man waiting by the phone for Ms. Right to call may seem ridiculous to some, but it's no longer far-fetched. If present trends continue, men will soon find themselves in a position that used to be associated with single women. At the very least, they will find out—if they haven't already—what it feels like to be the financially dependent partner in a romantic relationship, assuming they can find a woman who will take them.

While young women are increasingly willing to forgo Mr. Right for Mr. Right Now, it may be partly because they've simply given up on finding a man who meets their expectations. In places like New York City, where more than half of the women have college degrees and the median income of women between the ages of twenty-one and thirty is 17 percent higher than that of men, the women of that age bracket are learning that picking up the dinner check can backfire if their date's self-confidence is as flimsy as his wallet. As women, who already outnumber men, outstrip them in education and single homeownership nationally, the pool of eligible bachelors—or at least the kind of men that women want to marry—will continue to shrink, even as women's expectations continue to rise.

Nicole* was working on her master's degree in journalism in London when she decided to move to the Midwest to live with a man she had met earlier in a New York City bar. In the beginning, her lover was country-style charming and polite, "a blue-collar, hardworking, nice guy." Then things changed. On weekends, Nicole would find herself left alone while her boyfriend went drinking with the boys. When she confronted him, he clammed up. "Out here it's considered not manly to communicate," she says.

When Nicole pressed him to open up to her, his drinking intensified. "It got worse the longer we were together," she recalls. "It was his coping mechanism. It's the only way people here know how to cope. There's no feeling with anything except alcohol. Guys would rather run away or not talk. They think, 'Oh, I'll just not talk, and maybe it'll go away.'"

Even though she's moved on to a guy who seems to respect her, Nicole is resigned to the likelihood that her career will eventually become an issue. "It's a new problem because we have new opportunities now," she says. "On some level a man is going to be threatened by his equal or someone who might be better than him. Whether it's a threat to his education, or, 'Oh, I don't want an equal because that makes me feel less of a man and I want someone who's subordinate to me,' I think it's resentment of being outshined. It's hard for a guy to think, 'Oh, my partner does better than me on almost every level.' Men are not geared up to handle it. They don't know what to do with it."

Nicole thinks that educated East Coast men can be just as bad in a different way. "Anywhere you go it's difficult," she says. "Does an alpha really want another alpha? I've dated the guys with money—you meet someone with money who you think wants his equal, but at the end of the day he really just wants another Barbie."

Even after a storybook courtship and marriage, a sudden rise in a woman's income or education level is more than some husbands can take. Candace*, a thirty-year-old Ph.D. candidate at Texas A&M University, at first got nothing but encouragement and praise from her husband, Ray*, when she announced her intention of earning a doctorate in rhetoric and English composition. But it wasn't long before her spouse became moody and distant. When Ray was offered a contractor's job in Iraq, he jumped on it, even though Candace had recently become pregnant. For months while Ray was away they barely spoke, except for an occasional phone call. Then, one day, he showed up at the airport, drunk. After ranting about her "selfishness," Ray confessed to having numerous affairs while he was overseas. Three days before Christmas, he told her, "I've never loved you! I hate you! I'm leaving you!" As the relationship further deteriorated and the couple veered toward divorce, Ray tried to kill himself, more than once.

In the end, Candace realized that love and compatibility are not the same thing. "Men are intimidated by women who are confident and completely sure of what they want in life," she says. "Ray was obviously resentful of me—that I was successful and he wasn't. It's a new problem, and I'm hoping it doesn't get worse. It's wonderful that women are in the limelight. We need more women out there that show they can do it all, because they can."

Candace is hopeful that men can adjust to women's new empowerment, but she worries that the old stereotypes of masculinity are holding them back. "Men need to take responsibility," she says. "Men that are irritated with women who are in power are not taking responsibility." Still, she admits, "if a man isn't being the breadwinner, somehow, someway, it's going to bug him. Even men today still feel like, 'I'm a man, I gotta work.' I don't think it's accepted to have a man stay home while a woman brings home the bacon."

An article in the June 2004 issue of *Demography* reported that women's adjusted income on average rises by 50 percent if they marry or cohabit, while men's only breaks even. "There's a lot of evidence that suggests that married people are better off than others in a variety of ways, including financially," said Audrey Light, the economist at Ohio State University who conducted the study. "But if you examine the transition from being single to forming a partnership, you find significant economic benefits for women and virtually no benefit for men."

Even so, as more women's incomes rise to the level of their male spouse, Light predicts, the benefits for women could be neutralized or even reversed. Sociologists are still wondering how that will impact gender relations, but it's a safe guess that it won't do much to stem the rising tide of singledom.

Meanwhile, education is increasingly seen as a critical factor in whether men or women marry at all. Census data compiled by the National Marriage Project at Rutgers University shows that college-educated women are more likely to marry, and less likely to divorce, than non-college-educated women. It also found that, unlike in past generations, college-educated men are more likely to seek out a mate of similar educational and economic status. Women with higher incomes and college educations seek out men with

similar *or better* credentials. But as the pool of high-income educated men shrinks, women may increasingly find themselves forced
to settle for less or go it alone.

While well-off men will often date down, well-off women tend to date laterally or date up.

Like a lot of young professional women, Kristin*, a twenty-six-
year-old legal assistant in Atlanta, isn't very keen on compromising on
her career for a man. "Things like the glass ceiling are going away," she
says, but there's a price to pay. "Successful men are intimidated by
successful women. They go for the women that want to be housewives.
They want the ones who stay at home, who have no career or ambition. You can't put two successful, career-driven people together if
you want the nuclear family. It defeats the purpose." Kristin is convinced that things between men and women will get worse before
they get better. "In the future, women will have a lot of motivation to
get what they want—it's that instant satisfaction," she predicts.
"Women are going to get pushier, and that will be the new problem."

For men without college degrees, the prospects of finding a mate
are already much lower than for their educated brethren. Census figures show that 18 percent of men with less than four years of college
have never married, up from about 6 percent a quarter-century ago.
For men between the ages of thirty-five and thirty-nine, the percentage has jumped from 8 to 22 percent. Since 1979, the earnings of men
without a college degree have barely kept steady with inflation, while
women's have grown by 20 percent. Among men who never attended
college, income has dropped by 8 percent while women's has grown
by 12 percent. That trend is likely to gain momentum, thanks to the
projected growth of female-friendly industries, corporate initiatives,
and federally mandated training and networking programs designed
to shrink the disparity between male and female incomes.

Men who delay or avoid marriage tend to cite the same reasons regardless of their educational level—a fear of being changed or controlled, loss of freedom, and the specter of a costly divorce. Yet the increase in the number of men who have never married is steepest among those who have lost their jobs or never finished college. For women, though, holding off on marriage can actually have financial dividends. Christopher Jencks, a professor of social policy at Harvard, points out that, because a woman's income tends to level off and stay there after she has children, the longer a woman waits to marry, the higher her postnuptial salary level is likely to be. It all adds up to the transgenerational shift in female attitudes toward men and marriage that gives that *New Yorker* cartoon its satiric bite.

"Women are saying, 'I'm not ready, I want to work for a while, the guys I hang around with don't make enough money and they don't want a commitment,'" Jencks told the *New York Times*. "It's the same thing a lot of African-American women in poor neighborhoods are saying. But there's the difference that they're having children." Which is possibly one reason why only about 30 percent of black women are living with a spouse, as compared to 49 percent of Hispanic women, 55 percent of non-Hispanic white women, and 60 percent of Asian women.

The marriage-class gap has dire repercussions for men and women who are not in the upper tier. In her book *Marriage and Caste in America*, Kay Hymowitz describes how educated, upper-income men and women tend to see marriage as a first step and platform for the more difficult and expensive goal of raising a family, a luxury that families with two college-level incomes can usually afford. In cultures that regard marriage as the ultimate commitment, cohabitation is more circumstantial than elective. Lower-income couples often approach marriage and family in the reverse order—they are more likely to have children before marriage, a situation that puts undue pressure on relationships, which then often unravel, swelling the numbers of lower-income single-parent families.

The picture darkens even more when one considers that employment among men is slipping across all education and income levels. The *Father Knows Best* image of males as breadwinning patriarchs who genially preside over a tight-knit nuclear clan is being undermined by legions of men of all ages and socioeconomic levels who are divorced, are cohabiting, or are single and working only part-time or not at all.

Today, about 13 percent of all American men between the ages of thirty and fifty-five are out of a job—up from 5 percent in the 1960s.

Meanwhile, the percentage of employed women has been steadily rising. In the mid-1960s, 45 percent of women between the ages of thirty and fifty-four held a job; today that figure stands at 73 percent.

The newly unemployed men range from blue-collar workers who have been laid off in factory closings and are eking out a living on pensions and temp work, to dot-com executives in their thirties and forties who lost their positions when the Internet bubble burst in the 1990s. Some of the men have found themselves lacking the skills to rejoin the Information Age economy, while others have failed to find jobs that they don't consider demeaning or underpaid.

Many make ends meet by drawing on federal programs that were once a short-term bridge to a new job but for a new generation of unemployed have become an end in themselves. Federal disability recipients have swollen to a total of 6.5 million men and women, up from 3 million in 1990. Experts estimate that displaced male workers make up 25 percent of that number. Another 2 million men, arrested during the 1980s and '90s, are now back on the streets, looking for jobs they will probably never get because of their prison records.

Official employment numbers do not tell the whole story, since they don't include men who have stopped looking for work. These missing men live on the fringes of the modern workforce, spending their days reading, going to the gym, or searching the classifieds for jobs that never seem to suit them. The lucky ones have working wives to help pay the bills. But single men who never finished college, or who find themselves unemployed, middle-aged, and alone, will most likely stay that way.

ME TV

There is a woman at a motorized wheelchair and power scooter company in Texas whose professional title is "celebrations assistant." Her job is to shower confetti and praise on her fellow workers. She smiles and tells people they're doing great and passes out more than a hundred festive balloons a week. At the end of a hard day of making other employees feel good about themselves, there's nothing more important to her than a supportive email from her supervisor, because, after all, she's pretty special, too.

Celebrations assistant is a booming occupation. In companies large and small, on the coasts and across the heartland, employers are heaping employee awards, free vacations, and other perks on the people who work for them. Why? Because men and women in their twenties and thirties grew up with near constant praise from their relatives, teachers, and parents—when they stop getting it, they quit.

And those are the secure ones.

The display culture has become the culture of self-aggrandizement.

Time's Person of the Year for 2007 was—who else?—"YOU!" The point was underscored by a silver box on the magazine's cover that reflected the reader's own image. The editors explained that their choice was due to the explosion and mainstreaming of user-generated content—the billions of blogs, podcasts, jpegs, and video files being produced by "ordinary" (i.e., not yet famous) people, generated and edited on their PCs and laptops and distributed via the Internet to other YOU-sers, who then take the content as an excuse to post their own ratings and comments. A few months later, *Wired* invited visitors to its website to upload pictures of themselves. In July, the first five thousand to do so received copies of *Wired* with their own image on the cover under the headline "You Are Here." Again, the editorial premise was the increasing personalization of media and marketing, but the real hook was the illusion that each subscriber was cover-story material. Even the U.S. Postal Service has jumped on the personalization bandwagon: for a fee, yourstamps .com allows people to upload any image—including their own—to a website where the pictures are turned into individualized U.S. postage stamps. It turns out that Andy Warhol's prediction that someday everyone would be famous for fifteen minutes described merely the greenroom for a society that is insatiably and unabashedly obsessed with projecting itself onstage.

During the 1980s, when David Letterman started plucking people from the audience and inviting them to join the show, it became hilariously obvious that it was the context not the content that made TV so mesmerizing. It was like a veil being lifted from the national psyche: if a bucktoothed math instructor from Kansas could leave his seat and join Dave and get the entire studio audience to laugh and applaud, then *anybody* could. You didn't have to be smart or funny or beautiful to be a TV star, you just had to be *there*. In the age of digital media, "there" means anywhere and everywhere, faster than you can say "Look at *me*!"

If Letterman let the self-milking cow out of the broadcast barn, it was MTV's *Real World* that sparked the star-search stampede. Within a couple of years the networks were clogged with reality shows, from *Fear Factor* to *American Idol* to *Queer Eye for the Straight Guy* and *The Swan*. Back in the early '90s, when the phenomenon was just gathering steam, a few television executives predicted that the fad would quickly burn itself out. Today, a series called *The Search for America's Hunkiest Plumber* would not even lift an eyebrow. As Tila Tequila knows, it's only a matter of time before everyone gets their own show.

American society has become a solipsistic circus, and boomers, the postwar generation that rattled the cage of the status quo before becoming it, has transferred its applause addiction to the next generation. For men and women in their twenties and thirties, neediness doesn't end at the office. Along with their work, they bring it home. The same Gen Y- and X-ers who demand recognition from their bosses, expect constant reaffirmation from lovers and spouses. And because they have been told how great they are since they were babies, they are also more likely to distrust the praise they get as adults.

The cumulative effect of so much self-regard is a further erosion of the rules that once defined the mating game. New research shows that while men have always held the lead in self-centeredness, women—here as in just about every other arena—are catching up fast. In a cross-generational study released in 2007, Jean Twenge, a psychology professor at San Diego State University, compared the scores of 16,475 students who took the Standardized Narcissistic Personality Inventory, which asks people to respond to statements like "I think I am a special person." Twenge found that, on average, college student in 2006 were 30 percent more narcissistic than corresponding students in 1982.

"The data show that the narcissism seems to be increasing in both men and women, but the effect seems to be particularly strong in women," Twenge reports. "Even though women are often told to avoid the narcissistic men, it's also excellent advice to tell men to avoid the narcissistic women."

Men still score higher on the Narcissistic Personality Inventory than women, but the difference is much smaller than it was a generation ago. "Men are more narcissistic overall; it's that the change over the generations was more dramatic for women," Twenge explains. "So in 1982, men scored higher on the narcissism inventory than women, and that is still true—men still score higher—but that sex score difference is smaller than it used to be. Basically what has happened is that women have narrowed that gap. If you think about it kind of like the gender gap in pay—that gap has narrowed, and now it's the same thing in narcissism."

Women today are also more assertive than a generation ago. Studies show that the average college woman in 1990 was more assertive than 67 percent of all college women in the 1960s. The change in female assertiveness has been so dramatic that the statistical difference between the assertiveness of men and women no longer exists.

As one might expect, gender parity in narcissism and assertiveness is having a deleterious impact on the ability of men and women to navigate the give-and-take required for successful relationships. Women, for a variety of reasons, are still more likely to hold their partner accountable for their happiness than men do, even as they seem to be setting higher standards for what constitutes an ideal mate. If the man and woman of the house both work, she is likely to bear the brunt of housekeeping and child-rearing responsibilities, a situation that turns her into a tired, resentful spouse. He, on the other hand, has trouble coping with a partner who's often too stressed or exhausted to be as romantic or attentive as he would like. As expectations escalate, marriages are succumbing to centrifugal forces that encourage both sides to dig in their heels.

"One could certainly argue based on research evidence that women's list of what they want in a mate is longer than men's," says Twenge, who is the author of *Generation Me: Why Today's Young Americans Are More Confident, Assertive, Entitled—And More Miserable Than Ever Before*. "That may be for biological evolutionary reasons. Given that, you could make the case that women have become pickier, but you could say the same thing for men, because their narcissism has gone up as well. Obviously, in real life, as opposed to when you're talking about it in the abstract, it's a fine line to walk. On one hand, you don't want to give people the advice that they should marry the first nice person that comes along. On the other hand, people should not be holding out for the perfect woman or the perfect man—and I think that does happen a lot."

But, as Forrest Gump might say, perfect is as perfect does. Twenge has found that female notions of the ideal male often combine the best qualities of two completely divergent types of men. For many modern women, she observes, "a lot of the income expectations are still there—but then on top of that the guy's got to be my soul mate. And so I would agree that there are a lot of women out there that are asking men to be several contradictory things at once. It is pretty amazing how a lot of women in the same breath will say, 'Oh, I want a guy who's great with kids—but he also has to make a six-figure salary.' And, there are some exceptions, obviously, but most people who are making a six-figure salary are also working sixty to eighty hours a week. They're not going to help with the kids because they are not going to be there."

In fact, the very same qualities that some women find attractive in a man when she meets him might be the same things that will ultimately break them apart. "I think a lot of women are preconditioned by biology or society or both to look for the guy who's charming and confident and makes a lot of money and shows that off and is assertive," Twenge says. "And basically, what I've just described is a narcissist, and that's the guy they're going to meet if they hang out at the bar and wait for somebody to hit on them. Yet what a lot of women really want in the long term is the guy who's not narcissistic, who'll care about them, who'll listen when they talk and who will take care of children with them. And for that you're looking for a nonnarcissistic guy."

It doesn't help that men are psychologically conditioned to avoid behaviors traditionally associated with women. To help explain why some men are so resistant to updated definitions of "masculine" behavior, Twenge points to the work of Nancy J. Chodorow, the noted feminist and psychologist. In books like *Femininities, Masculinities, Sexualities*, Chodorow argued that polarized, rigid definitions of male and female behaviors are inherently flawed and are often distorted by the social and cultural baggage of the psychologists themselves, who until recently were almost always male. She also put a Freudian spin on theories about how boys learn to define themselves as men, especially when they spend so much of their childhood in the company of women.

"Chodorow says that because most children are raised primarily by women, and that the adult you have the most contact with happens to be female, girls have an easy time deciding what it's like to be a woman—they just look to Mom," notes Twenge. "But boys, either because Dad is not around at all, or is working all the time, have to define what it means to be male by defining it as 'not female,' and thus they look at the media to define it and they define themselves in opposition to what is female." And so, she explains, "that's where some of the gender hierarchy comes from and, that's also why boys like this stupid stuff, because they don't have realistic picture of what it means to be a man."

So is it any surprise that men get into trouble in a relationship when suddenly they're expected to embody many of the traits they've spent their whole life trying to suppress or eliminate? And who can blame women for losing their patience with guys who are unwilling or unable to do their fair share of what used to be called "women's work"? When both people in the argument have been raised to think they're always right, negotiation and compromise don't stand much of a chance.

Twenge has found that this selfish new breed of Americans, which she has dubbed "Generation Me," are often driven by unrealistic expectations of themselves and those around them. Generation

Me takes longer to finish college, and marries later than any previous generation—at age 27 for men and 25 for women (in 1970, the average ages were 23 and 21, respectively). They expect to have money and buy nice things but also want a meaningful, creative career. They distrust corporations and the government and tend to be politically independent. They get tattoos on their bodies to advertise their individuality, but also want to be taken seriously by their professional peers and superiors. And because they tend to put themselves and their happiness first, they are more likely to delay difficult decisions about their careers, marriage, and children. Once they do commit, their high expectations of how, and by whom, they should be loved means they are much more likely to end up where they started—on their own. The percentage of 15-to-24-year-olds living in one-person households has doubled since 1970, and the number of 25-to-34-year-olds living alone has nearly tripled.

Twenge rejects assertions by journalists and feminist writers who claim that young women are reverting to the stay-at-home status of earlier generations. She says that media interpretations of the 2002 U.S. Census figures that showed a decline in the number of working women with children less than one year old are a misleading spin on distorted facts. She points out that while employment rates for young women have fluctuated between 2 and 3 percent since 2000, the difference is statistically inconclusive at best since employment numbers for men showed the same dip. What's more, the percentage of working women with children in 2003 was at 55 percent, up from close to zero in the 1950s. Finally, steadily growing female enrollment in professional schools and the pressure on families to have two income earners in the household, she says, all suggest that the overall number of working women will hold steady or continue to grow in coming decades.

"These realities suggest we will never go back to stay-at-home moms as the majority of mothers," Twenge writes in *Generation Me*. "These stories continue to get press simply because they make media companies a lot of money. They might be based on flimsy statistics and nonexistent 'trends,' but women will pick up a magazine with an adorable child, dressed in white, who looks longingly up at his mother. Guilt sells magazines, but it won't pay the mortgage, so women's prominence in the workplace is here to stay."

Yet another sign that women's participation in the workforce is irreversible is the increasing importance of work as a component of female identity. Research shows that the correlation between self-esteem and socioeconomic status has increased for women, even as it has decreased for men. "Women's self-esteem is now more strongly linked to their work and education than men's is," Twenge reports. "Work, income, and education, once relatively unimportant to woman's identity, are now even more important to women than to men."

While a growing number of men are willing to help out with household work and child care, the percentage of stay-at-home dads is still relatively minuscule. Between 1998 and 2005, the number of single men adopting foster children more than doubled, to 1,483; yet single men still account for only about 3 percent of all adoptions. Until cultural definitions of masculinity catch up to current economic realities, Twenge sees more turmoil ahead. "There's lots of conflicting things, and guys are being pulled so many different ways, it's hard to tell how things will turn out," she says. "In almost every realm of life, from clothing to jobs, it's considered perfectly fine for girls and women to do male things, but it's not considered fine for males to do female things."

Still, Twenge sees reasons for optimism, particularly among younger men and women. "This is a generation that is very tolerant and is very open-minded about gender," Twenge notes. "I hope what will happen is that gradually there will be more acceptance for men taking on roles that have traditionally been female. That has happened already in some realms. For example, flight attendants were once one-hundred-percent female, and it's still a very small percentage, but more and more men are Mr. Mom and staying home with the kids. And there's really good data that more and more men are taking a more active role in child-rearing. So what I'm hoping is that those trends will continue."

And if they do continue, where will those trends ultimately take us? Twenge thinks part of the answer can be glimpsed in the results of a study in which she gathered 103 samples of 28,920 college students on two questionnaires that measured stereotypical feminine and masculine traits. The "masculine" scale was determined by the degree to which respondents identified with terms like "competitive," "independent," "never give up easily," "self-reliant," "forceful," and "ambitious." Beginning in the 1970s, women scored incrementally higher on the masculine scale with each passing year. By the 1990s, more than 50 percent of the women scored conclusively "masculine," a jump from only 20 percent in the 1970s. The average college woman in the 1990s reported more "masculine" traits than 80 percent of college women in the 1970s.

Today, college women overall score as high as men on masculinity tests, rendering the stereotypical definitions of "masculine" and "feminine" developed in the 1970s essentially meaningless. In the space of three decades, in other words, the traditional psychological distinctions between men and women have virtually disappeared. "The change was so large that by the early 1990s, men's and women's scores on the scale of so-called masculine traits were indistinguishable," Twenge reports. "The generational change in personality had turned the very definition of the scale on its head: clearly these traits were no longer masculine, but simply human."

UNHINGED

The politics of sex and desire in some ways resembles the debate between the theory of evolution and religious creationism. One side anchors its arguments in measurable, quantifiable phenomena—men

and women behave in certain ways because of the size and structure of our brains and bodies, which are in turn part of a biological
imperative that socialization and environment can alter but never
defeat. On the opposite side are those who put their bets on the
ability of man- and womankind to transcend biological fate and
reach for something higher. Rejecting the view of humans as mere
superevolved animals or complex machines, they argue that members of the species Homo sapiens are uniquely capable of understanding the implications of their actions, of judging right and
wrong, and are therefore not just capable but morally required to
remold society—and themselves—into something higher, better,
and, ultimately, more humane.

Are we slaves of chemistry or masters of our own destiny?

Are we helpless before our biological fate, or capable of redeem-
ing ourselves through a transformative act of faith?

The answer is still being debated. We know, for example, that
every fetus begins as a female and changes course only after the Y
chromosome triggers the production of a hormone called SRY,
which not only ensures that the baby's sex will be male but also
masculinizes its brain. We know that the interplay between the
conscious and unconscious aspects of sexual desire are different for
men and women. In most men—straight or gay—visual identifica-
tion of a potential sexual partner triggers a linear progression from
desire to arousal to climax. Women on the other hand have a much
more complex range of responses—climax might be a result of
physical stimulation, emotional connection, or some combination of
both. Sexual attraction, for a woman, might come only after other
psychological factors have initiated interest in a potential mate.
Tests have also shown that women are more likely than men to be
aroused by both heterosexual and homosexual erotica. At the same

time, gay and straight men share a narrower, more single-minded, spectrum of desire, despite the fact that their sexual orientations are inverse.

Are men and women biologically hardwired to act and interact in a predetermined way? Or do they have the free will to choose one way of behaving over another? Are they responsible for their actions, or just cogs in a biochemical matrix that is driven by the prerogatives of genetic reproduction and human evolution? And when neurologists say that gay men's brains are hardwired to respond sexually to other males, are they supporting the notion that homosexuality is part of the natural spectrum of human sexuality, or pinpointing the mechanics of a biological dysfunction?

Human sexuality, in fact, is so complex and varied that any attempt to define it in strictly scientific terms leaves out a huge part of the human experience. In America, Europe, and many other parts of the world, sex is no longer defined by activities link to reproduction, or even marriage. Masturbation, premarital sex, homosexuality, and other behaviors that were once considered taboo and unnatural have become socially acceptable or even desirable. Yet despite a greater understanding and open discussion of human sexuality—or perhaps because of it—the institution of marriage has never seemed more beleaguered or prone to failure. Today, nearly half of all American marriages end in divorce. Thanks in large part to the seismic shifts in gender roles and sexual options, the social, cultural, and legal bonds that tie men and women together have never appeared more tenuous.

The signs of marital disconnect are cropping up in unexpected places. Architects are reporting a sudden jump in the demand for homes with two master bedrooms. According to a survey by the National Association of Home Builders, 60 percent of custom houses will have dual master bedrooms by 2015. And a poll of 9,100 Canadian men found that nearly half had faked an orgasm. The reasons they gave included fatigue, impatience, and lack of desire. *Forbes* magazine announced the arrival of the "office spouse," a platonic partner who supplies the support and companionship of a spouse during working hours. According to a Harris poll, 17 percent of both married and unmarried respondents reported having an office-spouse relationship to help them get through the day.

With modern marriage on the ropes, an entire industry of referees and trainers has jumped into the ring. An endless stream of books and magazines promises to impart the key to togetherness, while "relationship coaches" give couples tips on how to keep the romantic fires burning. Rita De Maria, who dispenses advice for America Online and is the coauthor of *The Seven Stages of Marriage*, doles out "marriage busters" tips like "Put Logic Aside," "Peacekeeping Doesn't Pay," "Quit Nagging," "Stop Stonewalling," and "Ditch Unilateral Decision Making." If this all sounds like an excerpt from the Geneva Convention for prisoners of war, it might be because of a common goal of limiting unnecessary casualties on the battlefield.

Yet not everyone views divorce as necessarily a bad thing. In Chicago, a billboard sponsored by the all-female law firm of Fetman, Garland and Associates, proclaimed: "Life's Short. Get a Divorce." The ad, which featured its message flanked by photos of a muscular male torso and a female with beckoning cleavage in a black lace bra, loomed over a part of Rush Street nicknamed "The Viagra Triangle" because of its proximity to three trendy singles bars in the Windy City's Gold Coast section. The ad was ordered removed by the city for technical reasons less than a week after vocal protests by legal associations and promarriage organizations. But Corri Fetman, who took credit for the concept, made it clear that she was anything but repentant about giving the impression that, for some people at least, divorce is a good thing. She scoffed at suggestions that her ad would contribute to the divorce rate and vowed to forge ahead with more sexy ads plugging her craft. Divorce "promotes happiness," Fetman, a divorcee whose personal trainer's rippled abs appeared in the spot, told ABC News. "It promotes happiness and personal integrity."

But for David Blankenhorn, the author and promarriage crusader, nothing could be more misguided or untrue. As president of the Institute for American Values, Blankenhorn has made a career out of defending marriage and educating people on why he thinks it is possibly the single most important institution in American society. He likens Fetman's divorce ad to cigarette commercials that glamorize their products without mentioning the risks. Most damaging of all, he asserts, is the impression that divorced people are as happy, or even happier, than married people.

"What I'm trying to argue is that the real crisis is a breakdown in the male-female relationship, and the real institution that suffered has been the institution of marriage," Blankenhorn explains. "And we've all suffered, but mostly children. And so the thing to do is to reenvision and renew and reinvigorate the notion that men and women belong together, that's a fine way of life, it's a necessary way of life if we want to bring children into the world. And we need to do much better at it. You know, that's my secret plan to make the world better. I don't really see what the alternative is. People have often told me, 'Well, that's very idealistic, and it's unrealistic, in the sense that, how are you going to do that?' To which my response is, 'What's *your* plan that's more realistic?'"

Blankenhorn's views are grounded in the belief that marriage is both a critical thread in the social fabric and the ideal expression of love between a man and a woman. He also contends that marriage is intrinsically heterosexual and that same-sex marriages and single-parent families are detrimental to children and society because children need a mother and a father. In his lectures, books, and editorials, Blankenhorn, who describes himself as a liberal Democrat, takes pains to explain that he is not antigay per se but is merely defending the American family from cultural forces that threaten to tear it apart.

Marriage is good for kids, Blankenhorn asserts. Families with two daddies, two mommies, or only one parent are not. He scoffs at any solution that does not acknowledge marriage as the only viable and legitimate context for bringing children into the world. "I have never heard anybody suggest anything [else] that has any sense of realism to it," Blankenhorn says. "They say, 'Be nice,' or they talk about child-support enforcement, or mentoring programs . . . it's ridiculous! When you look at the size of the problem, and you look at who's available to do something about the problem . . . The strengthen-the-marital-relationship model may not work either, but at least, let's put it this way, if we were able to lower the divorce rate by ten or fifteen percent, and lower the unwed-child-bearing rate by ten or fifteen percent, that would be a dramatic improvement in child and social well-being. According to almost any measurement—I don't care, any social science, liberal, conservative—everybody would tell you that you would have a fundamentally better society if that happened. Which can't be said of any other of these ideas."

And how does he propose to get people to stop having children out of wedlock? "We just gotta say it's wrong," he says. "'Don't do it, please.' I think we should have much firmer policies on a lot of these matters, but we don't. We're the most libertarian society in the world. You know, in Europe—enlightened, secular Europe—they are much stricter than we are about all these assisted reproductive technologies. So, to me, it's just a disaster. We should just stigmatize it and say it's wrong."

Blankenhorn also takes issue with stereotypical depictions of men as uncaring or incompetent husbands and fathers. "Well, men are not as wired for that as the female typically, but they are wired for it!" he says. "I think men have a need and capacity to love their spouse and love their children. Steven Nock wrote a book called *Marriage in Men's Lives* where he said that men that are estranged from their spouses—I mean, you suffer, you suffer psychologically. Physiologically it's a deprivation. Men are also inclined to promiscuity, and male-male competition over things like women. So, it can go the other way with men, too . . . But there is definitely this template of the pair bonding, and of falling in love, and of wanting to love and nurture your offspring. I mean, it's definitely there. And if society stops caring if people do this or not, the women will probably keep doing it. Because I don't think we've found a way to completely screw up the mother-child bond."

The beginning of the end of marriage, Blankenhorn contends, took place decades ago as a result of various cultural forces. But while no single group is responsible for the crisis, it will take a concerted effort by all involved to reverse the tide. "We just have to say, 'We've taken some wrong turns as a society on this issue, sometimes with good intentions,'" he says. "In the seventies, when the divorce revolution first began, there was an outpouring of literature, from psychologists who said that this would be good for children, because if the happiness of the parent improved by virtue of getting rid of a bad relationship and entering a healthier relationship . . . Some people still think it! It was almost . . . you couldn't pick up a magazine without reading an article about this in the seventies. Now, anyone who has looked at this more than three minutes knows that it's a fundamentally misguided way to think about the problem. We now know as a society that that's a way too sunny way to view the subject."

Blankenhorn's prescription, however well intentioned, runs against a social current that is moving toward more—not fewer—alternatives to traditional notions of marriage and family. To get people to voluntarily abandon the option of divorce and single parenthood, you wouldn't just have to turn back the cultural clock, you'd have to break it and throw it away.

At the same time, recent advances in fields such as neurobiology and anthropological psychology reinforce the view that gender behavior is grounded in chemical and biological imperatives that date back to the origins of the human species. Viewed through this filter, many of the traits that have long been associated with men and women are determined by the chemistry and structure of the Stone Age brain; in other words, men gravitate toward guns and trucks, and women coo when they see infants, not on account of social conditioning but thanks to millions of years of natural selection. Thus, when a man falls for a curvaceous babe with large breasts and an hourglass waist, he is not being a sexist pig, but is actually responding to visual cues that subconsciously indicate the woman is fertile and therefore a good choice for mating and propagating his DNA. And when he forgets his wife's anniversary he is not being an insensitive brute but is merely confirming that men's brains are less able than women's to retain memories and process emotions.

And when his wife asks him for a divorce after thirty years of marriage, it turns out their marriage might well be a casualty of inevitable changes in her brain chemistry during menopause. In her book *The Female Brain*, Louann Brizendine describes the wrenching and—for men, at least—mystifying changes that can come along with the onset of menopause. After decades of successfully playing the dutiful wife, Sylvia was detaching from her children and arguing constantly with her husband, Robert. Hurt and surprised by his wife's sudden outbursts, Robert was still trying to understand what had happened to his once-compatible spouse when Sylvia announced that she was leaving him to go back to school and restart her life.

"Her ratio of testosterone to estrogen was shifting, and her anger pathways were becoming more like a man's," Brizendine writes. "The calming effects of progesterone and oxytocin weren't there to cool off the anger, either. The couple has never learned to process and resolve their disagreements. Now Sylvia confronted Robert with regularity, venting decades of pent-up rage. . . . Studies show that women who are unhappy with their marriages report more negative moods and illnesses during their menopause years. So when the hormonal haze lifts and the children leave home, women often find themselves more unhappy than they could allow themselves to realize before. Often all the unhappiness gets blamed on the husband."

"The dirty little secret of the divorce debate is that two-thirds of all divorces involving children are initiated by mothers," Cathy Young wrote in the *American Spectator*. "To many people, the idea that women are more likely to dump their spouses seems so counterintuitive that they are tempted to look for some alternative explanation. Maybe the wife formally files for divorce, but the husband has already moved out and is living with some floozy. Yet surveys of divorcing couples suggest otherwise. Consistently, at least two-thirds of the time, both spouses agree that the wife wanted to end the marriage—and usually not because of adultery, wife-beating, or other grave offenses, but over such things as "losing a sense of closeness" or "not feeling loved or appreciated."

In *Married but Not Engaged*, a book by the Christian writer Paul Coughlin and his wife, Sandy, the authors decry the tendency of the conservative clergy to treat men as sinners simply because they are male. They report that numerous readers have told them that they stopped going to church on Father's Day because they were tired of hearing themselves described "deadbeats" and being told that they are "insufficient" and "inadequate."

"Many have been shamed in the church for years with the unbiblical idea that women are moral and spiritual, that men are less intrinsically so, simply by being male," they write. "They also have been given the ridiculous message that if there is anything wrong with their marriage, it's up to the man to fix it, and if the problem persists, it's his fault because he has been unable and/or unwilling to be the spiritual leader of his home. One popular Christian counselor claims that in more than thirty years of counseling, he has never seen a marriage problem where the husband didn't bear most if not all of the responsibility!"

Are guys getting a raw deal? Anne and Bill Moir certainly think so.

In their book *Why Men Don't Iron: The Fascinating and Unalterable Differences Between Men and Women*, the Moirs make the case that much of the social reevaluation of the sexes is "heterophobic" and "anti-male," and that it undermines men's psychological and physical health. They argue, for example, that the dietary trend toward products that contain soy and linseed oil, both of which are high in estrogen, are literally feminizing men, and contribute to male afflictions such as low sperm counts.

The Moirs maintain that the reason women do 93 percent of the washing and ironing is less about male sexism than about masculine biology, which makes men better suited to do certain tasks than others. "Remember that a man needs more stimulation than a woman to motivate his brain, and this means that it is much harder for the male to cope with the mundane and the repetitive," they write. "Men get bored more easily. His biology has equipped him with sensation-seeking qualities that build empires and take him to the moon, but also make him shy away from dull tasks. The low serotonin and high dopamine addiction that is so useful at his work can be a disaster in the home because he simply can't concentrate as well as she does.

Domestic chores are simply not exciting enough a challenge to turn on his frontal cortex, and so he is likely to burn the shirt as his mind strays in search of something to relieve his boredom.

"He is the same with any repetitive task except those that stimulate his interest like the maintenance of a car or a boat."

Maybe, but anyone who has ever watched a golf game on television knows that men are just as capable of tedious tasks as women. And how does the Moirs' assertion square with the careful, laborious effort that master craftsmen put into making furniture, or the painstaking calibrations that scientists need to make when building enormous telescopes and subatomic-particle accelerators? It seems at least equally possible that the difference between, say, ironing a shirt and maintaining a sailboat is that men identify with boats because sailing fits into the acceptable cultural definition of what men do. For many guys, polishing the deck of a sailboat is "manly" work, while steaming the wrinkles out of his favorite sailing pants is not.

So, when ambitious, liberated women pair up with men who are allergic to household chores, conflict can ensue. Amanda* was still attending a state university in her native Northern California when she met what she thought was the perfect man. "He was good-looking, witty, naturally smart, a gifted artist, and had a great heart," she recalls. "The problem was he was completely dependent on his mother. She would drive for two hours to visit him at least once a month, if not more, and do his laundry, clean his house, stock his cupboards and fridge, plus she would foot the bill for all of it! He claimed to hate how overbearing she was, and that he wanted her to give him space, etc., but when it came down to it, it was obvious that he wasn't going to actually do any of the things she did for him on his own."

That included, unfortunately, earning enough money to pay for his comfy college lifestyle. "Ultimately, I ended up breaking it off with him. I loved him, of course, but I was so scared of eventually filling the role his mother had made him so dependent on. I never thought that I'd be facing such an issue: breaking up with a guy because his mom treats him like he's twelve and he is ok with that. I mean the man had to learn how to live on his own, how to grow up!"

Amanda is now single and hoping to meet a nice guy who isn't afraid of a washing machine or ironing board. "The scary fact is that more and more I hear of and meet men who have this strange codependent relationship with their moms. Why are these women completely handicapping their sons? They're never going to get grandsons if their sons can't find a mate."

And would those grandchildren be more inclined to iron their own shirts than their mama's-boy dad? Is there a true north of masculinity that overrides social norms, or is biology more malleable than previously thought? What is man's natural nature?

The Moirs blame "eco-feminism" for promoting the idea that men, who run the engines of corporate capitalism and the culture of materialism that they spawned, are chiefly responsible for pollution and the despoiling of the environment. The cultural bias in favor of vegetarianism and farmed foods and against beef, they contend, is a veiled condemnation of anything associated with fundamentally masculine behaviors and needs, including the zinc and protein in red meat that fuels male metabolisms.

"Eco-feminism knows that man is a predator, and that is the trait which condemns him," they write. "Men do look for a certain dominion over nature. That is part of a man's nature, and the root of the distaste for the *real* male is his competitive, striving, aggressive, dominating, demanding and predatory nature. The eco-feminist preference for a male who is purely a social construct is understandable, even if it goes against all that we know about male nature. But a rejection of his *natural* nature in favor of his potentially *social* nature (he can start by becoming a "moral vegetarian" perhaps) is more a matter of hope triumphing over reality. This is not to argue that the male should not on occasion temper his aggression; only to point out that the natural male cannot be got rid of by sweeping him under a social realist carpet woven by feminist-vegetarian communities. By denying the real nature of the male, the eco-feminists deny the real environment."

The Moirs accuse feminists of ignoring male biology and making a "conscious attempt to undermine male identity" as they pursue an agenda of "sexual imperialism." They warn that attempts by women to turn men into versions of themselves will only backfire and lead to frustration on both sides. "Old style sexism meant that a man stamped his view of the world upon women," the Moirs write.

"New-style sexism means that women are imposing their view of the world upon men, and this is the prevailing sexism in the unisex age: the age of the unsexed. Differences—real, substantive and determinable—in the mental worlds of the sexes are denied. It is a genderless dream, a world without sexual conflict in which fathers are mothers. . . . The New Man is a biological fantasy, a fancy of the New Woman."

CHAPTER 4

Mechanical Bulls

L ong before the first shots in the gender wars were fired, a solitary figure rode the plains. He galloped toward the horizon, toward the unknown, in pursuit of his destiny. Behind him was home: wife and family, the Colonies, Europe, the past. Ahead of him was adventure and adversity, untamed landscapes and savage natives, the unexplored future. Rugged and strong, quick on the draw but slow to back down from an argument, he was stoic, fearless, and self-sufficient. Equally adept with a branding iron and a gun, he moved with the herds, slept under the stars, and strummed lonesome ballads by a flickering campfire. He was a man of few words, but he knew how to use them. Sometimes he wore a sheriff's badge, but the law he most represented was moral, personal, absolute. It was easy to know who his enemies were and, when they faced off in the town square at high noon, easy to know who won.

As the front lines of civilization pushed west, so did he, helping to map the wilderness and clear the land for the next wave of settlers. Over time, as the trails became roads and the towns became cities, he grew restless and moved on, repeating the process, until one day he reached the Pacific and the end of the American frontier. Cowboys to this day remain synonymous with the West, the storied magnet and mecca of dogged, rough-riding individualists.

From the Lone Ranger to the Marlboro Man, from John Wayne to Ronald Reagan, the cowboy myth looms large in the American psyche.

Modeled on the Mexican *vaqueros* who were running cattle when the first white settlers arrived in the West, the cowboy became the embodiment of the American spirit: steadfast, fearless, dependable, quintessentially male. By the late nineteenth century, the cowboy was already an endangered species, but the legend has lived on in countless books, TV shows, and movies. A macho archetype that evokes nostalgia for a bygone way of life, the cowboy is as much a state of mind as a state of being.

But while the cowboy image has survived and thrived, real cowboys have not. The summer drought of 1886 and the winter blizzards of '86 and '87 decimated the cattle herds that gave cowboys their raison d'être. The Indian wars were over and the Industrial Revolution was looming. As the trees were felled for houses and the railroad brought people to live in them, the cattle drives dried up and it got harder and harder to find honest work.

By the 1890s, desperate, destitute cowboys had begun stealing the same cows they had once vowed to protect. In *The Cowboy: Representations of Labor in an American Work Culture*, Blake Allmendinger chronicles the alarming rise in cowboy crime. In the Montana State Prison, between 1870 and 1894, the number of convicts who described themselves as cowboys or herdsmen increased by a factor of twenty-four. Between 1892 and 1896 the number of cowboys in the Wyoming prison at Laramie more than tripled. All over the West, displaced ranch hands were using the skills learned on their jobs to bamboozle their old bosses. Those who didn't hang up their spurs or turn to crime were reduced to plying their trade at rodeos and dude ranches, teaching lasso tricks to paying city slickers.

Men stripped of work and dignity have little use for morals, or for the codes of civility that tenderfoots relied on to make their world seem safe. Besides, most of the new jobs were in factories, where a man's time was sliced and measured like a side of beef. Today those jobs are disappearing, too, and ordinary men are once again losing their livelihoods and self-respect. In an age when cowboy swagger has replaced substance and the good guys measure justice by the size of their gun, it's not hard to imagine a suburban desperado loping into the sunset, wondering how things got so dang turned around.

WESTWORLD

John Perry Barlow grew up in the company of cowboys. Born and raised on a windswept spread in Cora, Wyoming (pop. 89), he learned how to be a man from his father, Norman Barlow, a Wyoming state senator, and the men who worked his ranch, the Bar Cross. A former lyricist for the Grateful Dead, Barlow is a cofounder of the Electronic Frontier Foundation, an organization dedicated to protecting First Amendment rights in digital media. Equal parts libertarian evangelist, gentleman rancher, and "new media" soothsayer, he has been on the masthead of *Wired* since its inception and his "Declaration of the Independence of Cyberspace" is posted on thousands of websites.

For Barlow, whose business card carries the brand "Cognitive Dissident," the World Wide Web, at least in its formative days, had the same sense of boundless possibility as the rugged open spaces he knew as a boy.

He also suspected that the Internet's success depended on its ability to foster a sense of community similar to the one that helped people survive in a place where the average temperature in January is zero degrees Fahrenheit.

"It is one of the most macho places in the world, but in the better sense of the word," Barlow says. "We like to say that Sublette County, Wyoming, is where 'the men are men and the women are too.' It's kinda true. It's very demanding physically. It requires you to be able to suffer an awful lot of hard work under extremely austere conditions. It's very cold most of the time and you still have to go and show the character and willingness to stand up to your job, and you have to do it in spite of having to do it in a place that is functionally uninhabitable. It's a place where people's word becomes a matter of life and death. If somebody says they're going to do something and they drop the ball in a place as hostile as that, they could leave you in a life-endangering situation."

On the Bar Cross a man's role was not determined by what he wanted to do, but by what had to be done. Manly virtues like fortitude, integrity, and reliability were not taught; they were necessary components of existence. Barlow, now in his fifties, is bemused by what appears to him as a kind of pandemic of male immaturity. In Wyoming, "I was surrounded by men," Barlow recalls. "The people who worked there and my father and everybody—these were all unmistakably men. Nobody was ever going to think of Norm Barlow as a boy. He had boyish traits, like me. Real men are complex, multidimensional."

And what exactly is the difference between a boy and man? "The difference is, for one thing, it's a kind of gravitas," he opines. "For another, it's character—knowing this is someone you can trust. It's intuition that this other person is somebody whose word is extremely important to him. Integrity is huge."

Maybe it is that constant presence of nature, both beautiful and dangerous, that fostered a sense of responsibility to others, of helping those in need, that still defines the cowboy code. "There's this sort of notion of the insensitivity of men," Barlow says. "But when people would get hurt or sick or something like that in Wyoming, they didn't even have to ask. And people didn't have to make a big fuss about it, they'd just be there, right away. They'd just turn up and they'd be available because that was just part of what one did. And whatever disagreements you might have with the other person were irrelevant, because you felt this sense of interdependency. In a fundamental way your very manhood was on the line if you didn't bring up your side of the equation. I think dignity has a lot to do with it.

"When I was growing up, first of all the culture itself had this incredible pantheon of real men as its cultural icons," Barlow says. "And men of various sorts—whether it was Humphrey Bogart or Gary Cooper or Steve McQueen. Even James Dean, as young as he was, was a man. Jimmy Stewart. Clark Gable. Cary Grant. Due to a variety of different cultural transformations, we forgot, as a society, how to teach manhood."

Barlow has done his share of mentoring over the years, but one young man stands out. In 1977, a mutual friend with ties to the Wyoming Democratic Party gave his number to Jacqueline Kennedy Onassis, who was having trouble finding a suitable summer camp for her son, John F. Kennedy, Jr. "Jackie had first sent John out to a Youth Conservation Corps camp in Yellowstone," Barlow remembers. "Like a good Democrat, that was a predictable thing to do. But she had to do something, he was doing things like pouring glue down the mail chute, which at 40 Fifth Avenue simply wasn't done. He'd just gotten out of Secret Service protection—and most of the adult males in his life had been Secret Service agents, or at least most of the men who were close at hand. So she had sent him out to Yellowstone, and that didn't seem to work at all—for one thing, he was way too vulnerable to the press. And he had nothing in common with the other kids who were there."

Their mutual friend suggested that the Bar Cross was just the kind of place to keep John Jr. out of trouble. "So one night I'm sitting at my desk," Barlow recalls, "and the phone rings and I hear this breathy voice, 'Hi, this is Jacqueline Onassis.' And I said, 'In the entirely unlikely event that this is not some kind of joke, what can I do for you?' And she explained the situation and asked me if I would give John a job working on my ranch for the summer."

Barlow made a point of treating the former president's son like any other ranch hand, including giving him chores like digging postholes and draining sanitation tanks. "He took to it real well," says Barlow. "He didn't brag. He didn't strut. He didn't impose himself. He really was not like other kids in the Kennedy family, and a lot of that has to do with the fact that he was Jackie's son, but it also had to do with the fact that at a critical juncture in his life he picked up a lot of values that were Wyoming-like. He was quiet in that way, and he had that same understated wit, he knew a little bit goes a long way. I thought he just became more himself. I think there were changes, but it was subtle. He hadn't been around a lot of man stuff. He was raised by women. I think it was a factor. The Kennedy family ended up giving me more credit than I think I deserved. He came back from Wyoming so improved in their minds that they ended up sending me several hundred Kennedy cousins, who were quite a bit less promising."

John returned to the Bar Cross several times, and he and Barlow stayed close. When JFK Jr. married Carolyn Bessette in 1996 on Cumberland Island, off the coast of Georgia, Barlow was one of the few non–family members present.

"I was also a person he would call when he wanted to sort stuff out," Barlow says. "He wasn't sure whether he wanted to go to Harvard or Brown, he didn't think he deserved to go to Harvard. And he was admitted anyway and that was something of a shock. He called me up at one point and told me that he'd decided that he could easily be a great man but it would be a more interesting accomplishment to be a good man, and it didn't look like the two were compatible. In the beginning, I was like a father to him of a sort, and then he was like a brother to me, and towards the end, in many respects, he was like a father to me. He was the guy I would turn to when I felt I needed to be more graceful."

A personal sense of grace is on the long list of things that Barlow finds sorely lacking in most of today's young men. He traces the source of the current malaise to the closing of the American frontier, when American men, domesticated and saddled with monotonous factory jobs, lost their natural edge. "The Industrial Revolution was already an emasculation—and a big one," he declares. "When you're working for the man, you are less than a man. At the beginning of the twentieth century, forty-five percent of the American workforce was in agriculture—they were working for themselves. And at the end of the twentieth century, less than two percent were working on agriculture. Big, big shift there."

So, where, as Paula Cole sang in her 1997 hit, have all the cowboys gone?

In Wyoming, where wearing boots and a Stetson hat may or may not be a fashion statement, the buckaroo spirit is part of the local lore, passed on from generation to generation like the proper way to saddle a horse. "Cowboy mythology to a large extent is based on cowboy reality," Barlow observes. "Now, I don't know how much cowboy reality is based on cowboy mythologies. There's been a feedback loop going on all along, at least during my lifetime, between the myth and reality."

Cowgirls were changing, too. Barlow remembers his first encounter with feminism, which came when he went east to attend Wesleyan College in Connecticut and found himself smack in the middle of a gender shootout. "It was ground zero of the feminist movement," he recalls. "I was sympathetic with its fundamental purpose. I didn't want women to feel 'less than'—because women didn't where I came from—and I was kind of appalled at the degree to which they seemed to feel that way in society in general. And, sure, I wanted to fix that, but then immediately women started doing this dreadful thing where they were imitating men at their worst, and making themselves into bad versions of men—violent, angry, humorless, angry men—and I hated that.

"But at the same time I felt, all right, there are aspects of me that are not thoughtful male aspects. And surely I've done things in my time that are exactly the kind of thing that pisses women off. So, you know, I set out early to become kind of a Wyoming equivalent of a sensitive New Age guy. I didn't feel like anybody was trying to take anything away from me. The way I interpreted the feminist movement was that it would help me to be more conscious of what I wanted to be conscious of anyway. There was a positive element. But I had no idea that it was going to become so angry, or so inclined to emasculate."

Even so, the fact that women are coming into their own online—and everywhere else—is no surprise to him. Barlow remembers how, as recently as the late nineties, the Internet was being depicted as yet another male-only club that was hostile to the participation and interests of females. "I said clear back in 1998 that women would have a lot to do about the Web," he recalls. "Everybody was saying this was going to be hard on women, the Internet was going to be unfairly angled toward men, which at that time it was a little, because you still had to be kind of a geek to even get on it. But I said don't look at it now, look at it down the road when the interfaces are more invisible. And then you've got a social environment where authority is based on consensus, and it can't be imposed, you can't rely on force. The whole thing is made out of relationships, and I ask you—who is going to do well in that environment?"

One part of cyberspace where men still have a numerical advantage is YouTube.com and similar video sites. An Ipsos Insight Web traffic report for the *New York Times* showed that 64 percent of all male Internet users polled had watched a video online, as opposed to only 51 percent of females. Helen Smith, a psychologist in Knoxville, Tennessee, who publishes a blog on popular culture and society at drhelen.blogspot.com, cited comments by Debra Aho Williamson, a senior analyst with eMarketer, which issued a similar report, suggesting that men are more visual and use the Internet for relaxation and entertainment, while women are more likely to use the Internet to accomplish tasks and for work.

"Hey, what if men are more visual and want to de-stress on the internet and have a good time watching videos, so what?" asked Smith, in a column titled "Men Just Want to Have Fun." "I think it's great. The reason? If men don't go to therapy (and why should they?) or talk much to their girlfriends or wives (again, why should they if they are not getting any satisfaction from it?) and need a way to connect, laugh, be silly, etc., then maybe the internet offers the perfect way to do that. TV pitches their advertising and shows mainly to women because they know that women control most of the purse strings in the country. The internet is still a bit like the Wild West, where even men can still find sites and blogs that are accepting of masculinity and don't portray men as either buffoons, chauvinists or both. Sure, some of these sites like Blogging Heads TV are still salivating over trying to get female viewers to show how 'progressive' they are, but I say, what's wrong with having guys as viewers and readers? They're an important demographic too."

An important demographic that, as Smith points out, is too often portrayed as populated by villains, fools, or both, a demographic that goes online for "fun" while women get things accomplished, a demographic that uses technology as an escape, a refuge from the stress of negative stereotyping. A demographic that plays games in a digital world where you get hurt but never feel pain, get killed but never really die.

But even before the Internet became the latest realm where men are losing ground to women, they were already on the defensive, caught in the crossfire between a shrinking pool of positive role models, feminist tracts that blamed them for everything that was wrong with the world, and a growing sense of their own expendability. As the social value of men became less obvious, many took cover behind caricatures of their own masculinity. Too often, that insecurity has only served to exacerbate the very behaviors that women find so despicable.

"Part of the problem," says Barlow, "is that there are some other things that we associate with men at their worst which became so dominant in cultural perceptions of manhood they kind of crowded out all the virtues. Lust, the capacity for violence, a capacity for mindless and occasionally dangerous competition. Cruelty. Insensitivity. Arrogance. All of which are qualities which I think you find in broken manhood. When manhood is not properly formed, or is under cultural stress, then you start to get these behaviors, and if you take that list of male liabilities you'll find that they map really well for male behavior in certain oppressed groups. Men who feel themselves to be culturally powerless."

MIND GAMES

Barlow is not alone in noticing the phenomenon of mainstream males behaving in ways that used to be associated with disenfranchaised outsiders. Mahzarin Banaji, a professor of psychology at Harvard University, has observed a pattern in American men that resonates with her own experiences as an immigrant from India. "This is something I've been tracking anecdotally for a number of years," she says. "I am becoming more certain that there's something to this hypothesis that women are, psychologically speaking, immigrants in the world of higher education, and immigrants know that they have to bust their ass. Women are everywhere. You advertise a job for an assistant and it's the women who apply, you ask for volunteers, and it's the women who do. The world as men have known it is changing. What used to come easily, because of the tail wind that carried them faster—isn't blowing quite like it used to."

Based on her experiences with male students at Harvard, Banaji believes she may have found some clues to the future of men in her own past. "There's an interesting parallel here with the ethnic group that I come from in India—the Parsi Zoroastrians, who settled in India around the ninth century. Tanya Luhrmann, an anthropologist, noticed that Parsi women seemed to be more dominant, psychologically and socially stronger as personalities. In trying to make sense of this, she was led to the conjecture that Zoroastrian men, who had identified with the British men who controlled India under British rule, were left emasculated in a new independent India. Whatever the reason, it is true that after Luhrmann pointed this out, I did a mental check of every Zoroastrian family I've known and lo and behold, her hypothesis of female dominance did seem to hold up. And so I just wonder, when one's group's stake in the world drops, if one of the ways in which members of those groups react is by becoming less participatory. They disengage."

The disengagement Banaji talks about can range from a subtle withdrawal to, literally, dropping out—from high school, from the workforce, or from a society that no longer seems to understand or value you. She believes part of the key to this puzzle may lie in research conducted by Stanford University psychologist Claude Steele.

"The concept that Steele uses is 'disidentification,'" Banaji explains. "He talks about it in the context of blacks, when it comes to academic achievement, and women, when it comes to mathematics— and he says that when any group is viewed as not being up to snuff at any skill, its members underperform when they are reminded of their group membership. If I'm a girl, for example, I'm just not going to invest in math. Why do it? There are all these other things I can do in which my group isn't viewed to be weak, less good. In the case of African-Americans, there are role models for the group in the worlds of sports and music and even media, but not in the world of academic achievement. And [Steele] says, 'Look'—he gives his own example, he's an African-American—and he says, 'I was terrible at playing French horn, but it's no great loss when I disidentified with music, not to the world of music or to me.' But when you disidentify with academics, you are basically opting out of life in some major way. It's going to affect everything for the rest of your life; it's not like playing French horn."

Steele's research, which was conducted at the University of Michigan and Stanford during the 1990s, initially emerged from an interest in trying to understand how race might affect the academic performance of African-American college students. But it soon evolved into a general theory of "stereotype threat," meaning that negative assumptions about a person or group can affect their performance regardless of their race or social status. "Everyone experiences stereotype threat," Steele wrote in the *Atlantic Monthly*. "We are all members of some group about which negative stereotypes exist, from white males and Methodists to women and the elderly. And in a situation where one of those stereotypes applies—a man talking to a woman about pay equity, for example, or an aging faculty member trying to remember a number sequence in the middle of a lecture—we know that we may be judged by it."

Stereotype threat has been shown to create stress among those who experience it, particularly if that threat occurs in a realm where they are expected to do well. A male football player, for instance, is likely to feel much more stress in a game against a female football team than, say, in a cooking competition. For the males, losing to women in a cook-off might not matter much, but losing to women in a football game could undermine their identity and sense of self-worth. The higher the stakes, the greater the stress level. To reduce the stress of stereotype threat and to "realign his self-regard," a football player who loses consistently to a female team may learn to care less about football in general. This psychic adjustment, or "disidentification," is a coping device that reduces the pain of failure by lowering the stakes of success. Steele and his colleagues have used this idea to help explain the gap in SAT scores between white and African-American students. But if negative stereotyping was an outgrowth of cultural and environmental cues rather than genetic or racial predisposition, they wondered, could disidentification also be observed—or induced—in groups that were not ordinarily considered victims of discrimination? To find out, Steele and his colleagues told a group of white male math students that they were about to take a test in which Asians usually did better than whites. Another group of white math students were given the same test without being told that Asians usually scored higher. Since white males were not known to have any group inferiority in math, social stereotyping (in this case, the expectation of failure suggested by the researchers) could be the only explanation if the first group of students scored lower than those who were not told that Asians usually did better on the test. "That is just what happened," Steele reported. "Stereotype threat impaired intellectual functioning in a group unlikely to have any sense of group inferiority."

Today, with women gaining on men in almost every arena, and the negative stereotyping of American males approaching a kind of cultural crescendo, men could be starting to exhibit some of the same symptoms of performance stress and disidentification that Steele observed in African-Americans a decade ago.

"So, this is just a hypothesis," Banaji ventures. "But what if what we are thinking about women and math and African-Americans and intellectual pursuits is happening for mainstream men generally? What if they are sensing that the world is changing? And it is changing fast enough that it isn't the world of their fathers, it isn't the world they might have imagined it would be for them. What if the path ahead for them is not so clear? And that's not even taking into account the fact that masculinity, as we've thought about it, is itself a challenged concept. It's being challenged in every way, from who goes off to war, to who brings home more money, to whom you take directions from at work. Sure, the number of women in male-dominated professions is still small, but their numbers are growing in every sphere of achievement, in nearly every profession. The enclaves that were all male are no longer all male. I can imagine that men today are experiencing something that no other men in the past have. And it's a change that is soft enough, slow enough, that it can't be verbalized. It's not easy to name what's different, that the world isn't as easy as it used to be, as convenient as it was expected to be. One of the real, and sad, possibilities is that men may disidentify with hard work. I'm not one to be worrying easily about the shifts in the resources of a privileged group—and I certainly don't mean to imply that I think women control the world's resources!—but I do sense that something is shifting for men. In our thinking about women's rights and women's access to resources, it is important not to lose sight of the fact that men are adjusting to a new world with new power structures and that we ought to be having the conversations to flesh it out, to do research, to prepare for it. The loss of power is never a pretty sight."

But this does set the stage for some pretty interesting research. Banaji, along with fellow psychologists Anthony Greenwald of the University of Washington at Seattle and Brian Nosek at the University of Virginia, is one of the creators of the Implicit Association Test (IAT), a social cognition tool that juxtaposes positive and negative words with other words or images in order to measure automatic, or implicit, feelings and attitudes that might contradict a person's conscious opinions and beliefs. For instance, by measuring the difference in the time it takes for a person to match the word "good" with an old person's face versus the time it takes them to match the same image with the word "bad," and then switching and re-sorting the variables with younger faces, Banaji and her colleagues have shown not just that many younger people harbor an implicit bias toward age but that some older people do, too.

One of the implications of IAT research is that our implicit attitudes are often shaped by environmental factors and by the contexts in which we perceive others and ourselves. In other words, individuals who have absorbed a cultural bias will add it to their automatic assumptions—even when it undermines their own sense of self-worth. Research has also shown that implicit biases can be predictive of behavior; for example, someone with an anti-Asian bias is more likely to discriminate against Asians, or less likely to hire or promote an Asian, all other qualifications being equal.

From the start, Banaji and her colleagues have focused on the ways that implicit attitudes have contributed to discrimination against women and other minority groups in the workplace and in social, civil, and political settings. But now it seems that the IAT, by going beyond the things people will admit or may even be aware of, might yield interesting insights into the psyches of American men. As a Harvard professor, Banaji has noticed a difference in how male and female students regard extracurricular activities or special projects that might give them an edge over their peers, and what she finds has given her pause.

Is it possible that male students at the most elite college in America are beginning to show signs of a syndrome once associated with women and disenfranchised minorities? Banaji, for one, is beginning to think so.

"It's true that my view is slightly biased, in that psychology as a field draws more women than men to it," Banaji notes. "But what I notice is that, even given that base rate—whatever it is, 65 to 35 percent, or whatever that number is—my experience is that when I advertise some kind of opportunity . . . twenty people will show up, and nineteen of them will be women. Or I'll say, 'There's a book I'm writing, and I'm trying to hire somebody who can read these chapters and give me some feedback, I'll pay you a measly eight dollars and fifty cents an hour, so who wants to do it?' I'll get applications and they will be predominantly from women—at rates higher than their numbers in the population of psychology majors."

Are Harvard men simply too arrogant to think that they need to try harder to win? Maybe. But the behavior that Banaji has observed is exactly what one would expect from a gender that has disidentified with excellence and is no longer willing to do whatever it takes to remain academically aggressive, despite—or perhaps because of?—having reached the pinnacle of American education.

In a study titled "Who's in Charge? The Effects of Situational Roles in Automatic Gender Bias," Jennifer A. Richeson of Dartmouth College and Nalini Ambady from Harvard used implicit bias to investigate the degree to which status affected male perceptions of the opposite sex. The researchers enlisted sixty European male and female participants whose automatic gender-related attitudes were assessed in cross-gender interactions where the female participants were given roles whose status was either superior, equal, or inferior to that of the participating males. The results, the authors reported, "revealed that the social roles of the females affected male participants' gender attitudes. Specifically, male participants who anticipated an interaction with a female superior revealed negatively biased evaluative attitudes about women. By contrast, males who expected to interact with a female equal-status partner or subordinate revealed attitudes that were biased in favor of women. This finding highlights the importance of situational factors in the generation of implicit attitudes regarding social groups. Specifically, the present data points to the influence of situational status on males' attitudes regarding women."

In a nutshell, men who interacted with women they perceived as being of equal or lesser status were more likely to show a positive attitude toward women in general. When a woman was perceived as having a higher social status than a man, his impression of women become more negative. The implication is clear: as women's status in American society continues to rise, relations between men and women will continue to erode because men's attitudes toward women will become progressively more negative. But what the study does not measure is the effect that contact with higher-status women has on the men's impression of their own sex. If human males behave anything like monkeys, then the higher the status of females around them rises, the more likely they are to behave like females themselves. *And as their impression of females becomes more negative, so will their opinion of themselves.*

Banaji wonders if men are being hurt by the lingering cultural assumption that they are in charge, an assumption that no longer matches reality and is preventing men from seeing how much ground they have already lost to women—women who are more motivated and driven to succeed because of the historical subjugation of their gender. While Banaji and her colleagues already know that many men and some women share an implicit bias toward females, they have not yet tested how men may implicitly be losing their grip on the male gender-role associations to which they consciously adhere. She is now curious to know if her anecdotal impressions of men at Harvard would be confirmed by an IAT that measured implicit male attitudes toward success, status, and achievement—values that once defined the masculine psyche but may no longer operate as key motivators for young American men.

Banaji suspects that part of the answer may lie in the social context that defines how men and women see themselves. It's possible that men might not have a socially acceptable way to internalize, or even name, what they are collectively feeling. "There's a women's movement that gives a name to the thing they feel," Banaji says. "When you ask women, they say, 'My group is discriminated against.' And men can't say that. And yet there is discrimination against boys. For one thing, we must have valued women more than men, because we didn't used to send them off to war. We're willing to say that men can die for their country, but women can't. And women have been saying, 'No, we want to do that, too.' So I do think that there is a certain way in which the male role is becoming silently redefined, and the women's role is being redefined in a very verbal, public way. Men in the past only knew how to do one thing—and when that thing is taken away, they don't know what to do. There are men who can become dads, of course, but there's that identity thing. They can be quite good parents, if they put effort into it. There are dads like that, but it's not something that they've been trained to do as men."

Conversely, women—like immigrants and minorities—might be exaggerating their behavior to compensate for their sense of being outsiders. Could this partly explain the very unladylike behavior of female soldiers like Megan Ambuhl, Lynndie England, and Sabrina Harman, who shocked the world in 2004 by torturing and humiliating Iraqi prisoners at Abu Ghraib? One could sense a collective shudder in men worldwide: *Is this what women are capable of when they join the ranks of men?* Banaji's explanation is less sinister, but barely more reassuring. "I bet women, just like any immigrant group, feel that they'd better show that they're like the boys," she says. "But I do think that women are just as likely to be bad soldiers as men. And it's because we've internalized it—we're part of that group. We've become the zealots."

That zeal is driving younger women to pull ahead of their male counterparts in the quest for excellence. At the Newton North High School in Newton, Massachusetts, and other educational institutions across the country, it is no longer enough for young women to be as good or better than boys; they are now competing with other girls for whom anything less than academic and athletic perfection is tantamount to failure. Even as these supergirls' parents sometimes worry that their overachieving daughters are flirting with "anorexia of the soul," these young women have no intention of slowing down to let the boys catch up.

Carson Christus, a senior at Bernards High School, in Bedminster, New Jersey, can barely imagine a time when boys were automatically assumed to be better at academics and sports than girls. "It's definitely changing," she says. "I guess that in previous generations it was, like, girls thought they were going to stay home while the guys went out to make all the money. Now it's, like, one of my closest friends at school wants to be the head of a company when she gets older. And that is something you wouldn't have seen ten years ago."

"There's always been guys who wanted to be CEO of some major corporation, but you're definitely seeing that girls are more organized, they're sometimes more studious—the girls just care more," observes Carson Christus. "The guys, like, they just go to school because they have to."

A stellar student and varsity starter on the girls' field hockey team, Christus was granted early admission into Columbia University for the fall of '08. Besides carrying an A-minus average, she was a New Jersey Horse Show Association champion equestrian, a winner of her school's Presidential Fitness Award and Community Service Award, and a member of the choir and the Knitting Club.

Christus thinks that, while girls have definitely advanced, boys' attitudes haven't kept up with the changes around them. "I think it's gotten to the point where girls know that guys aren't better at everything," she says. "I think guys still try to act like they are, but they're almost getting to the point where they have to reassure themselves. Because it's getting true that girls are just as competitive as guys in sports, in school, and in life, I guess. It's a big step for guys because things have been the other way for a long time."

But while the swelling flocks of superachiever girls don't make it any easier for boys to find their footing, young men are losing traction against something that goes way beyond the upward trajectory of the opposite sex. Most of all, men are failing to live up to themselves. "It's not even like falling behind somebody, it's about falling behind yourself—it's a kind of inner abdication," John Perry Barlow laments. "And when they do assert themselves, they assert themselves in this idiotic macho way, like a gangster."

Or, if they don't mind wearing jockstraps in public, they can become Jackasses.

First seen in the MTV series *Jackass*, which premiered in 1999, as well as in two subsequent movies and the spin-off TV shows *Wildboyz* and *Viva La Bam*, Jackass culture blends one dose of skater punk with equal parts Peter Pan–sexuality and an almost primordial delight in the rituals of pranksterism and self-inflicted pain. *Jackass*, which featured Johnny Knoxville and his merry crew getting shot by paintball bullets, setting themselves on fire, and wiping out on skateboards, bicycles, and exploding rockets, touched a nerve in boys of all ages. *Jackass* and its spawn were instant hits because millions of males related to the spectacle of a bunch of guys existing in a kind of perpetual spring break with no apparent goal other than to have some laughs at each other's expense while wearing little or no clothing.

At its best, Jackass culture showed a bunch of nonaggressive men who, by rejecting any and all gender codes, felt free to behave—or misbehave—any damn way they wanted. Like the British "lads" who emerged in Europe in the 1990s, Jackasses simply refused to grow up. But Knoxville and his tattooed tribe brought something special to the mix—a disregard for personal safety that verged on the masochistic. *Viva La Bam*, which centered on Bam Maguera, a rambunctious twenty-something who constantly terrorized and tortured his lovably goofy parents, was the tamest of the bunch. And while *Jackass* ended with a legal disclaimer that warned viewers not to try the stunts they were watching, it was *Wildboyz* that took the Jackass daredevil ethos to the max. The show, which debuted in 2003 and moved to MTV-2 in its third season, followed *Jackass* alumni Steve-O and Chris Pontius as they traipsed around Africa and Asia, repeatedly putting themselves in harm's way—that is, in the way of the local fauna. The boyz, whose on-camera stunts included being stung by Emperor scorpions, nearly attacked by wild jaguars, nipped at by hungry crocodiles, and bitten by black bears, repeatedly risked their lives for the sake of a gag. In one of their most outrageous stunts, Steve-O and Pontius dressed in seal costumes and jumped into open water just feet away from a great white shark.

But why stop there? *Scarred*, a new series from MTV for the 2007 season that focuses on the casualties of stunts gone awry, skips the humor and goes straight to the pain. One episode showed a one-minute clip of Nova Scotia skateboarder Bruce Treby separating his small and large intestines after slipping off a metal railing and smashing into the concrete below. The twenty-one-year-old became an Internet celebrity of sorts after the clip was posted on YouTube and downloaded thousands of times by fans who apparently revel in the visual splendor of physical trauma.

Masochism, narcissism, and vandalism are merging with new media as teenagers, mostly male, use videocams and cell phones to record themselves hurting each other or themselves and then post the clips for all to see on the World Wide Web—knowing that it could result in punishment. This digital exhibitionism is intentionally viral and self-promotional. In Deer Park, New York, five teenagers were arrested for "fence-plowing," which typically involves young men hurling themselves at a wooden fence with enough force to break through it. Authorities speculated that the boys had been influenced by a video clip by twenty-five-year-old Adam Schleich-korn, the self-proclaimed "God-father of fence-plowing," whose fence-plowing video got a 3½-star rating on YouTube and attracted 70,000 viewers.

This pandemic of male self-battery may have a psychological subtext that is directly tied to the crisis in male identity. "Masochism presents a model of a power that can strengthen itself by self-renunciation, that can advance itself by acts of self-denial, even self-mutiliation," Nick Mansfield writes in *Masochism: The Art of Power.* "In this way, power can display all the imagery and rhetoric of subversion without ever being remade. . . . Masochism destabilizes what are represented to be fundamental sexual and cultural investments."

"Gangsters" and "jackasses" both devalue human life, albeit in completely different ways. Gangsters trivialize life by threatening the lives of others; jackasses trivialize life by needlessly jeopardizing their own. Gangsters are boys pretending to be men; jackasses are men pretending to be boys. Behind the shaky façade of fearlessness lurks a sense of heedless risk that can only come from the deep conviction that there isn't much to lose in the first place.

"In the end, being a man means that you take yourself seriously, and you take other people seriously," Barlow says. "When I think of the men that I knew in Sublette County, there was, and continues to be, a kind of fraternity of hugely high regard for those qualities in one another and in that an ability to maintain them. There's a kind of stewardship of character that takes place in the whole society."

But how can men take care of others when they don't even know how to take care of themselves? "Men don't want to take responsibility," Barlow observes." And at the same time you've got men becoming not only vestigial human beings, but if you look at the stuff that they're entertaining themselves with it's all stuff that is trivial. It's refusing life. You escape from reality in a video game. Or you pick up a copy of *Maxim* and read that and fancy yourself to be going out with Christina Aguilera and driving around in a Lamborghini."

Or, if you are Brody Jenner, you plan a whole career around being "the guy who got Nicole Richie to eat." Jenner, who is the

twenty-four-year-old son of Olympic gold-medal-winning decath-
lete Bruce Jenner, has parlayed a brief stint in the short-lived reality
show *Princes of Malibu* (and an impressive batting average with
B-grade TV starlets) into an offer for his own MTV reality series.
Jenner knows that in a celebrity-soaked culture the appearance of
fame is as good as the real thing. He has set his sights on stardom by
simply being, well, *himself.* After all, why go to the trouble of actually doing something when merely existing is enough? Not that
Jenner lacks ambition. Like cowboys and cybernauts, he knew that
the surest way to make a mark is to stake out uncharted terrain. So
when his efforts to leverage his father's athletic accomplishments
didn't click, he and his then best friend and business manager,
Spencer Pratt, cooked up the idea to make him the first man in history to get Nicole Richie to stuff her face. "Such an idea is many
things—perverse, postmodern, proof that apocalypse predictors
shouting nonsense on streetcorners are on to something," David
Amsden wrote in *Details,* "but to Jenner and Pratt, it was a business
plan." True, getting Nicole Richie to pig out is big news. But by being good-looking and sleeping with the right people, Jenner has already turned himself into a marketable commodity. Or, as he puts
it, "To make good TV, you have to have bitches, cars, and money."
And who can blame him, growing up as he did in a culture where
press clips pass for values.

**At a time when their real power is ebbing, men are willing to
make do with the external signs of upward mobility.**

In an age where sex, power, and materialism rule, it's not just
men but masculinity itself that has become commoditized, packaged, and predigested for the masses. Lulled into complacency by
Budweiser ads—and Budweiser itself—most men are all too happy
to gorge on reassuring platitudes and pretend that the mindless vio-

lence and materialism engulfing their gender has nothing to do with them.

"The NASCAR dads feel really threatened," Barlow observes. "They feel so threatened now that they're starting to manifest most of those unempowered male behaviors. Increasingly there's no difference between the NASCAR dads and the dysfunctional ghetto guys. And they're substituting stereotypes of masculinity for reality. Well, real men don't do that. Men are confused about how to be a man, so now there are 'man rules.' We never had rules. Nobody had to tell you."

To illustrate his point, Barlow returns to the cowboy archetype as portrayed by Gary Cooper in the movie *The Virginian*. "There's a scene where there's this kind of bully asshole guy who's just always trying to pick a fight. He's kind of a punk gunslinger type, and he gets into an argument with the Virginian, who's quiet and courtly and a cowboy—he's got all that quiet cowboy courtliness. And the guy calls him a son of a bitch. And the Virginian looks at him for a long time, and finally he says, 'If you want to call me that, smile.' And that's it. He didn't say, 'I'm going to kick your ass for calling me a son of a bitch.' He just made it clear that that was not how he expected people to behave and if that behavior went on, then the shit would hit the fan."

PANDORA'S BOX

For a long time it looked as though quietly brave gents like the Virginian had vanished with the cowboys, never to return. Then, almost a hundred years after the end of the great westward expansion, a man rode a rocket into the stratosphere, marking the first human foray into outer space. Suddenly there was a new place where men could go to test their limits and prove their mettle—the final frontier. At first it seemed as if the American Pioneer was getting a second chance. In Tom Wolfe's *The Right Stuff*, and the movie version that followed, the astronauts were lionized as twentieth-century pioneers, with the grit, courage, and brains to go where no man had ever gone before. It was the dawning of a new age for mankind, but also for men, who now dreamed of building frontier outposts on the moon and beyond. America and the rest of the world swooned, and John Glenn, Neil Armstrong, and their fellow spacemen became international superstars.

But not everyone was ready to turn on the applause machine. For feminist critic Susan Faludi, the entire U.S. space program was just another stop on the long masculine journey to Nowheresville. According to Faludi, the Mercury and Apollo astronaut's trajectory from cosmic explorers to global celebrities is a tragic arc that robbed them of their manhood by making them glorified passengers on a flight that was mostly controlled by computers at Houston's Space Command Center. In her book *Stiffed: The Betrayal of the American Man*, the U.S. space program becomes a metaphor for the cultural emasculation of American men, who had been turned by NASA into feckless fodder for "an ornamental age."

"The astronauts were billed as reincarnations of Daniel Boone, setting out across a new wilderness to inhabit virgin lands," Faludi writes. "But their manifest destiny, it seems, was to travel in media space and open up a new entertainment age. They weren't the first media-destined icons of the western frontier; Sitting Bull and Wild Bill Hickok had performed their last acts as sideshow attractions. But the astronauts heralded a time when the sideshow would as never before supplant the main event."

America's astronauts, in Faludi's view, were doomed even before they lifted off the launchpad. John Glenn and all the rest were, in the beginning at least, willing participants in their own emasculation, not just because they agreed to "pilot" ships that were actually steered by computers, but ultimately, and most egregiously, because they allowed themselves to become *famous*. "The ghost of celebrity had haunted the manned space program from the start," Faludi asserts. "They grinned and waved morning, noon, and night, homecoming queens on a space-age float. . . . The astronauts had gone off to be new frontiersmen, but they had come back as space-age equivalents of pinup girls."

Grown men turned into objects of adoration and public affection? Outrageous! Faludi coyly presents the story of the fallen space angels like an American tragedy, but the subtext is Greek drama, where fallen heroes get exactly what they deserve.

The "sideshow," in Faludi's disdainful calculus, negates the "main event," namely, the fantastically difficult and heroic effort of sending men into outer space and bringing them back. By that logic, aren't the baseball champions who parade down Wall Street after winning the World Series doing a disservice to themselves and their sport? Was Albert Einstein, greeted by noisy crowds in 1921 when he toured the U.S. to give lectures on his Theory of Relativity, a pinup physicist? In that case, aren't the millions of men who post their own pictures on MySpace or stream homemade videos across the Net vying for a chance to be display culture victims, too? After all, what are the Web browser and the media player if not digital windows that frame anything and everything for crass, mindless viewing?

Et tu, YouTube?

But why is it that when men become media "pinup girls" they are demeaned and sacrifice their masculinity; yet when women become construction workers they are empowered and retain their femininity? Faludi has a handy explanation for this one-way definition of gender emancipation. By the end of the twentieth century, she argues, consumer and media culture had trapped both men and women in a world where celebrity was valued over substance, representation mattered more than production, and appearance trumped substance. This was bad for both sexes, Faludi allows, adding: "But at least 'femininity' fit more easily into the new ethic—the sort of femininity that was a continuation of the supposedly feminine 'vanity' to which women had once been relegated. Whether this was the only role women wanted or not—and, as the success of the women's movement made abundantly clear, most didn't—it was still, for women, a familiar role, with familiar rules and perks as well as debits. Women could take consolation in the assurance that, no matter how demeaning their objectification, it at least would not threaten their sexual identity."

In other words, women are free to allow themselves to be objectified through their "supposedly feminine 'vanity,'" and free to reject it as they please. Men, on the other hand, in being forced by the display culture to embrace feminine "vanity," have been stripped of their masculinity.

Men, of course, have an option: they can opt out and simply refuse to play the game. That was the dubious course taken by Buzz Aldrin, the second man to walk on the moon. Overshadowed by a showboating Neil Armstrong, and tired of "selling the moon," Aldrin, according to Faludi, did the only thing a self-respecting rocket jockey could do: he quit the space program. But not before answering endless questions about how it *felt* to walk on the moon drove him, literally, to a nervous breakdown. "At a media appearance a year into the circuit, the how-did-it-feel question came one time too many," Faludi writes. "Aldrin stammered, his throat went dry, and the room swirled, almost as if the feminizing implications of the query had reduced America's new hero to the status of a Victorian lady in need of smelling salts." Aldrin's wife, Joan, came to his rescue, we are told, doing "her best to offer comfort and steered him to the nearest bar."

And they say chivalry is dead!

Faludi's retelling of the Apollo space mission perfectly illustrates the dilemma of the modern American male: if he clings to traditional notions of masculinity, he is derided as a clueless caveman; but the moment he deviates from the masculine norm he is lambasted for being a feminized sissy. It is unseemly, not to say contradictory, for women to be outraged when men say women are becoming masculinized by moving into realms that used to be dominated by men, and then accuse men of being unmanly for doing the opposite.

It didn't start out that way.

The term "feminism" was coined in the 1880s in France as *feminisme*, a combination of the French word for woman, *femme*, plus *-isme*, a reference to the social and political ideologies of socialism and communism, which were also forming at the time and which shared a critical stance toward capitalism and the goal of liberating exploited workers and empowering the oppressed and disenfranchised masses. The Socialists also envisioned an egalitarian society where all forms of discrimination would be abolished and women and men would flourish together as equals. But the early association between feminism and Marxist ideology has turned out to be a mixed blessing. While the moral and economic critique of capitalism articulated by Karl Marx and Fredrick Engels gave feminism intellectual heft, its lingering association in some minds with communism has made it easy for opponents to paint feminists as radical leftists out of touch with the U.S. mainstream.

American feminism found its voice when the Fourteenth and Fifteenth Amendments to the U.S. Constitution granted black men the right to vote. Elizabeth Cady Stanton and Susan B. Anthony were among those who argued that women were entitled to the same legal and political rights as men of any color, particularly the opportunity to participate in the democratic process. This first stage of feminism coincided with the Industrial Revolution, when automated manufacturing jobs and a budding consumer economy were undermining the social strictures of agrarian life. The feminist demand for equal opportunity and civil protections was reinforced by the increased mobility and productivity of the female factory worker, who now had a viable alternative to child rearing and housekeeping as a way to contribute to her family.

During World War II, a shortage of men needed to build weapons for the Allied effort cemented the image of the woman worker, encouraged and epitomized by government-sponsored icons like Rosie the Riveter. A poster from the 1940s showed a short-haired woman in a blue denim shirt flexing her biceps under the slogan "We Can Do It!" In 2000, a Rosie the Riveter memorial dedicated to the 18 million women who, during the war, worked in steel mills, lumber mills, aircraft factories, offices, and hospitals was unveiled in Richmond, California, on the former site of the Kaiser shipyards.

The Sexual Revolution of the 1960s, along with "the pill" and other contraceptive devices, ushered in feminism's second phase. For the first time, sex and reproductive responsibilities were separated and women were free to enjoy intercourse without fear of pregnancy. For some feminists, this also meant that women were free from men, while others argued that men were now held responsible for women's sexual gratification as well as their own. Social activists of both genders called for an egalitarian alternative to bourgeois marriage and strictly defined gender roles. Bras, which once symbolized the self-sufficiency of modern working women, were denounced as psychologically restraining devices and burned.

In the beginning at least, many men had no problem with this. Idealists regarded women's rights as a just cause grounded in basic human rights. The emancipation of the no longer "weaker sex" was part of a social evolution that would liberate men, too, and lay the foundation for a utopian, truly democratic society. Men with less altruistic motives embraced the practical benefits of the new woman—"free love," abortion as an alternative to pregnancy, and a generation of females who no longer saw marriage and motherhood as the only path to personal fulfillment.

The Sexual Revolution did transform sex, marriage, and gender roles forever, but not necessarily in the ways that early enthusiasts might have predicted. For women, freedom from economic reliance on men brought with it a new pressure to find financial security through their own careers, which for some meant delaying or eliminating the option of having a family. Men, for their part, discovered that "free love" wasn't free; in exchange for the possibility of casual, premarital sex, women were released from their obligation to be mothers and housewives—and compliant lovers. As the crusade for women's rights moved from the courtroom to the bedroom, orgasms became a political issue. Radical feminists such as Mary Daly and Marilyn Frye called for a complete separation of the sexes, while others questioned the validity of gender identity itself. Somehow, as idealistic rhetoric became social and political reality, men noticed that equality didn't *feel* all that equal. While liberated males came off as softer, diminished versions of their gender, liberated women were organized, efficient, ambitious, and more than willing—and able—to take men on as equals in every sphere of modern life.

The women's movement proved adept at not just lobbying for women's personal freedom but also at instigating a wide array of social initiatives and protectionist legislation. As feminism's radical fringe became increasingly aggressive and antimale, a broad sociohistorical critique of male dominance emerged. Men were responsible for not just the degradation and enslavement of women, but also for war, famine, and the destruction of the environment. Men who objected or took offense were branded as reactionaries and misogynists. Hemmed in by the polarizing images of preening metrosexuals on one side and chauvinist cavemen on the other, most men found their options narrowing just as women's were expanding.

It was this growing sense of one-sidedness, this blanket demonizing of all things male that turned a famously feminist man into a promale crusader. Warren Farrell, whose 1975 book *The Liberated Man* defined the sensitive male, had made an about-face by the time he wrote a new introduction eighteen years later. "Feminism's shadow was that it only saw men's shadow side," he wrote. "Feminism's deeper shadow was its propensity to sell the theme of woman-as-victim and man-as-perpetrator."

That realization was the impetus for Farrell's *The Myth of Male Power*, his 1993 book that sought to reframe the battle of the sexes as a conflict in which both sides had suffered casualties and both now had to give some ground to broker a just and lasting peace. Farrell soon found that this was a message many feminists did not want to hear. In the introduction to *The Myth of Male Power*, Farrell describes his transition from feminist poster boy to postfeminist pariah.

"For three years I served on the board of directors of the National Organization for Women in New York City," he writes. "As I explained women's perspective to men, I often noticed a woman 'elbow' the man she was with, as if to say, 'See, even an expert says what a jerk you are.' I slowly became good at saying what women wanted to hear. I enjoyed the standing ovations that followed. The fact that my audiences were about ninety percent women and ten percent men (most of whom had been dragged there by the women) only reinforced my assumption that women were enlightened and men were 'Neanderthals.' I secretly loved this perspective—it allowed me to see myself as one of America's Sensitive New Age men. Feminists who asked me, 'How can we clone you?' reinforced that secret pride. And invitations for new engagements following each speech allowed for some financial security. . . . When women criticized men, I called it 'insight.' When men criticized women, I called it 'sexism.' Soon the men were no longer expressing their feelings. Then I criticized the men for not expressing their feelings!"

Farrell decided that the only way to break the gridlock was to give men a place where they felt safe to express themselves. Instead of forcing men to admit their crimes against womanhood, he encouraged them to talk about their deepest concerns and fears. "I heard things I had never heard before—and that forced me to reexamine my own life and motives," he writes. "The combination created a new dilemma. . . . Now when women asked, 'Why are men afraid of commitment?' Or feminists said, 'Men have the power,' my answers incorporated both sexes' perspectives. Almost overnight my standing ovations disintegrated, as did requests for me as a speaker. My financial security was drying up. I would not be honest if I denied that this tempted me to return to being a spokesperson only for women's perspectives. I quickly discovered it took far more internal security to speak on behalf of men than to speak on behalf of women. Or, more accurately, to speak on behalf of both sexes rather than on behalf of only women."

Farrell wasn't alone in trying to rebalance the gender equation. But by the end of the millennium the battle of the sexes had moved, polemically at least, from all-out war to the brink of mutual assured destruction.

If the first casualty of war is the truth—and the need to mobilize the troops against a clear target sometimes takes precedence over fact—then it shouldn't come as a surprise that the factual fodder for the gender wars is too often distorted by exaggerations, errors, and an almost willful disregard of common sense.

"American feminism is currently dominated by a group of women who seek to persuade the public that American women are not the free creatures we think they are," Christina Hoff Sommers writes in her book *Who Stole Feminism? How Women Have Betrayed Women.* "The leaders and theorists of the women's movement believe that our society is best described as a patriarchy, a 'male hegemony,' a 'sex/gender system' in which the dominant gender works to keep women cowering and submissive. The feminists who hold this divisive view of our social and political reality believe we are in a gender war, and they are eager to disseminate stories of atrocity that are designed to alert women to their plight."

The possibility that feminism may have opened a Pandora's box for both sexes was vilified by feminist hardliners as nothing more than a systematic attempt by the male-dominated establishment to revoke the hard-won gains of the women's movement. Likewise, the "postfeminist" women who rejected the feminist label or declared feminism's mission accomplished were just unenlightened dupes of the masculine industrial complex.

"Women's advances and retreats are generally described in military terms: battles won, battles lost, points and gains in territory gained and surrendered," Faludi writes in *Backlash: The Undeclared War Against American Women*. "The metaphor of combat is not without its merits in this context and, clearly, the same sort of martial accounting and vocabulary is already surfacing here. But by imagining the conflict as two battalions neatly arrayed on either side of the line, we miss the entangled nature, the locked embrace, of a "war" between women and the male culture they inhabit. We miss the reactive nature of a backlash, which, by definition, can exist only in response to another force."

True enough, but once the dogs of gender war have been unleashed, it's hard to call them back. As students of military history know, armies have a way of marching ahead with their own momentum, greedy for more territory even after the objective has been attained, even when inevitably, as Faludi correctly points out, both sides are forever transformed by the conflict. Too often the desire to "win" muddies the battleground until victory becomes difficult, if not impossible, to define.

"The sexes are at war," Camille Paglia declares in her collection of essays *Sex, Art, and American Culture*. "Men must struggle for identity against the overwhelming power of their mothers. Women have menstruation to tell them that they are women. Men must do or risk something to be men. Men become masculine only when other men say they are. Having sex with a women is one way a boy becomes a man."

The confrontation that Paglia describes is one in which men are psychological weaklings, ruled first by their mothers and then by the opinions of other men. Never mind that women have at least as much to do with defining masculinity as men do, and that male identity is forged by the intertwining—if sometimes contradictory—desires of both sexes. By invoking a Freudian struggle between sons and mothers, she is dividing men from their feminine selves and denying them the right to define themselves. But her real target is the notion that men are capable of making moral judgments or exercising even the most basic level of self-control.

In a conflict that is being waged on all possible fronts, for Paglia even a college fraternity party is enemy territory. "College men are at their hormonal peak," she writes. "They have just left their mothers and are questing for their male identity. In groups, they are dangerous. A woman going to a fraternity party is walking into Testosterone Flats, full of prickly cacti and blazing guns. If she goes, she should be armed with resolute alertness. She should arrive with girlfriends and leave with them. A girl who lets herself get dead drunk at a fraternity party is a fool. A girl who goes upstairs alone with a brother at a fraternity party is an idiot. Feminists call this 'blaming the victim.' I call it common sense."

The message here is clear: under that swaggering veneer, all young men are hormonally deranged, drooling would-be rapists, and all women are potential targets for animalistic male aggression.

The problem with this scenario is not that women shouldn't be wary and conscious of their surroundings at booze-soaked frat parties, or that rape isn't a reality and a crime. Rather, it's the familiar characterization of men as monomaniacal sex machines who have no control over their urges. The transgressive nature of male sexuality is prejudged and generalized as loathsome and subhuman. Women are deemed guilty only if they fail to see how treacherous and low men are by nature. A person who puts his hand into a lion's lair is stupid because lions are dangerous, unpredictable animals, and some people—members of a higher, if physically weaker species—are smart enough to know better. Paglia's "common sense" suggests that girls shouldn't go upstairs with a brother at a frat party for exactly the same reasons.

The possibility that a coed might lead the way to a frat boy's room because she *wants* to have casual sex, or that a man might be just as nervous and hesitant as the woman, is not even worth mentioning. Never mind that women can be sexually just as predatory or promiscuous as men. There is room for only one victim in a mind-set where men are reflexively typecast as the source of any danger, threat, or problem.

"It is inarguable that men have suppressed women and women's voices in a variety of ways—sometimes forcibly, more often through economic pressure and the planting of self-limiting doubts and fears," David Loftus writes in *Watching Sex.* "But few have noted the silences imposed on men: how men's tenderness, our peaceful side, our vulnerabilities have been ignored, devalued, and systematically bred out of us. We were given language to describe strength in terms of physical achievement, victory in terms of sports and war, manhood in terms of violence; but we did not learn—nor did we often seek—a language to describe strength in terms of patience, victory in terms of conquering fear (of intimacy, for example), manhood in terms of loving a child, a sibling, a parent, a spouse."

CHAPTER 5

Punked

The bond between father and son is primordial, immutable, and mutually transformational. Fatherly guidance not only teaches a boy how to be a man, it also provides the psychic blueprint for how he will see himself and raise his own children. In Cormac McCarthy's harrowing and heartbreaking novel *The Road*, a man and his young son wander through a postapocalyptic wasteland of dead cities and hollow-eyed cannibals. Aware that "the boy was all that stood between him and death," the man devotes his entire existence to protecting his son, foraging for food, using his own body to warm the boy, and fending off crazed attackers with his waning strength. The man is willing to die for his son, who believes that they are "carrying the fire," seeking survival and redemption in a world that has been consumed by a catastrophe of biblical proportions. The only iota of hope in McCarthy's bleak wasteland comes from another man, a man with children of his own, a man who is also willing to carry the fire.

When the trust between fathers and sons is broken, so is the compass that steers them in their relations with other men and women, and society itself. Absent dads leave a void that lasts a lifetime and can never be completely filled. In the growing literature and social awareness of dysfunctional men and boys, the importance of fathers and strong male role models is pervasive and unequivocal. Decades of research have shown a strong correlation between fatherlessness and underperformance. While growing up without a dad is no guarantee of failure, it is one more hurdle for any boy who hopes to become a success.

In their influential book *Raising Cain: Protecting the Emotional Life of Boys*, Dan Kindlon and Michael Thompson point to "compelling new evidence that having a father in the picture, especially an involved one, is good for kids: they tend to be smarter, have better psychological health, do better in school and get better jobs." Kindlon and Thompson cite a study conducted by Northwestern University and the University of Michigan that tracked more than a thousand families over a period of twenty-seven years with the goal of identifying what factors were most influential in determining their chidren's education levels, IQs, occupations, and incomes. "What they found surprised them," write Kindlon and Thompson. "Of the dozens of factors they considered, father attendance at PTA meetings was the most influential in terms of the child's income at age twenty-seven. . . . Children whose fathers were both emotionally close and highly involved had greater educational attainment, and they were less likely to commit delinquent acts, such as vandalism or selling drugs. These influences were not seen for mothers' involvement. This is not because mothers aren't important but because mothers don't differ much in their level of involvement, so when a father is highly involved, it's a big plus."

Yet today the chances of a young man being raised without a dad are greater than ever.

Worldwide, between 10 and 40 percent of children grow up in households where the father is absent.

The continuing drift toward divorce and single parenthood means that an ever larger percentage of the young men in America are being raised without a biological father. According to census figures, the percentage of "traditional" households—i.e., married-couple households with or without their own children—declined from 40 percent of all U.S. households in 1970 to 23 percent in 2003. Over the same period, the proportion of single-mother families grew from 12 to 26 percent, while single-father families grew from 1 to 6 percent. Overall, the odds of an American child growing up with one parent, usually the mother, are now about one in four, or twice as likely as in 1970.

This trend is bad for boys and bad for America. Seventy-five percent of American children raised in a one-parent household will experience poverty before they turn eleven years old, compared to only 20 percent of children with two parents. Males who are raised without the presence and involvement of their fathers are more likely to have emotional or behavioral problems, more likely to commit crimes and engage in drug abuse, more likely to have problems at school or drop out, and are more likely to succumb to low self-esteem, depression, and suicide. A report by the Board on Children, Youth, and Families by the Division of Behavioral and Social Sciences and Education by the National Academy of Sciences concluded that, contrary to popular belief, adolescence is a time when many youths are in particular need of parental guidance. Fathers play critical roles as sounding boards and as archetypes that help shape the moral and emotional development of young men and keep them from drifting into asocial behavior and emotional isolation.

In the most extreme cases, troubled young men will take their own lives. The National Centers for Disease Control and Prevention report that 86 percent of all adolescent suicides are committed by boys. Joan Ryan, a reporter at the *San Francisco Chronicle*, was flabbergasted when she ran across the statistic in a column about a University of California student who shot himself in 2006. "The number floored me, particularly as the mother of a son," Ryan wrote in an article she subsequently penned for the paper. "Yet not a single e-mail, phone call or letter about the column mentioned the striking statistic. It occurred to me that if 86 percent of adolescent suicides were girls, there would be a national commission to find out why. There'd be front page stories and Oprah shows and nonprofit foundations throwing money at sociologists and psychologists to study female self-destruction. My feminist sisters and I would be asking, rightly, 'What's wrong with a culture that drives girls, much more than boys, to take their own lives?' So why aren't we asking what's wrong with a culture that drives boys, much more than girls, to take their own lives?" Ryan notes that the Center for Adolescence at Stanford, a nationally recognized clearinghouse on teen behavior, has no one on its long roster of experts who can speak on the topic. Ditto for the American Association of Suicidology, an organization dedicated to suicide prevention since 1968. She worries that the higher survival rate for girls who attempt suicide is at least partly a result of behavioral codes of masculinity that discourage men from discussing their problems for fear that it will be interpreted as a sign of weakness. She argues, correctly, that boys haven't been given the same psychological and social latitude as girls, and that, while the influence of mothers is important, diligence from dads is absolutely essential.

"Just as we enlisted fathers to empower their daughters, we need them now to empower their sons," Ryan writes. "We mothers can tell our sons to talk about their feelings, to teach them the signs of depression, to say it's ok to ask for help. But they learn how to be men from their fathers."

As the magnitude of America's masculine emergency sinks in, men and women are mobilizing on a number of fronts. Mothers, sisters, and wives are beginning to discern a pattern of neglect and discrimination that threatens the men in their lives and the next generation of boyfriends, husbands, brothers, and sons. Concerned fathers are realizing that just being there and playing catch on Saturdays isn't enough anymore. A grassroots consortium of parents, community leaders, and men, united by their conviction of a looming catastrophe, is making use of the media to amplify their message of awareness and action. They are writers, educators, community leaders, and clergy. They are male and female, young and old, straight and gay. And just like the men who are at risk, they transcend race, ethnicity, and socioeconomic class.

For men like Glenn Sacks, fatherhood has become nothing less than an activist obligation, a call to arms, his weapons being TV, print, the Internet, and the weight of public opinion. In his TV, radio, and public appearances, Sacks focuses on what he regards as a systemic bias against men and boys that ranges from negative depictions in media to the way that fathers are stigmatized and marginalized in the aftermath of divorce. "If there are two sexes, why is there only one kind of sexism?" asks Sacks, a divorced father of two and a former public school teacher who claims a website readership of 5 million. On his nationally syndicated radio show, *His Side*, Sacks takes on gender and family issues from "an unabashedly male point of view." Sacks, who calls himself a "defender of the much maligned American male," opens his show pledging to mobilize men against the "unfair attacks and insulting stereotypes that we constantly endure."

A major sore point for Sacks is ads that play up the pejorative image of men as clueless, helpless, or hopeless, undermining their credibility as people and as parents. In 2004, he launched a campaign against a Verizon commercial called "Homework," in which a bumbling father who tries to help his small daughter with homework is treated with contempt by both the girl and her mother. "The thing that really pissed off my readers about it is the way the father was being humiliated in front of his daughter," he recalls. "It's the kind of thing that happens with divorce, where the father is maligned to the kids, et cetera. But anyway, it really got people pissed, and we did a campaign about it." After receiving hundreds of letters and a drumbeat of negative publicity, Verizon yanked the ad. "It struck a chord with these people," Sacks says. "They're just tired of seeing men always portrayed as idiots and clowns, particularly fathers being portrayed as idiots with their children." In 2007, Sacks fought to prevent Arnold Worldwide, an agency he accuses of creating antimale ads "that make men look stupid," from getting a $150 million contract for Volvo. Arnold's previous ads for Fidelity Investments included "Ping Pong," in which "a father plays ping-pong with his eleven-year-old daughter, beats her, and goes into a mocking, in-your-face celebration as his daughter has the 'my dad is an idiot' expression on her face"; and another, called "Kid's Toy," which depicts a man "who makes a fool of himself playing with a kid's toy in a doctor's waiting room as a little girl and two women watch him with contempt." Arnold got the Volvo account anyway, but Sacks reports that Volvo executives called to assure him that their new ads would not be demeaning to males.

Sacks is adamant about the destructive effects on boys who are raised without fathers. "You know, teen drug abuse, school dropouts, juvenile crime, and teen pregnancy—the rates, even if you control for race and for socioeconomic factors, they're highly correlated with fatherlessness," he says. "And then there are a lot of studies which have shown that fatherlessness is the number-one predictor of those pathologies, which means that you could have a middle-class kid without a dad and he's in more danger than a lower-class kid with a dad."

While agreeing that the increasing number of kids growing up without their dads is a serious problem, Sacks takes issue with the accepted wisdom that it's always the man's choice. "There's this assumption that people make that if dad's not there it's because dad doesn't want to be there, and sometimes that's true, but sometimes dad's not there because mom doesn't want him to be there," Sacks says. "The vast majority of divorces are initiated by women, particularly the ones that have kids involved, and some men are abusive, although there are women who are abusive, too, and we don't really talk about that. A lot of times it's the woman more often than the man who's initiating the breakup of the marriage, and then once the marriage breaks up, if she doesn't want him to continue to see the children, a lot of times it's very difficult for him to have a meaningful role in their lives."

Once a couple has split, Sacks contends, the legal system is skewed against fathers maintaining a close relationship with their children. "The courts don't enforce visitation orders very well. They do it very indifferently, and that's even if you can get a lawyer and get your way into court," he says. "The standard custody arrangement gives dad only a few days a month with his kids, a situation where you can't really be an effective parent. False allegations are a big problem, false allegations to domestic violence, to a lesser degree to child sexual abuse . . . Certainly there are men who beat their wives or who molest their children, but false allegations are a huge problem, and those are separating a lot of fathers from their children. You know, I get letters from guys all the time, all day long, who are trying to be fathers to their kids but they aren't allowed to! Somehow nobody ever talks about them."

Sacks blames a social predisposition to treat men as unworthy parents, betrayers and incorrigible philanderers who have no interest in maintaining close ties to their children. "In my view, the feminists did a lot of good things during the sixties and seventies, and since then they've done some good things, and I think they still occasionally do good things, but I think that they've also jumped the rails, and a lot of the stuff they do, particularly in family law and domestic violence, a lot of the stuff they do is very destructive and unfair," he says. "I think that in a lot of ways it's a betrayal, because in the seventies, the feminist thing was: women are going to have their careers, and men are going to spend more time at home, and men are going to have more time with the children, and men will have the time to be more involved fathers because they'll no longer have the burden of supporting the family themselves. And now, whenever there's any kind of legislative attempt to try to make it so that fathers can have more time with their children after divorce, or fathers can have joint custody after divorce or fathers could have shared parenting after divorce—the feminists, all the time, right down the line, they fight it like crazy! And, to me, that's just a total betrayal."

There is ample evidence that men are capable of being terrific parents. Each year in the United States more than 100 million Father's Day cards are bought and delivered to 66 million dads. But few know that Father's Day was originated by Sonora Dodd, as a way to honor her father, the Civil War veteran Henry Jackson Smart, who had made great sacrifices to raise his daughter after becoming a widower. In order to give all Americans a way to show love and respect for their dads, Calvin Coolidge made Father's Day a national holiday in 1924.

Fifty-three years later, dutiful dads, and probably more than a few single moms, were turning out in droves to buy a copy of *The Dangerous Book for Boys*, a compendium and handbook of adolescent male pursuits that contains instructions on how to make a paper airplane, hunt and cook a rabbit, and play Texas hold-'em poker, among other traditionally masculine must-knows. Within months of its 2007 publication, the book had sold half a million copies and was on track for an estimated total circulation of 4 million. By neatly packaging the knowledge that was once considered purely masculine, passed from father to son, man to man, the book was meant to tap boomer dad nostalgia for their own presumably idyllic childhoods. In a time of hyperviolent video games and nonstop Instant Messaging, the marketing reasoning goes, a book like this evokes a gentler, more innocent and playful kind of boyhood. It also, on a more subliminal level, conjures a bygone era when there was such a thing as male-only activities. Needless to say, *A Daring Book for Girls*, with chapters that discuss "Five karate moves every girl should know," was already headed to bookstores. The intended target audience of *The Dangerous Book for Boys* was dads, who, presumably, would buy the book, sit down with their sons, and teach them what it used to be like to be a man. Instead, thousands of copies are being given directly to thirteen-year-olds, who are, inadvertently, receiving the message that the way to become a man today is something you figure out from a book.

In certain circles, fatherhood has become fashion chic. *GQ* has identified six different "dad styles":

- Thirty-six-Holes-a-Weekend Dad (Hermès)
- Tribeca Dad (Varvatos)
- Intellectually Superior Dad (Ivy League sweatshirt)
- Hipster Dad (CBGB T-shirt)
- Sexless Dad (Crocs with socks)
- Capitulation Dad (wife's bathrobe)

Celebrity papas pose proudly with their broods, and a study by the University of Maryland found that between 1965 and 2003 the average number of hours dads spent on child care increased from 2.5 hours to 7 hours a week.

Sacks finds it grossly unfair that the very men who are trying the hardest to break old stereotypes of male behavior are the ones being punished by a system that discriminates against divorced dads. "The feminists told us they wanted us to be more-involved fathers, and that that was what was good for us, and for the kids and for women and whatever," he says. "And a lot of us guys have done it, including me: I have been the primary caregiver for my kids for the last nine years. And then the moment you get divorced, though you want to be able to continue parenting your children, the feminists do everything they can to put roadblocks in your way. And I just think it's a terrible thing."

BLOOD BROTHERS

The streets of Harlem, U.S.A., are teeming with men. They are all ages and races, but mostly they are young and black. Some saunter past the chain stores, shuttered buildings, and hip-hop boutiques, joking and laughing with their posse of friends; others slouch in doorways, speaking in low voices to get the attention of the ladies. But most walk alone. They patrol the sidewalks warily, watching everything from some interior distance, baseball caps and hoodies pulled down over their faces, hiding in plain sight.

Harlem is not known as a place where people go to look for hope, but that's exactly what I found on the corner of Martin Luther King Boulevard and Madison Avenue.

I was there to meet Geoffrey Canada, the founder, president, and CEO of the Harlem Children's Zone. Housed in a tidy brick-and-glass six-story building, the HCZ offers smart-parenting classes, a K-through-12 charter school called the Promise Academy, and tutoring, mentoring, and antiviolence counseling. Canada is courted by corporate chieftains and national politicians and has been profiled by *60 Minutes, CBS This Morning, NPR,* and *Nightline,* not because he is engaging and sincere—which he certainly is—but because of his single-minded determination to prove that even ghetto youths can flourish and grow into successful, fulfilled human beings.

Founded in 1970, Harlem Children's Zone, Inc., is a pioneering nonprofit, community-based organization that works to enhance the quality of life for children and families in some of New York City's most economically depressed neighborhoods. Canada's formula is subversively simple: designate a sixty-block area as a "Children's Zone," then rally local civic leaders, corporate sponsors, and an army of volunteer professionals in health, education, and social issues to collectively cultivate the growth and well-being of every child in the Zone, from birth to adulthood. HCZ's centers serve more than 13,000 children and adults, including over 9,500 at-risk children with an emphasis, as the mission statement on its website explains, "not just on education, social service and recreation, but on rebuilding the very fabric of community life."

Canada, who grew up in the South Bronx, is also the author of *Fist Stick Knife Gun: A Personal History of Violence in America* and *Reaching Up for Manhood: Transforming the Lives of Boys in America.* Tall, lean, and fit for fifty-five, with a shaved head and graying goatee, he combines the brainy intensity of a college professor with the polished aplomb of a career diplomat.

Canada has no doubt that men are in a crisis, and that the problem cuts across race, geography, and socioeconomic class. It concerns him that young American males are increasingly raised without a man in the house. He has witnessed at close range how the lack of male role models—men who can relate to and rein in a young man's wilder impulses—can have dire consequences for boys and their communities. Same-sex mentoring, he says, is both essential and irreplaceable when it comes to setting boundaries for young males.

"It is my belief that if you had a society where fathers ended up being the primary parent in the family, and mothers were disappearing from the household, we might have a problem with girls in America," he says. "We might suddenly find out that men really couldn't help girls make the transformation into women. I am convinced that while it's certainly not impossible, it's very, very difficult for women to help boys, who are vulnerable to a lot of pressures on them to act in some very old, stereotypical ways when it comes to violence, and drugs, and alcohol, and sex. The message is constant, it is very negative, and it is very powerfully constructed. I think it is very difficult for a woman to help vulnerable boys make that transition into manhood."

Canada worries that much of contemporary youth culture is only making matters worse. Music, which once provided an uplifting counterweight to the grim realities of urban life, has become an amplified feedback loop of anger and despair. Rap and hip-hop, which have huge appeal for young people of all races and classes, have repackaged promiscuity and materialism as components of personal fulfillment. Too many rock and rap videos and song lyrics celebrate contempt for authority and kowtow to the twin gods of bling and booty.

"I think this culture is very toxic for men," Canada says. "I just think it's the worst for guys who are lost. Music has always showed African-Americans the light. During slavery times, people sang 'all your days are going to get better.' In the civil rights struggle there was always 'we shall overcome' . . . Stevie Wonder, James Brown . . . The music said to folks, 'Here's a way, hang in there.' This is something totally different. It points the way to darkness. It really does. I was young when rock and roll first started. It got to be a pretty big deal, but there were always other really strong musical forces at the same time. This stuff has really eclipsed everything. And I think this message goes much further, out beyond the African-American community."

But most damaging of all is the lack of images that might guide young men away from caricature and toward character. In both TV and film, the depiction of masculinity is one that emphasizes the harsher, meaner dimensions of manhood. From the broads-and-booze mentality of SPIKE TV to the ritualized bloodletting of movies like *American Gangster*, men are constantly being told that sex and violence are the only masculine behaviors that count.

"I just think these kids get lost in a series of images and messages which suggest to them that men are this tough, hardened, cold, exploitative kind of folk," Canada observes. "And if you never see a man as loving and caring and faithful, as someone who nurtures you, it's not easy to figure that stuff out on your own later. I think men have lost their roles. It used to be where it was clear it was about having a job and providing for your family. I think men struggled—we maybe weren't the most enlightened folk, but at least we knew who we should be. I think that's much harder to know now. The communities I work in, where men don't make as much money as women, where they're not employed as often as women are . . . You begin to say, 'Well, if I'm not the provider, if I can't afford the apartment, I can't pay the rent, then I'm not even the protector in that sense.'"

If the role of provider and protector is out of reach, then men will turn to areas where they still have an advantage, even if pursuing that image is ultimately self-defeating and self-destructive. "There's a definition out there that others have created," says Canada. "This whole exaggeration of what it means to be a man—I think it's sort of like a virus that infects our boys when they are very young. And you throw in that very volatile mixture of handguns, drug sales, sexual bravado, and you've got a mess. And that's a lot of what I see."

In his award-winning documentry *I Am a Man: Black Masculinity in America*, the director, "antisexist activist," and former Northeastern University quarterback Byron Hurt examines how slavery, sexism, and the threat of violence have shaped African-American notions of manhood. In interviews with black men and women in more than fifteen cities, Hurt illuminates the insecurity that drives ghetto gangster bravado. "It's about the storm we feel inside," Hurt explains in a videoclip that appears on his own website as well as on YouTube. "One of the things that people have done in every form of slavery," notes former Atlanta mayor Andrew Young, "is to rob the male of his masculinity." Because black men had to "earn their masculinity," as one interviewee puts it, being a man, being cool, has become an ultra-important component of black male identity. Their aggression toward women is a way of unshackling themselves from a matriarchal legacy that undermines their self-esteem. And as men of every race and socioeconomic level are forced to "earn their masculinity," they, too, have become obsessed with proving their manhood.

There is a moment in the development of young men when they reflexively test their powers. They will push against parents and society, and if there is no one in their lives strong enough to push back, they will define themselves in accordance with the cultural messages that surround them. "I see a lot of thirteen-year-olds who are bigger than their parents, their mother, and they are not scared physically anymore," Canada says. "If you have lots of great skills, you can still keep that kid under your control. But here you have a kid that has a candy store open for them that's all filled with bad stuff. And he's got this five-foot-three person telling him that he can't go in the candy store. And he thinks, 'You know what? I'm going to visit that candy store, I'm not going to get stuck here'— *totally different* than if he's got that male figure being there."

What's missing in the hyperaggressive archetypes of pop-culture masculinity is a definition of manhood that says it's at least as manly to be considerate, to care about your family and your community, to show vulnerability and compassion. "I think what happens," says Canada, "is that our boys have begun to think that being a man has all to do with whether or not you're tough and hard, and cold, and maybe even heartless, and nothing to do with what a man really does when he raises his family: the sacrifice, the love, the concern, the nurturing and all of that sort of stuff. I think it's been a problem for a long time. I think the problem is clearer in groups like African-Americans, but I think it's really becoming an American problem. You see it on your campuses across America: the ones who are succeeding, they're mostly all girls. You look and see who's really in trouble and you keep seeing guys, guys, guys."

Canada likens the state of many young urban males to a kind of "post-traumatic stress," in which they are dealing with the constant threat of poverty and isolation and physical violence, torn between irreconcilable definitions of being a man.

"You get a sort of ripe environment for this set of contradictory values that have nothing to do with family, success, health," he says. "All this stuff ends up killing men quicker, they destroy men's emotional equilibrium."

"This exaggerated sort of testosterone-fueled image that men have of themselves—no one can live up to those kinds of stereotypes."

Part of the problem, Canada maintains, is that men have been left behind in the evolution of the sexes. As socioeconomic conditions have changed, women have redefined themselves. Men, meanwhile, are still clinging to outdated, unsustainable notions of manhood. "There has not been a redefinition of masculinity in any conscious way," Canada affirms. "We have redefined women's rights, there has been a very conscious redefinition. Women can be all of these things now. Growing up, little girls are told, 'Of course you can be a scientist, an astronaut, you want to play professional basketball, golf . . .' So we have begun to redefine what women can be. But we have not redefined men at all. We have nothing to say to these very vulnerable populations. I'm talking about the population I know well, which are these poor, inner-city kids. Instead of people opening up the definitions of what they can be, they have been so narrowly defined . . . You can be a brawler, or you are going to hustle. If you decide that you want to be a student, you are going to get ridiculed, beaten down, harassed, intimidated, robbed. So you get one group that is opening up the definition of womanhood. 'Look,' society is telling them, 'these are your choices: don't worry, if you don't want to wear dresses, you don't have to wear dresses, you can go out and wear pants and play basketball and that's cool, people can't say anything about you.' It's not that way for guys. Homophobia is bigger than it's ever been before. You are in such a tight box."

Canada's experiences with inner-city youths has taught him that the key to change lies in motivating boys to be better versions of themselves, something that they can only learn from other males—men that they look up to and respect, men who can show them an alternative version of themselves and help them achieve it. It starts with telling young men that they matter. "I think the issue is that we have created a belief structure in this country that says that men are irrelevant," Canada says. "If you want to get a sense of the currency out there, you just think back to the Million Man March, think about what that tapped into. It was the first time that this group had heard anyone express concern about them as a group that needed help. And I will tell you, both men and women responded to the fact that guys need help! 'My husband, my brother!' Well, that's a moment that's passed; and the incarceration cycle doesn't help the situation. But one way we can begin is with early, early intervention. I know that you can spot these boys who are going to be in trouble by the third and fourth grade. And we know—when you see the percentages that come from these communities, no one is ever surprised."

Canada thinks it might be high time for a Million Man March for American men of *all* stripes, of *all* colors. The disengagement and disillusionment of young men can't be healed or averted by suppressing their natural urges, but it might be possible to channel their male energy in ways that appeal to their sense of masculine pride. "We need today's equivalent of the Boy Scouts," Canada says. "When I was growing up, nobody wanted to be a Boy Scout because we thought that was corny. But they had the Sea Cadets—everybody wanted to put on those uniforms, and walk around, and, you know, well, it seemed like such a male thing, you could get a uniform and play soldier. I don't know that it's got to be military. Martial arts are another way it could go. You go into those karate schools and you see a different relationship [between men]. How can you be a man with power and have respect, mercy, compassion, all of that sort of stuff? It's perfect. This is not personal, and you can still be physical. So I think that is an area to look at. I think we need to retrain all the cultures. Who better to deal with issues of values and morality and family than these people that the kids are desperate to get recognition from?"

Nothing will change, however, if men do not step up to help each other, to lend a hand to those who are stumbling or in danger of being lost. "If we are to save the next generation of young boys, they need to be connected to men so that they see examples of the possible futures they might live out as adults," Canada writes in *Reaching Up for Manhood.* "I think all of us must do more to help children at risk, especially our boys. Mentoring is a critical activity that can help support children and can make the difference between a child succeeding or failing."

DEMON DAYS

When fathers fall short, the road to manhood can be full of potholes and sharp turns. Jay Bakker has spent most of his life sorting out conflicting feelings toward his dad, Jim Bakker, the televangelist and disgraced leader of the Praise The Lord club. During the 1980s, Bakker and his wife, Tammy Faye, ruled a ministry that boasted 13 million viewers, raked in up to $1 million a week in donations, and included a Christian theme park, Heritage USA. That world disappeared forever in 1987. Jay Bakker was twelve years old when his father resigned from the PTL amid allegations of sexual and financial scandal. The trauma of his father's arrest and the family's ostracism from the religious community led Jay to quit school and turn to drugs. Jim Bakker was eventually convicted of fraud and served five years in prison before being paroled in 1993 for good behavior. The following year a now clean and sober Jay Bakker founded his own ministry, Revolution Church, an alternative, nondenominational congregation built on a philosophy of acceptance and inclusion.

Tattooed and pierced, and with a taste for black T-shits, Jay is the subject of a six-part documentary series, *One Punk Under God—The Prodigal Son of Jim and Tammy Faye*, that aired on the Sundance Channel in 2006 and 2007. The show follows Jay as he preaches to the faithful in Atlanta, revisits the ruins of Heritage USA, and struggles to rekindle a relationship with his estranged father, who has remarried and has a new TV program based in Branson, Missouri. Jay comes across as a man who has had to rebuild his sense of himself, the world, and even God from scratch. It's clear that his father's fall from grace not only tore his family apart, it opened a rift between himself and his faith, a void that could only be healed by redefining God. Upon the ruins of his father's empire, Jay Bakker built Revolution, a church that could embrace them both.

In *One Punk Under God*, Jay is visibly nervous as he drives to visit his father, whom he hasn't seen in two years. "I hope now that we can have a relationship again, especially with my mom being sick," Jay says to the camera. "After the scandal, I saw the hypocrisy of the church—I grew up with a lot of people who didn't know who God was. I have learned from some of the mistakes of my dad, and I don't want to repeat the same thing."

The screen shifts to Amanda, Jay's wife, who has stayed home in Atlanta. She adds: "I think his expectations have gotten to Jay, because he has an idea of his dad and their relationship, and then he goes and the reality of it sometimes doesn't match up, and that's been hard on Jay. He wants to have a close relationship with his father, and it's sometimes not there to have."

After a painfully awkward greeting, Jim takes Jay on a private car tour of Branson. They talk briefly about Jay's mother, who is ailing, and clash over Jay's liberal views on homosexuality. They reconcile in private, behind closed doors.

Later, as the cameras roll, the elder Bakker introduces Jay to his studio audience, adding, "He's trying to hide the fact that he's my son, so he has tattoos." Jay responds by pointing to his PTL tattoo.

"When our world fell apart, Jaime [Jay's given name] was about ten years old, and so I didn't get to raise him after that," Jim Bakker says as both men choke back tears. "I was very upset about it." He looks at his son. "You said, 'Dad, when you get out of prison I want to go to Disneyland with you, and I don't want anybody else, not my sister, not my cousins, just you and me.' And we spent three days. I'll never forget when you left and you cried and you hugged me. And you cried and you said to me . . . do you remember?"

"I said one day . . ."

"You said, 'All I ever wanted was one day alone with my dad.'"

"Yeah. . . . It was a good day."

Afterward, Jay reflects: "My dad's a pretty sincere guy, you know, when he's on TV. It's almost a release for him. So, that's almost like his counseling, I guess. I don't know. It's what he does, and he's good at it. . . . I made a lot of realizations on this trip. I used to have a hard time when he didn't agree with me or he was worried about something. But now I realize that he respects me—finally, now that I'm thirty, an adult.

Like Jay Bakker, Joe Loya had to forgive his preacher father before he could heal himself, but not for the same reasons and not in the same way. Loya, who grew up in the Hispanic barrio of East Los Angeles, was seven years old when his mother was diagnosed with a terminal kidney disease. During the long illness that followed, and after her death, Loya's father began to physically abuse Joe and his younger brother. As the beatings became more frequent and severe, Loya realized that a showdown was approaching.

"I was sixteen," Loya recalls. "I had a concussion, so the world was very wobbly to me at that time. But it wasn't wobbly enough for me not to tell my brother to lock himself up in the bathroom. I went to the kitchen and got a knife. And when he came back and was getting ready to get to round two—I mean, he was coming in, and he was getting ready to beat me. He was taking a weight set apart, so something was going to happen. What exactly was going to happen

I didn't know, but this was a new level of improvised savagery. So I just said fuck this, and I got the knife. I charged him, he charged me, we wrestled, and then I stabbed him in the neck."

Loya was able to escape to his aunt's house and he and his brother were eventually placed in a foster home in Pasadena. Loya's dad survived, but his father's physical and psychological abuse had left Joe humiliated and angry. One formative episode stands out in his mind. It was the day he told his father, whom Joe later found out had himself been beaten as a child, that he'd been roughed up by some bullies on the way home from school. "I was a skinny, nerdy, bookish boy," he recalls. "So I go home, where my dad is studying the Bible, preparing for his Sunday mass lesson, and he sees me walk in with my torn sweater, broken glasses, and he said, 'What's wrong?' And I said, 'These guys beat me.' And the sight of his defeated son, his Mexican defeated son, was so painful for him to witness, and to have to cope with, that he got up, slapped me in the face, and said, 'Get in the car.' And we went driving around looking for the guys, because, he said, 'You're going to fight them individually, and if you lose, I'm going to beat you.'"

"This hypermaleness, this sort of demented maleness was beat into me, literally beat into me," says Joe Loya.

"I couldn't feel safe in my fragility, so, you know, you put up a front. I had a very, very strong will, and I thought of myself as being very strong, and I would eventually create that in myself."

By the age of twenty-six, Loya had transformed himself into the kind of person other people feared. He robbed banks, sometimes as many as four in a single day. In 1986, Loya was arrested and convicted. He served two years, was released, and quickly resumed a life of crime. In 1989, he was apprehended again and served an additional seven years in federal penitentiaries in California, Kentucky, and Massachusetts. Even during his incarceration Loya was angry and prone to violence against his fellow inmates, behavior that landed him in solitary confinement.

It was during a stint in "the hole" that he had a hallucination of a pale, bald boy, a childhood friend of his who had died of leukemia. The vision of his dead friend triggered a flood of memories from Loya's childhood, and he realized that the boy had come to remind him of what he'd become—and who he still could be. For the first time, he met an adversary that he could not intimidate or defeat. The pale little boy terrified him because he realized that seeing him so vividly meant he was on the verge of losing his mind. "I was so scared, so humbled by this," he recalls. "I had to adjust my sense of self. I had to admit that I might be able to control other men, I might be able to walk into a bank and control people, their movements and their fear, but I cannot control my mind. So all sense of Joe Loya being in control, of Joe Loya being able to control, evaporated."

Out of this bottomless pit of despair thoughts and words began to bubble to the surface and, for the first time in many years, he began to write. He wrote about his dead friend, and his family, and the young man he once was, and the sociopath he had become. Loya began a correspondence with the writer Richard Rodriguez. In his letters, Rodriguez encouraged Loya to keep working on his biographical manuscript, which in 2004 was published as *The Man Who Outgrew His Prison Cell: Confessions of a Bank Robber.*

"My writing was an unmasking of myself," Loya wrote. "No more hiding behind a façade of bravado. I was committed to disarming my rage so that I might eventually have a chance to live a normal life and stay out of prison. Organizing my blemished narrative on the page allowed me to grasp how my anger and violence had always disguised immense wounds, and had been mostly a profound grief for a life gone terribly awry."

Today, Loya is a different man, married and living in the San Francisco Bay area with his wife and their young daughter. His writing

has been published in newspapers and magazines across the country
and he often speaks in prisons to tell others his story.

Asked if he wished he had had a son, he replies, "Ah, boy—you
don't know how much I did not want a son. I was praying that I did
not have a son. You know, the world makes boys badly, it makes men
badly. And no matter how good I did, my boy was going to suffer in
this world. I just felt like the world was going to compete in such a
violent way against all the lessons I would try to teach him. It was going to be hard for him to become the man that I would encourage
him to be. And even if he was a good man, there are not a lot of
places for him to go! I come upon a lot of guys who find out I was in
prison and they 'man up' in some way that's really uncomfortable for
me. Because they figure this guy's a man's man, and so I need to be
more male. And it's amazing, because they're guys that would never
be like that, and their posturing would never impress anyone I ever
knew who was really hypermale, but they man up around me, and it's
really embarrassing. Because I'm not that guy anymore. I do not vali-
date it, and in many ways, if people listen to me talk, I'm often derid-
ing it. And this is what I'm saying: my son would have to face the
male ethic everywhere he went—even those places that you would
think might be natural havens for men who are trying to be peaceful.
Some of the most intense male, bad-male energy I've felt is when I
visited an abbot in a monastery! A Catholic monastery in Long Island. So this is what I'm saying. I would grieve for my son because of
the world he would be born into. And I mean it. The world makes
men badly. And I did not want my son to be part of that."

In Loya's view, men in modern society are dealing with many of
the same internal conflicts as the prisoners in America's jails. He
sees ordinary males responding to their own insecurities and fears
by adopting an aggressive, tougher-than-thou attitude, which in
turn has spilled over into the media and onto the streets. "The hypermasculine ethos of prison has come out," he says. "You see it, for
one thing, in the influence of prison garb on hip-hop, especially in

videos, the big blue jacket, the baggy pants, the influence of that ethos, the posturing, the words, the outright physical antagonism, humiliation, the rapping thing where they're yelling at each other and calling each other punks, all that. The prison ethos makes sense because so many of the people making these videos are influenced by so much of the population that was in prison."

There is also violence, Loya believes, in the way that men talk to one another, in the very words and expressions that they use to communicate. He finds the American vernacular peppered with martial metaphors, verbal cues that accentuate conflict and domination. "It's the way we talk about things, the way we set things up," he explains. "Even like 'I had to fight my worst self' or 'I'm wrestling with my demons.' It's all very exciting and interesting to hear someone who has never really fought with anything to be saying something like this, but look at the language we use! It's very forceful—it's a fight, it's combat, it's warfare. . . . And in order for us to change, we need to change the way we talk about manhood. We need to change the way we talk about ourselves."

The male ethos of the soldier goes beyond words, Loya maintains, affecting almost every aspect of a man's social and emotional life. "Just look around," he says. "It's a very martial world. Games are more violent, everything is bulked up. It's like anything that we touch is influenced by the martial metaphor, the soldier metaphor. Even police have been militarized—they look like soldiers now, like SWAT teams, and all that. The martial has always been around, but now there are so many ways in which martial has seeped in, because the world has become more complicated."

For Joe Loya, the way that men treat their sons is part of a chain of male energy that is passed from generation to generation. And unless that chain is broken, the anger and humiliation experienced by one man will inevitably resurface in his children.

"My dad was utterly humiliated as a child," Loya says. "And one thing I know is: he utterly humiliated me as a child. And what happens with that humiliation is that it becomes really congested, and if you don't have a way to work it out it will harass you, and it can fuck you up two ways: it can fuck you up psychologically, so you become passive-aggressive, you can't develop intimacy with people, you become an asshole and you treat people shitty because you're afraid that people are going to humiliate you. And you just become . . . an asshole, or a person who doesn't know how to connect with people. Or you become violent, and you get it out of you by attacking other people physically or verbally, you become abusive that way, in a truly violent way, not just an aggressive way. And that's exactly the way my brother and I went: he went aggressive in his relationships with people, I went violent in my relationships with people. And so, you need to act on it. It harasses you, and you end up dealing with it in one of two ways. And with me, because I was a doer, and because I had a strong will, I stabbed him. And then I had a taste of blood, I felt so emancipated, so powerful. It felt so wonderful to knock this bully off that pedestal."

"We can't blame my pop for my criminal behavior," Loya writes in *The Man Who Outgrew His Prison Cell.* "I take responsibility for my choice to commit those crimes. However, we can blame my father's fist in my mouth for altering my imagination, my idea of what was possible when I felt my world was out of control. He gave me occasion to contemplate committing violence on others whenever I felt they were stopping me from achieving some satisfaction in my crummy life. We can blame his banging my body with a metal teapot for giving me a stark example of terror and overkill."

The fact that there are fewer and fewer fathers in the lives of young men is only contributing to the problem, Loya believes. Men discipline children differently, and without male authority and support, young men are more likely to be defensive and reactionary, more likely to feel that they need to be aggressive in order to protect themselves from other men and from the world at large. Loya credits his foster father, Bob Storm, with offering him a positive role model that would later help him redefine himself as a better man.

"I think boys, because boys now do not have a father, they need to compensate for that in the world by picking up on male themes, and making them hyper," Loya says. "Because they feel amputated—cut off from a certain fatherly condition, a socialization that they missed. I'll give you a perfect example. When you go into gang neighborhoods, or you go into prison, and you see the white guy who's part of a Mexican gang, or the light-skinned Mexican who's part of a Mexican gang—you can be sure he's the one that in order to make it into that group had to make himself appear even crazier. Or he had to put more ink on his body. There was something that he needed to do to compensate, because he was almost like the convert. He's saying to them, in essence, 'I might not be you, and you look at me as different, so in order to belong I'm going to hyper it.' And I think that's what boys have been doing in the world because they don't have fathers, and probably they know that's what they're missing. They're sort of social amputees in a way, because they're missing this one heavy element of socialization. It's just like the guys in prison who are handicapped—the ones that have one arm a little shorter than the other, or the ones that have a stutter—these people, they're the ones you have to look out for, because they're going to compensate. There's something about that dynamic that I think is active in boys becoming men over the last thirty years."

Men are not the only ones who have been transformed. One of Loya's epiphanies in prison was that maleness is "performative," something that can be observed, learned, and emulated. As women become more empowered and move into traditionally male realms, Loya has noticed an increase in masculine-style posturing among females.

"Most of my friends, my close friends, are females," he reports. "And it's been interesting to come from where I came from and see so many women struggling with their own maleness. I have a lot of female friends who are really brilliant, really beautiful. Most of them are white, and several of them are really rich. And all of them have great educations—from Oxford, Harvard, Princeton. And the one thing that has demented them in a way, in their relationships with their bosses, in their relationships with husbands and boyfriends, is the stuff that they have to struggle with in themselves that is male. They feel that men are not recognizing their maleness, the maleness part that they have themselves, so they try to pump it up. I even have a friend who says, 'I need to man up.' And I say, 'Don't use that phrase!' The metaphors are there for these women, and they are as demented by maleness as men are. Not as much as men, but they are terrorized by maleness. I end up giving counsel to women about how to change that dynamic in them, and oftentimes it resembles the advice I'm giving to my male friends."

Loya, for his part, has found redemption by heading in the opposite direction. "The thing that helped me is that I went female," he explains. "I'm in my mother phase now. For so many years I was influenced by my father's dynamics, but now I'm in my mother's phase. I'm more loving, I'm more peaceful."

Toward the end of *The Man Who Outgrew His Prison Cell*, Loya reveals a more sensitive dimension of himself, putting a whole new spin on metrosexual grooming habits. With his prison release date approaching, he happened to see a makeover session on *Oprah*. The makeovers were for battered wives who wanted to feel attractive again. "Most men fantasize about getting laid or getting high when they get out of prison," Loya writes. "But as my release day neared, I fantasized about getting a facial. This from a man who once bit off a piece of a guy's ear because he had sold my *Playboy* magazine."

For Loya, getting a facial was less an act of vanity than a cleansing ritual that would symbolize his rehabilitation and return to society.

"I didn't presume that I'd be made handsome by the facial," writes Loya. "In fact, I was sort of put off by the whole Palm Springs treatment I'd seen in magazines—red mud caked on the face and cucumbers worn on the eyes like matching monocles. I just wanted to wipe clean the grime that had become caked on my face in those dungeons. And it would be a real challenge to see if I could allow myself to be touched without flinching. I wanted to prove, right out of the joint, that I could accept a softer version of myself."

Later, in an article for the arts journal *The Big Ugly Review*, Loya looked back on that episode. "Five years out of prison, I still hadn't gotten a facial," he confides. "But when I threw a party to celebrate my release from parole, a friend gave me a gift certificate for one at a European-style skin care salon in Berkeley. A tiny facial gun gently suctioned clean the pores on my nose and cheeks—which felt like small kisses, under the warm bath of light. As I lay relaxed on the table, I could not miss the irony that a gun had been used to accelerate my downfall, and now another kind of gun was being used for my cleansing."

CHAPTER 6

Fight Club

On a balmy June evening, in the dimly lit basement of a church on the Upper West Side of Manhattan, several hundred well-dressed men and women faithfully gathered to commune and worship. But they were not there to pray, or to succor the needy, or collect alms for the poor. They had come to drink beer and cheer as Yohei "The Specimen" Nishiyama, Chris "Mr. Classic" Romulo, and a dozen other muscled young males punched and kicked with the single aim of knocking their opponent unconscious. Since 1997, in a neighborhood known for yuppie couples and family-sized apartments, the Friday Night Fights, an "Old School Fight Club" that features a DJ spinning rap and pop hits between bouts, has hosted a series of sold-out matches. Held at the Church of St. Paul the Apostle, these fight nights are attended regularly by at least one of the parish priests.

Between bouts, as 50 Cent blasted from the speakers, Philip Swain, an architect who lives downtown, surveyed the crowd, which, noticeably, was about 30 percent female—and many of these ladies were on the arms of buff men. "I'm surprised that women are interested at all," Swain remarked afterward. "They must be the type that are into muscle-heads. The guys that they're with want to be perceived as tough guys who can dominate, but the only guys who can actually do that are in the ring."

Those pumped-up wannabes have plenty of company these days, and some of them are joining the fray. "How can you know about yourself if you've never been in a fight?" Brad Pitt asks Edward Norton in *Fight Club*, David Fincher's 1999 cult film about a secret society of mostly white, middle-class men who beat each other senseless for the pure blood sport of it. Based on the nihilistic novel by Chuck Palahniuk, *Fight Club* was both a mirror and a catalyst, reflecting a pent-up rebellion against a perceived emasculation of the modern man, and it gave a name to a phenomenon whose time had come. Organized amateur bouts like the one at St. Paul's exist today in every major American city, and underground fight clubs—held in parking lots, empty buildings, and suburban backyards—are spreading to places like Rexburg, Idaho (pop. 18,000), where about a hundred students gather once a week for impromptu punch-ups. In nearby Idaho Falls, a community Web forum proposed (without a hint of irony) starting a local fist-fest "to settle disputes among consenting adults and reduce aggression."

> **User #1:** I don't see anything wrong with it. If there are two consenting adults who want to beat the crap out of each other, then let them! Who is it hurting?
> **User #2:** Technically, it's hurting two consenting adults . . . but I digress . . .
> **User #1:** Yeah, but that's their choice. Who is it hurting besides those two consenting adults? No one.
> **User #3:** Where do we go to fight? I am in a bad mood and would love to smack someone around. But it would be my luck the dude was as gifted as myself and knew how to fight too. LOL. I would probably get my teeth knocked out. But I guarantee I wouldn't be angry at anything anymore.

The U.S. Department of Education says that in 2004, violent incidents were reported in 74 percent of all primary schools, 94 percent of all middle schools, and 96 percent of all high schools.

Violent crime, after dropping during the mid- and late 1990s, is creeping back up in many cities. While crime rates are still down overall, murder, robbery, and gun assaults have increased by rates in the double digits between 2004 and 2006, particularly in medium-sized and midwestern cities.

In places like Sioux Falls, South Dakota, fight night can be any-time. Mark Uttecht, a website designer, says his hometown is a place where random violence between males is business as usual, particularly in and around local bars, where alcohol fuels the fisti-cuffs. "The testosterone boys get really bored," explains Uttecht. "And if there's nothing going on with the girls, the next best thing is to pick a fight with other guys."

Finding a provocation to brawl isn't hard, or even necessary. "Fights break out spontaneously all the time," Uttecht says. "I was out one night with a friend. He sat down in a chair at a bar, and some guy sitting at a table behind us got mad at him even though nobody had been sitting there. So then this guy and a friend of his tried to grab the chair from him. And I saw my friend put his finger against the guy's chest to stop him and the next thing I know the first guy had smashed my friend's head with a bottle and he was fly-ing across the floor. The cops came and broke it up but nobody got thrown out. Then my friend bought the guy who started the fight a drink. I know, it doesn't make any sense. They just wanted to fight, because I guess they weren't going to get laid or anything so the next best rush for a guy is to beat up another guy. My brother and my friends can tell you the same story. And it gets worse than that. After a while it dawns on you—I'm not like those people. But at the same time it's weird, because, most of them, these are really nice guys, with good jobs and families."

If they are young, they are also likely to have computers, and a streak of online exhibitionism. Video clips of underground fight-club bouts have been sprouting up on YouTube, Photobucket, MySpace, and other video sites. In Brisbane, Australia, parents and educators were outraged after grammar school students posted clips of two students slugging each other until one boy fell to the ground. At Lee Senior High School in Sanford, North Carolina, fifteen boys were suspended and arrested for staging fights in the school lavatory and posting them online.

These incidents occurred the same year that a troubled loner at Virginia Tech opened fire on fellow students during morning classes, killing thirty-three and wounding fifteen before taking his own life in the deadliest shooting rampage in U.S. history. The gunman, Cho Seung-Hui, a twenty-three-year-old resident alien from Korea who attended the school and lived on campus, left a note that railed against "rich kids," "debauchery," and "deceitful charlatans." More than a year before the shootings, Cho had been dropped from an English class by the department head because she was so concerned about the "disturbed" nature of his writings. One classmate described Cho's plays and essays as "very graphic" and "extremely disturbing."

Less than three months later, pro wrestler Chris Benoit strangled his wife and smothered his seven-year-old son before hanging himself from a weight-lifting machine in their Fayetteville, Georgia, home. Benoit, an acclaimed star of Extreme Championship Wrestling, World Championship Wrestling, and World Wrestling Entertainment, had allegedly been undergoing treatment for low testosterone levels, a side effect of the overuse of anabolic steroids, which can also cause depression and erratic mood swings. An autopsy revealed that Benoit had been injecting himself with testosterone shortly before his murderous rampage, and had also taken the narcotic painkiller hydrocodone and the antianxiety drug Xanax, fueling speculation that he had killed his family and himself in a fit of "roid rage."

The Benoit tragedy is consistent with a pattern of violent behavior linked to the use of anabolic steroids, a synthetic form of male hormone that boosts energy and promotes the growth of lean muscle. Over the past two decades, steroids have become the scourge of professional and amateur sports. In the 1930s, scientists discovered that steroids could facilitate the growth of muscle in laboratory animals. Since then more than a hundred different anabolic steroids have been developed, including oxymetholone, oxandrolone, methandrostenolone, and stanozolol. First used by Soviet weightlifters in the 1950s, anabolic steroid use quickly spread to professional athletes in other sports and countries. In 1988, Richard Pound, the vice president of the International Olympic Committee, declared that the use of steroids had become "endemic" among weight lifters and threatened to recommend that weight lifting be dropped as an Olympic event. At the Summer Olympics in Seoul the same year, Canadian runner Ben Johnson was stripped of his gold medal in the 100-meter dash after testing positive for steroids. In 2004, Congress passed the Anabolic Steroid Control Act, which added eighteen substances to the list of banned steroids, including androstenedione, also known as "andro," and tetrahydrogestrinone, or THG. The law was designed to cover "pro-steroids," which are chemically related to steroids banned in 1990, and produce similar effects after metabolizing inside the body.

"Steroid use by young people is a serious health issue," declared Delaware senator Joe Biden, who sponsored the bill. "A lot of kids don't know how harmful this stuff really is. It's not only a health issue but also a values issue. If kids think that all the best athletes are 'on the juice,' what does that teach them? I think it teaches them that they should use steroids or steroid precursors to get ahead and win the game; that cheating is OK."

Steroid-doping scandals have tainted baseball, cycling, and other pro sports. In 2005, Mark McGwire, Jose Canseco, and five other baseball players were subpoenaed to testify before Congress on steroids. During his testimony, McGwire, who broke the single-season home-run record by hitting seventy in 1998 for the St. Louis Cardinals, was evasive about his use of steroids, even though he had previously admitted to a journalist that he'd taken androstenedione, a legal over-the-counter muscle-enhancer banned by the NFL and the IOC. In 2007, McGwire, who was accused by some pundits of hurting baseball by casting doubt on his late-career achievements, failed to win election to the baseball Hall of Fame. The following year, Roger Clemens was called before Congress to testify about allegations that he had been injected with steroids and human growth hormonal.

Androgenic anabolic steroids, a.k.a. "Arnolds," "gym candy," "pumpers," "roids," stackers," "weight trainers," and "juice," are synthetic variants of the male hormone testosterone, which has attributes that are both androgenic (referring to the physical changes that occur in young men during puberty) and anabolic (meaning that it builds muscle mass). Proponents say that steroids help them build lean muscle, decrease recovery time between workouts, and increase strength, endurance, and aggressiveness. Steroids are most commonly used by bodybuilders, law enforcement officers, security guards, and workers in other occupations where muscle size and strength are considered important. Doctors sometimes prescribe steroids for men or women in cases of testicular or breast cancers, low red-cell count, delayed puberty, to counteract muscle atrophy due to AIDS, and for other conditions. Steroids can be taken orally, in a patch, or by injection, either in six- or twelve-week treatment cycles, or in lower doses over longer periods.

Side effects from long-term usage can include elevated cholesterol levels, severe acne, thinning of hair and baldness, high blood pressure, liver disorders, and impotence.

In males, steroids can produce a loss of sex drive, diminished sperm production, breast and prostate enlargement, and decreased hormone levels.

Women taking steroids may experience menstrual irregularities, infertility, and such male-gender effects as facial hair, diminished breast size, and a permanently deepened voice. In both sexes steroids may cause mood swings, manic behavior, impaired judgment, depression, nervousness, irritability, delusions, hostility, and hyper-aggression.

Possession or sale of an anabolic steroid without a valid prescription is illegal. Conviction of possessing illicitly obtained anabolic steroids carries a maximum penalty of one year in prison and a minimum fine of $1,000. Trafficking can result in five years in prison and a $250,000 fine.

Yet despite the risks, steroid use has been steadily rising—as many as 3 million men have swallowed or injected them in the past twenty years in this country. The National Institute on Drug Abuse (NIDA) estimates that between 1 and 6 percent of athletes in the United States, or several hundred thousand people ages eighteen and older, use steroids at least once a year. One of the most alarming aspects of the steroid epidemic is its spread to middle and high school–age athletes who want to emulate their high-performing sports heroes, even if that means flirting with lifelong damage to their bodies.

Even thirteen-year-old boys have gotten the message that ripped abs and bulging biceps somehow makes them more of a man. Evidence suggests that young boys bulk up because they believe they will gain respect from their peers and become more attractive to the opposite sex. A study of middle and high school students conducted in 1999 found that anabolic steroid use had increased significantly since 1991, the first year that steroid-use data was collected on younger students. An estimated 10 percent of all adolescent males have used some kind of body-enhancement drug or natural supplement.

The main rationale for taking steroids is to improve performance in sports and increase body strength. But the psychological motives for steroid use by men and women of all ages is revealing. According to research by the NIDA, most steroid users, to one degree or another, are victims of muscle dysmorphia, a behavioral syndrome in which a person has a distorted image of his or her body. Men with muscle dysmorphia think that they look small and weak, even if they are actually large and muscular; women think that they look fat and flabby even if they are actually lean and muscular. Others who abuse steroids have a history of physical abuse. In one series of interviews with male weight lifters, 25 percent of those who used steroids had memories of childhood physical or sexual abuse; the abuse level was zero among those who did not use steroids. Of women bodybuilders who used steroids, half reported that they had been raped. They believed that being bigger and stronger would make them more intimidating and less vulnerable to potential predators. Collectively, these interviews paint a picture of people who use muscle as a prop to compensate for some weakness that they feel inside. If bulking up and other hypermale pursuits are essentially a reaction to feelings of vulnerability, then it's pretty obvious that we live in a society rife with insecure men. And as women continue their march toward social, economic, and even physical parity with men, that insecurity will only grow.

Steroids, of course, are just one indicator of the tectonic shift toward more muscular, hypermale bodies. There is now a performance-enhancing drug for nearly every aspect of a man's life as marketers have been quick to capitalize on the average male's quest to become a bigger, stronger, leaner, more potent version of himself. From the Abs Diet to Bowflex, from metabolism jumpers like Hydroxycut to hair-loss solutions like Rogaine, making men more "manly" has become a multibillion-dollar business. In 1999 alone, American men spent $2 billion for gym memberships and another $2 billion for home exercise equipment. An estimated 100 million Americans purchase dietary supplements each year, with annual sales increasing 80 percent between 1994 and 2003 to $14 billion. Never mind

that research has shown many over-the-counter dietary supplements, including so-called metabolism boosters and fat burners
like ephedra, to be ineffectual or even dangerous. In 2004, after
ephedra was linked to a number of deaths, the FDA banned the ad-
ditive on the basis that it presented "an unreasonable risk of illness or
injury."

In magazines and on male-oriented cable channels and websites, not to mention gazillions of spam e-mails clogging millions of
computers, ads for *Girls Gone Wild!* videos are outnumbered by
pitches for products designed to give men a leg up at the office, on
the golf course, and in the bedroom. A commercial for Extenze, a
"natural male enhancement," reminds male viewers that they have
"nothing to lose, but a lot to gain." Sildenafil, marketed by Pfizer
under the brand name Viagra, was approved by the FDA in 1998 to
treat clinical erectile dysfunction, a condition associated with older
men. Instead, it was embraced by males of all ages as a chemical
shortcut to porn-star sexual prowess. Pitched by the likes of Bob
Dole and Brazilian soccer star Pelé, the "little blue pill" had annual
sales of $1 billion during its first three years on the market and was
soon joined by its pharmacological cousins, Cialis (tadalafil) and
Levitra (vardenafil).

More recently, Androgel, a testosterone supplement created by
the Belgian-owned company Unimed, was developed with an eye
to the estimated 5 to 13 million American men over the age of
forty-five who potentially suffer from "andropause," or lowered
testosterone levels. With its promise to increase bone density, improve mood, boost energy levels, and restore sexual vitality, Unimed
is aiming at a market estimated to be worth at least $2 billion
annually.

Ironically, the harder men try to distinguish themselves from
women by getting ripped, juiced, and randy, the more susceptible
they become to female-oriented marketing techniques. It has not
been lost on advertisers and the media that the same chiseled, hy-

permasculine bodies that men increasingly feel the need to achieve are just as attractive to gay men as they are to women. "Images of masculinity that will do double (or triple or quadruple) duty with a variety of consumers, straight and gay, male and female, are not difficult to create in a culture like ours, in which the muscular male body has a long and glorious aesthetic history," Susan Bordo observes in *The Male Body: A New Look at Men in Public and in Private*. "That's precisely what Calvin Klein was the first to recognize and exploit—the possibility and profitability of what is known in the trade as a 'dual market' approach."

In the decline-of-men markets of the twenty-first century, in other words, everybody really is buy-sexual.

But Madison Avenue's fervid embrace of beefcake has cost men much more than a ballooning balance on their Macy's charge card. When Calvin Klein figured out in the eighties that eroticized images of muscular men would sell underwear to men and women, straight and gay, he not only let the macho gay aesthetic out of the closet and into the shopping mall, he opened the door to the not-so-brave new world of straight male neurosis. As it became acceptable for near-naked male bodies to be ogled in ads and in the media, most men only felt a creeping sense of self-consciousness and inadequacy. While images of men had changed, masculine codes of behavior and sexuality had not. Masculinity had been repackaged but not fundamentally altered; guys were still expected to act like men, but now they had to look like Olympic gods, too. Almost overnight, men found themselves saddled with the responsibility of needing to look like a sex object, but without the freedom—or, in most cases, the desire—to act like one.

While female forays into male domains has accorded women confidence and empowerment, the beautification of the American male has brought with it only unease and paranoia, along with a slew of body-image and eating disorders that used to be associated exclusively with women and gay men. We now know the real price that men have paid for the right to flaunt their Calvins: today more than a million men have been diagnosed with dysmorphia, anorexia nervosa, and bulimia. Millions more are quietly infected with a diminished sense of self and a chronic fear of not measuring up.

In a culture where ripped abs and bulging pecs are de rigueur for males in movies, TV, and advertising, men have come to consistently overestimate the body dimensions that women find most attractive. In their book *The Adonis Complex: How to Identify, Treat, and Prevent Body Obsession in Men and Boys*, Harrison G. Pope and Roberto Olivardia, both of the Harvard Medical School, and Katherine A. Phillips, of Brown University's School of Medicine, describe their research into "a secret crisis of male body obsession" that "afflicts millions in our society and around the world."

The authors cite studies showing that the percentage of men who are dissatisfied with their bodies has risen steeply in recent decades, from 15 percent in 1972 to 43 percent in 1997. A 1997 *Psychology Today* survey of 548 men found that a solid majority were concerned about the way they looked. While 89 percent of the men said that they wanted models in magazines to "represent the natural range of body shapes," more than half of the respondents were unhappy with their own abdomens (63 percent) or weight (52 percent). Men also expressed dissatisfaction with their muscle tone (45 percent) and their chest (38 percent). Fifty-two percent reported dissatisfaction with their weight; 58 percent reported having dieted to lose weight; and 30 percent said that they smoked primarily to lose weight. Another study found that men were more likely than women "to want to look attractive to the opposite sex" and occasionally passed up dinners or romantic opportunities in order to work out at the gym, in effect choosing to look good for their girlfriends rather than have sex with them. The trend proved consistent in most foreign countries, including Venezuela, where 47 percent of the men polled admitted that they "constantly think about their looks."

In order to measure the difference between men's body ideals and reality, the authors of *The Adonis Complex* asked college students in three countries—the United States, Austria, and France—to choose from a chart of twelve male body types. When asked which body type they thought women would find most attractive, the male respondents on average singled out those with 30 pounds more muscle than their own. When asked to choose a body type that they would themselves prefer to have, the men pointed to bodies that had about 28 pounds more muscle than their own. When women were shown the same male-body-type chart and asked to pick the one they liked best, their choices were well below the level of muscularity that the men assumed women would prefer. "In other words," the authors observed, "there was a difference of 15 to 20 pounds of muscle between what men *thought* women wanted and what women *actually* wanted!"

The dramatic shift in male body consciousness, the authors contend, correlates with cultural and social changes that have occurred in the past thirty years. For instance, by comparing male centerfolds in *Playgirl* magazine from the 1970s, 1980s, and 1990s, Pope and his colleagues found that the average hunk had lost twelve pounds of fat and gained twenty-seven pounds of muscle. The researchers found a similar trajectory in popular women's magazines by analyzing the frequency of "undressed" (defined as "anything too risqué to be seen on a city street") men and women in back issues of *Cosmopolitan* and *Glamour*.

"The proportion of undressed women of both magazines has remained fairly steady over the past thirty to forty years, oscillating at around 20 percent," they wrote. Over the same period, the proportion of undressed men has "skyrocketed," from as little as 3 percent in the 1950s to as high as 35 percent in the 1990s. "Research shows that sociocultural influences, such as the media, tend to make women feel worse about their bodies, and preliminary studies of these influences suggest the same is true for men. In addition, there seems little doubt that over the last generation our culture has placed a growing emphasis on male body image—as exemplified in toys, comic books, magazines, newspapers, television, the movies and advertisements of all types."

The message to men that they are expected to be physically flawless is communicated almost before they can talk or walk.

During the past thirty years, the plastic muscles on popular action toys have steadily expanded to steroidal proportions. One study suggests that the hypermasculinity of action figures is setting unrealistic ideals for boys in the same way that Barbie dolls have done for young girls. In order to illustrate how distorted body self-images are inculcated in young boys, Pope and his colleagues collected toy action figures from the 1960s through the 1990s. The earliest iteration of GI Joe action dolls, they found, had physical dimensions that were roughly proportionate to a man with a 32-inch waist, 44-inch chest, and 12-inch biceps. By 1974, GI Joe's biceps had grown to the equivalent of 15 inches and he had developed noticeably defined abdominal muscles. Both those figures, however, "were shamed" by the Salute to GI Joe doll released in 1991, which had a 29-inch waist and 16.5-inch biceps, "approaching the limits of what a lean man might be able to attain without steroids." GI Joe Extreme, a doll released in the mid-1990s, had body proportions equal to a 55-inch chest and 27-inch biceps, "bigger than most competition bodybuilders."

The authors found a similar pattern of muscle inflation in other popular toys, ranging from *Star Wars* heroes to Batman. "All have physiques suggestive of steroid-using bodybuilders," they concluded. "And some—like the Wolverine—exceeded even the outer limits of what drugs can do."

As a result, males are experiencing body-image anxiety at increasingly early ages. As the pressure to have a chiseled, ultramale physique filters through the zeitgeist, even slight imperfections become intolerable. The American Society of Plastic Surgeons reports that 70 percent of all patients who underwent breast reduction surgery in 2006 were boys between the ages of thirteen and nineteen. That number is equal to the total number of men who had the procedure in 2004, and represents 70 percent of all men who had cosmetic surgery of any kind in 2006, or an increase of 21 percent over the previous year.

"Muscle preoccupations are much greater in young men," Pope and his colleagues write. "Growing up in recent years, these younger men have been saturated with steroid-pumped media images and aggressive advertising from the new body image industries. They perhaps have also experienced 'threatened masculinity' as a result of eroding traditional masculine roles. Older men, who grew up in the sixties and seventies, weren't exposed to these societal influences in their youth, and consequently don't have as many muscle hang-ups."

The authors of *The Adonis Complex* conclude that the two main factors contributing to the current male malaise are anabolic steroid use and the dramatic shift in gender roles that has occurred over the past four decades. They report that the risk of eating disorders for gay and straight men are now nearly identical, and that both groups suffer from various levels of dysmorphia and body-image problems for the same reasons: "to compensate for their perceived lack of manliness."

The researchers also concluded that the correlation between social changes brought on by the women's movement and hypermale depictions of men in the media and advertising was too convincing to dismiss. "The interval from the 1960s to the 1990s has seen history's most dramatic advances for women, and in parallel, the most striking changes in cultural attitudes towards men's bodies," they write. "As women have advanced, men have gradually lost their traditional identities as breadwinners, fighters, and protectors. Women are no longer so dependent on men for these services. Accordingly, as the importance of these other identities has declined, the relative importance of the male body appears to have increased, although men may not be fully aware of these motivating forces."

Which is not to say that some women aren't doing their part to convince men that old gender stereotypes still apply. A series of interviews conducted between 2002 and 2006 by psychologists at UCLA found a correlation between muscularity and frequency of sexual encounters. The study asked 788 heterosexual college students—509 women and 279 men—to look at pictures of men with varying levels of muscularity. The men were asked to rate themselves physically and then report on their sexual activities. Women were shown the same pictures and asked what kind of men they were most likely to have short- and long-term affairs with. The men who described themselves as "more muscular than average" had twice the number of sex partners as those who were of average or below-average muscularity. At the same time, 61 percent of the women reported that their short-term partners were more muscular than their long-term partners. The findings were interpreted by some to mean that bulked up men did better with women than their less-buff brethren. But the data also implied that less muscular men were better equipped, psychologically if not physically, to initiate and maintain long-term relationships. The exact reasons for this were not clear, but it makes sense that bodybuilders, who are more likely to suffer from dysmorphia than other men, might crave and pursue multiple sex partners as a way to reaffirm their male egos. Is the serial conquest of chicks just another series of "reps" in the psychological quest to bulk up?

Even if this were true, of course, it's unlikely that men would admit it to researchers—or anybody else, for that matter. Women, say the authors, "have learned in recent years to be more candid about their body image concerns—and they've grown stronger in their ability to reject societal messages that appearance is all-important. But men lag far behind in this respect; the Adonis Complex, like the forces behind it, remains in the shadows."

The male *omertà*, the unspoken code of silence that prevents men from talking about their problems, let alone seeking help, is as prevalent as ever. A 2006 study of 285 college men by psychologists at Ohio State University found that young males feel pressure to have a perfect physique not just on account of depictions of lean, muscular men in advertising and the media but also as a result of pressure from family and friends. As a result, their obsession with dieting and working out often interfered with other parts of their life. "They start to believe that the only attractive male body is a muscular one," Tracy Tylka, the lead researcher, told *Live Science*. "And when they internalize that belief, they judge themselves on that ideal and probably come up short, because it is not a realistic portrayal of men."

The liberation of the sexes, in a sense, has backfired for both genders: women are still seen as sex objects, but now men are, too. "Instead of seeing a decrease in the objectification of women in society, there has just been an increase in the objectification of men," Tylka said. "And you can see that in the media today."

Unlike women, though, men are stymied by ingrained codes of behavior that prevent them from asking for help, or even admitting that there's a problem. In his book *Real Boys: Rescuing Our Sons from the Myths of Manhood*, William Pollock writes about the "Boy Code," a set of powerful injunctions on male behavior that tell a man he must be stoic, stable, and independent, he must be daring and attracted to violence, he must avoid shame or a loss of control at all costs, and must never ever exhibit any behaviors that might be even remotely interpreted as feminine. This is not about being from Mars, because both sexes reinforce the message: real men don't cry or back down from an argument—or eat quiche (because it's too fattening?). These codes are so strong that men are loath to admit, sometimes even to themselves, that they exist.

"The first rule about fight club is you don't talk about fight club," the narrator of Palahniuk's black-eyed tale of all-male melees explains. "The second rule about fight club is you don't talk about fight club."

PLUMAGE

The quest to find our inner beast, the struggle to reconcile the two sides of masculine identity—one savage and dangerous, the other controlled and compassionate—is one of the oldest themes in human history. Ancient peoples from Africa, Asia, and Mesoamerica all practiced rites of duality and worshipped gods that were part animal, part human. In the nineteenth century, Robert Louis Stevenson turned that ontological tension into timeless literature with the publication of *The Strange Case of Dr. Jekyll and Mr. Hyde.* Based on a dream that Stevenson had one night, the novella is the tale of a scientist who concocts a potion capable of dividing the dual nature of man into two completely separate personalities. While often described as an allegory of the eternal battle between good and evil, it is also a metaphor for the tension between the instinctual and the intellectual, the barbarian and the gentleman. Jekyll is thoughtful and sensible, while Hyde is impulsive and murderous. The good doctor is racked with guilt and regret for an experiment gone awry, but Hyde is powerful and decisive; he is all id, free of morality and remorse, driven by instinct, beyond sin or redemption or fear.

Men yearn for the clarity and intensity of their wild nature almost as much as they fear it.

For theologians, the feral, unfettered male is in league with the devil, but biologists see something much more practical. For them, the roots of male aggression reach back to the evolutionary imperative to reproduce. The crux of Darwin's Theory of Natural Selection rests on the ability of any species to gain a competitive advantage from the genetic variations, or "alleles," that occur naturally in its offspring. Individuals with variations that enhance their ability to mate and reproduce are "selected" by nature because those traits make them more likely to survive and pass their genes on to the next generation. Sexual selection, which is a subset of natural selection, focuses on the strategies used by each gender to fend off or eliminate sexual rivals.

In his book *The Dark Side of Man: Tracing the Origins of Male Violence*, Michael P. Ghiglieri explains that the two main methods of sexual competition in nature are the "pretty male strategy" and the "macho male strategy." Pretty males win by making themselves more attractive to females, which means having more of the traits that females look for in a mate. Macho males compete by either defeating sexual rivals or preventing them from mating with females. Some females use a "supermom strategy," in which they compete on the basis of the efficiency of their reproductive abilities.

Females and males can both use "macho" or "pretty" strategies, and in some species females compete more violently for sex than males. In the Australian rain forest, the female cassowary, a six-foot-tall bird with three-inch claws, battles other females for the chance to mate with as many males as possible. The males, who are one-third smaller than the females, are stay-at-home dads who dutifully guard the eggs until they hatch and then raise the chicks and teach them how to fend for themselves.

In the animal world, males have a mixed record when it comes to caring for offspring. Most leave the little ones to be hatched and raised by the females, but there are notable exceptions. African bullfrogs have been observed to dig canals during the dry season to save their babies from dehydration, and the Siberian dwarf hamster acts as a midwife for the female, not only cleaning the newborn and cutting the umbilical cord with its teeth but caring for it afterward as well. Emperor penguins, as famously documented in the film *March of the Penguins*, hold eggs on their feet for up to nine weeks to keep them warm before hatching. But the ultimate New Man dad may be the sea horse. After fertilization of the eggs, the male sea horse becomes "pregnant" by carrying the female's eggs in its stomach pouch. When the hatchlings are ready, the male experiences contractions, "giving birth" to as many as a hundred tiny sea horses. Human males are not so sympathetic, yet researchers have detected a drop in testosterone and a rise in levels of prolactin, a hormone usually associated with lactating females, in some men as their pregnant partners near birth.

Among nonhuman mammals, females are limited by the number of offspring that they can bear and nurture to adulthood, while males seek as many partners as possible. The greater the gap in the "parental investment" between males and females, the more intense and violent the competition between males.

"Unlike gorgeous male birds, most male primates are drab," Ghiglieri writes. "In surveying three hundred published reports of mating behavior among higher primates, physical anthropologist Meredith F. Small found no examples of females preferring specific types of males. Instead, females simply mate with those males who are victorious in dominance fights with other males—mainly because these are the only males on their feet in the mating arena. In short, the 'pretty male strategy' is close to meaningless to polygymous male primates, who instead use the 'macho male strategy' to the hilt. It also seems meaningless to females, because their only option is the male who possesses the guts, savvy, and strength to be physically present."

Because the macho strategy calls for mating as many times as possible, it favors and reinforces greater size, strength, and speed, as well as the use of weapons, fighting skills, cunning, and, when necessary or advantageous, cooperation with kin in coordinated combat against enemies. "It is macho male selection that leads to war, rape, and most murder in nature," Ghiglieri writes.

But what happens when strength, speed, and brawn are no longer features of the macho male strategy and instead become manifestations of the pretty male strategy? What are the ramifications when the same hypermasculine traits and behaviors that our primate cousins use to achieve and maintain social status appear in modern human males as signs of insecurity and weakness? As the social and economic balance of power shifts away from males, and guys preen and flaunt their muscles in the hopes of hooking up with the opposite (or same) sex, are women becoming more macho than men? And are there any historical examples of threatened males trying to compensate for a perceived encroachment on their masculine turf?

The answers are, respectively: probably and definitely.

As technology has freed them from some of the strictures of reproductive biology, and as economic empowerment has ended their dependence on men, women are increasingly willing—and able—to tread on traditionally male territory. According to the National Federation of State High School Associations, about five thousand girls wrestled in 2006, nearly five times more than a decade earlier. As girls practice and compete with girls in hands-on matches, coaches and parents report that it is the boys who seem to be the most intimidated. Women are also becoming a factor in high-risk pastimes like skydiving, Indy car racing, and rock climbing, among other extreme sports.

Girls are losing their gun-shyness, too. Women are the fastest-growing segment within the shooting sports and now account for

16 percent of the nearly 21 million active hunters in the United States. A study by the National Sporting Goods Association released in 2006 reported that 2.4 million women hunted with firearms the previous year, a 72 percent increase since 2001. More than 5 million women enjoy recreational shooting, a 50 percent increase since 2001.

Women ages 18 to 24 represent the fastest-growing group of female hunters and shooters, followed by those aged 35 to 44.

In a study published in the journal *Gender and History* in 2005, Andrea L. Smalley traced popular attitudes toward hunting and gender by examining the editorial content of *Field and Stream* and *Outdoor Life* from the late nineteenth century to the present. Smalley found that nineteenth-century sportswriters "actively promoted a hetero-social image of their sport that downplayed any exclusive relationship between men and hunting. It wasn't until after World War II, which had introduced millions of women to work in wartime industries, that male sportswriters began to argue that hunting was a fundamentally male activity that women could never master or fully appreciate. "Demobilization and the resulting loss of intense male relationships could threaten to 'feminize' men," Smalley writes. "This threat prompted the post-war revival of 'virile' activities, such as violent sports. The post-war return to 'normality' in gender relations provided a rationale for women's exclusion, not only from public roles, but also from the hunting field." Sport hunting allowed the returning war veterans "the chance to recapture at least some sense of their profound battlefield experiences," experiences in which their role as heroic, gun-toting warriors was unambiguous and uncontested. American GIs had defeated powerful enemies in Europe and the Pacific, but it was the changes waiting for them on the home front that would shake their sense of manhood and put them on the defensive.

Some sixty years later, some young women have gone so far into boy territory that they need help finding their way back. In the British reality TV series *Ladette to Lady*, eight swearing, drinking, smoking, ill-mannered girls are given a five-week crash course at Eggleston Hall finishing school in how to behave like "real" ladies. In this updated, yet curiously retrograde, twist on Bernard Shaw's *Pygmalion*, now gearing up for its third hit season on Britain's ITV and the Sundance Channel, the "ladettes" are tutored in posture, cooking, grooming, elocution, and floristry as they compete for a prize awarded to the most Eliza Doolittle–like graduate of Eggleston Hall.

Though the frat-girl foul-ups are played for laughs, the social subtext is dead serious. In the United States, girls now account for 25 percent of all violent crimes committed by adolescents, including those involving firearms. In a 2006 study of violent crimes committed in Britain and Scotland, violent crime by females had increased 50 percent over the previous four years alone. A separate report found that the number of women in Scottish prisons has doubled in the past decade.

Vince Egan, a forensic psychologist at Glasgow Caledonian University, blamed female empowerment and binge drinking for the surge in female aggression. "It's drink and girl-power," Egan told *The Scotsman*. "Everyone thinks of the Spice Girls being an empowering thing. Suddenly there is a collective view that girls are here to do everything they like, but unfortunately that also gives them the right to do stuff that is just as idiotic as men do."

GUNS N' ROSES

The notion that males are inherently aggressive and violent—and that military and sexual conquest go hand in hand—is etched in our consciousness, and quite possibly in our family history. Temujin, a.k.a. Genghis Khan, the Mongol warlord who forged the world's largest land empire in the early 1200s, is considered one of the most ruthless and bloodthirsty warriors of all time. Yet to modern Mongolians, Genghis Khan, which means "Universal Ruler," is the father of their nation—literally. "The Genetic Legacy of the Mongols," a study published in the *American Journal of Human Genetics* in 2003, estimated that Genghis Khan has more than 17 million living descendants spread across a large swath of Central Asia and China and that as much as 16 percent of the Mongolian population carries his genes.

From a biological standpoint, war is usually initiated and waged by men, because they are the only ones with anything to gain from it. "War is typically men's ultimate reproductive gamble," writes Ghiglieri. "Many researchers agree that the goal most worth the lethal risk of war is women or the resources that attract or support more women and their offspring. That *something* men—or male apes—seek through war is selfishly expanding or securing their own families. It is macho male sexual selection in its ultimate manifestation as the highest-stakes reproductive risk that men can take. . . . In contrast, a woman can gain nothing by making war that she is then capable of defending or retaining and that is also worth her risking death. This is because, according to the primeval conditions under which war evolved, a man could accrue more wives through war and thus raise his reproductive success by an order of magnitude. A woman, no matter how successful she might be in war, could barely improve her reproductive success at all with more husbands, being limited most by her own body. Worse, she would unnecessarily face death for little or no gain."

In an era when many women regard childbearing as an option rather than an obligation, the motive for women to wage war should be less than ever. Yet, following the trajectory of murder rates, extreme sports, and hunting, the number of females who opt for a career in the military has risen dramatically. By 2007, 160,000 female soldiers had been deployed in Iraq and Afghanistan. By comparison, 7,500 women served in Vietnam and 41,000 in the first Gulf War. Today one of every ten troops in Iraq is a woman. In 2004, the world was shocked by revelations that several of the U.S. troops involved in the humiliation, abuse, and torture of Iraqi prisoners at Abu Ghraib prison were women. Photos of machine-gun-toting female soldiers standing over clumps of naked male Iraqis were greeted with disbelief in America and around the world. At the same time, there were signs that the effects of sexual assaults by male soldiers and officers combined with combat fatigue were appearing as a unique form of post-traumatic stress disorder (PTSD) among female enlistees.

As the gender wars have moved to the modern battleground, the traditional definition of the warrior has come under attack, with mounting casualties on all sides. The National Center for PTSD in Boston reports that both men and women who join the armed forces have higher rates of a history of sexual and physical abuse than the general population. A 2007 report by the Mental Health Advisory Team, Operation Iraqi Freedom, found that one in ten soldiers who spent an average of fifty-six hours outside a fortified area showed signs of acute stress, anxiety, or depression. When combat conditions and sexual politics are added to the mix, the results can be less than optimal in a profession where the operatives need to be completely focused on the enemy.

Yet despite the risks and pitfalls, senior military officers and Defense Department experts remain committed to the sexual integration of the armed forces. Their reasons are more pragmatic than egalitarian. Colonel (ret.) Michael A. Andrews, a Virginia-based Defense Department consultant and former U.S. Army tank brigade commander who served in Vietnam, Korea, Europe, and the Middle East, has had a front-row view of the shifting gender balance in the military for the past three decades. In 1974, while still a graduate student at Duke University, he wrote a paper that was published in the influential journal *Military Review* titled "Women in Combat?" In it he suggested that military duty should, in effect, be gender blind. "I received a lot of hate mail for that article," Andrews recalls. "What I said in this paper very simply was that it's irrelevant whether a soldier is male or female, what we ought to do is enforce the standard of the military occupational specialty. Therefore, in some specialties, such as armor, it takes a lot of upper-body strength to lift a projectile, and so on, but it doesn't matter whether they are male or female—we should test them, and if they pass the requirement then they should qualify for the military occupational specialty."

Andrews's opinion was at least partly based on personal experience on the battlefield.

"I have frequently used my own example. I thought I was a pretty fit guy, and during a very long hard day in Vietnam, and in the middle of a very intense, close fight, I couldn't pick up a wounded soldier. I could not lift him. So a man can be weak also. So the whole point of the paper was that."

In 1978, Andrews found himself embroiled in military gender politics again at West Point, which had just been ordered to admit women cadets for the first time in its history. Andrews, who was there as a faculty member, was recruited to join a committee tasked to figure out how women would be integrated into what had historically been an all-male military school. "It was absolutely earth-shaking," Andrews says of the emotional debate that ensued. "There was tremendous reluctance and resistance to do this."

Years later, he got his answer when the intelligence officer assigned to his brigade was a female. "Because of my background on this subject, I watched her very closely, and she did a good job," he says. "Eventually I had several women on my brigade staff."

It's been fascinating for me to observe this over the past thirty years. I think that women right now in the military are playing a tremendously significant role."

Advances in military technology are triggering changes that go far beyond the Army's new wrinkle-free, digital-pixel-camouflage, Velcro-fastened uniforms. Upper-body strength is irrelevant when attacks are increasingly launched by watching a screen and pressing a button. A. Alexander Long, a software engineer at Stellar Photonics, an advanced weapons firm in Redmond, Washington, believes that traditionally male attributes will matter even less as battlefield tactics move away from offensive strategies and toward defensive technologies that minimize civilian casualties.

"If you look at warfare from a historical perspective, you go from the cavemen, who were throwing rocks and spears, to the Romans, who were throwing rocks with catapults, to World War I and II, when bombs and guns were throwing rocks, too, in a way," Long says. "Today, though, we're not throwing rocks, we're directing energy—particle beams, lasers. It's more about technology than brute force."

For Andrews, the full inclusion of women into the armed forces is not just inevitable, it's essential. "I like to think almost cosmically about societies and civilization," he says. "Not any ten-year span or twenty-year span but the whole history of mankind. From what I've seen in the last thirty years being in the military, it is unquestionably a very myopic perspective. Someday we'll all be wearing unisex uniforms, someday it'll all be point, click, delete. The things that we have experienced in the last twenty or thirty years are embarrassingly primitive compared to what's ahead. And, in my opinion, the future success of the Army, and the U.S. military, depends on shaking off some of these near-term considerations and getting to a bigger, broader, wider-range perspective. The Army is in trouble, the nation's military is in trouble. We can't survive using fifty percent of the population. The military just cannot do it without both genders. It will be one-hundred-percent integration, and it's not very far off."

Andrews does not put much stock in the conventional wisdom that women, if allowed to wage war, will make kinder, more compassionate soldiers than men, or that, when they come face-to-face, they will hesitate to pull the trigger. "When I was writing this paper, back in 1974, I came across an article by Margaret Mead where she said that it would be an absolute disaster if women were allowed to become soldiers. Because, she said, from an anthropological perspective, they may very well be too vicious, they may very well be too good at it, because they would fight for their children and their homes—without treaties, without quarter, without compromise—and it would be even more vicious than what we have today."

In Mead's *Cooperation and Competition Among Primitive Peoples*, there is an essay by Ruth Landes on the Ojibwa Indians of Canada. Landes reports that a tribal man's motives are stereotyped, and consistent from one period of his life to another, but not so for a woman's. "There is a considerable group of girls and women who like to live alone or in the company of other women," she writes. "These girls have to develop certain masculine techniques in order to maintain themselves. Not all these women are permanent bachelors, but they live alone for as long as they choose. Women who have learned male hunting techniques and male attitudes regarding private property also have visions pertinent to men's work. Such women are given the same recognition as men. Female shamans are solicited to cure and teach men and women alike, and female warriors are given the male title of 'brave.' "

"Some of the most competent officers that I know today are women, and it will always be that way," Andrews says. "We have to transcend, and those who continue to dwell on it are small-minded people who just don't see a bigger, broader perspective of the mission. I believe there certainly are small-minded guys who because of their background or whatever don't think beyond the physical dimension. But their contributions to us are limited and will always be at the very lowest levels of the military organization. Our success depends on the kinds of skill sets that transcend brute physical strength"

Andrews believes that military history shows that the essence of the warrior is not limited to the strength of his armor or his ability to kill, but lies also in his willingness to sacrifice himself to protect others. The instinct to defend one's family and loved ones, Andrews points out, "is not owned or defined by either gender. Women might not be wired to kill for sex, but they are just as capable of sacrificing themselves to protect their homes and families. Will the women warriors of the future prove to be even more fierce than men? And can men find masculine affirmation in ways that are not dependent on aggression and domination? What's certain is that men and women will be finding the answers together."

The greatest danger facing any society, Andrews contends, "is that its warriors lose touch with the society that they have sworn to protect."

"If the warrior isn't representing the society and doing whatever the society tells him to do but instead becomes so elite or so detached or so much of an animal or a misfit or someone that is looked down upon, or someone that is not part of the society—that is the most horrible thing that can happen."

Andrews tells a cautionary tale about the Roman centurions, the soldiers of the greatest army of its time, which had conquered most of the known world. During the height of the empire, their legions were sent to the farthest frontiers of Rome, and because of the politics and military demands being made on that far-flung empire, they began to have extended tours of duty, seldom if ever returning to their home. Cut off from their wives and family and their country, the centurions mixed with the local people, starting new families in the places they were posted, and eventually their allegiance was no longer to Rome but to the people they had been sent to subdue.

"The greatest fear I ever had as a soldier was to become isolated from the society I was sworn to defend," Andrews says. "And that would be horrible, because that would make you a mercenary, it would make you a killer. And so what we need to be is more inclusive. The greatest danger is to be disconnected from your own society. And therefore, more women is great. We want a standing army, we want professional people, but at the same time we don't want them to be exclusionary, we want them to be representative of our society. And I'm for everything that can do that: I'm for the draft, I'm for women, I'm for minorities. Everything that we can do to make our army more representative of, and more accountable to, the people is good. And more women is better."

The makers of GI Joe obviously agree. The GI Joe 25th Anniversary set released in 2007 includes a formidable crossbow-toting counterintelligence agent named Shana M. O'Hara (codename: Agent Scarlett). She was born in Atlanta, and her father and brother were both martial arts instructors, her bio, posted on GIJoe.com, informs us. A karate black belt at age fifteen, she graduated from advanced infantry training and Ranger school, covert ops school, and Marine sniper school and is qualified as "expert" on the M14 and M16 assault weapons, the M700 Remington sniper rifle, power crossbow, throwing stars, Ka-bar, and garotte. Concludes her dossier: "Scarlett is confident and resilient. . . . It's remarkable that a person so deadly can still retain a sense of humor."

If the warrior class is no longer the exclusive domain of men, and if the well-being and long-term security of the United States in fact depends on the full acceptance of what Andrews calls "the other fifty percent," then society must not just be willing to give women the equal right to fight, it must also be willing to value equally the lives of its male and female warriors.

"Back when I wrote that article about women in combat, somebody came out with a counterargument, saying that no society would intentionally brutalize its young women by sending them to war," he recalls. "And my response was: How about a society that's willing to brutalize its young men—what's the difference?"

But if women can be as lethal as men, and if being a man and a warrior are no longer synonymous, how does the male warrior define himself? When war, physical bravado, and even the ability to kill are no longer defined by gender, men must find a deeper, less obvious meaning in the warrior's stance.

MANIMALS

They attack without provocation or warning, sometimes in the dead of night, but also in broad daylight, terrorizing and leveling entire villages. They murder male and female, old and young, and frequently turn on their own friends, siblings, and parents. In Jerusalem, Yossi, a thirty-three-year-old male, charged and killed Atari, a forty-six-year-old female he had known his entire life. In Africa, a single male demolished dozens of huts and uprooted trees while his companions looked on. Violent incidents are also on the rise in Sri Lanka, Thailand, and India, where thousands of people were forced to flee their homes after a series of life-threatening raids. The aggressors are elephants, and their rampages in Africa, Asia, and other parts of the world are viewed by scientists as signs of an alarming breakdown in pachyderm society that is pitting elephants against people and each other.

Since the mid-1990s, when trainers and game reserve wardens first noted the phenomenon, attacks by elephants on humans and other animals have reached crisis proportions. Between 2000 and 2004, 300 people were killed by elephants in the Indian state of

Jharkhand. In Assam, 239 people have been killed by elephants since 2001. In one incident in 2006 in Bangladesh, five people were killed. Victims are usually trampled, but enraged elephants have also been known to hold down their victims with their trunk or a foot before impaling them with their tusks. In South Africa, over the past decade, elephants have been charging at people on safari and raping and killing rhinos by the hundreds. In one South African park alone, three young males attacked and killed sixty-three rhinoceroses. At another South African reserve, 90 percent of deaths of male elephants are attributable to other elephants, compared with only 6 percent in most stable elephant communities.

Animal experts at first assumed that the unprecedented attacks were due to hormonal imbalances or increased crowding and loss of habitat to humans, but new theories paint a much more complex picture. A 2005 essay published in the journal *Nature* by Gay Bradshaw, a psychologist at the environmental sciences program at Oregon State University, and several colleagues, suggests that the rampaging elephants were suffering from a form of post-traumatic stress. Bradshaw, who is the author of *Elephant Breakdown: The Psychological Study of Animal Cultures in Crisis*, makes the case that animals are emotionally much more like humans than previously thought. "Stress, trauma and other social disruptions—what biomedical research has identified as having profound influences on human psychology, physiology and behavior—holds for other social animals such as elephants," the scientists wrote. "Culls, translocations and captivity create chronic stress, decrease fitness and undermine socialization capacity, thereby reinforcing maladaptive behavior."

In the matriarchy of stable elephant herds, young females and males spend most of their time under the care of their mothers and other females. But as males near adulthood they are normally taken away by the older bulls for a period of all-male socialization before being returned to the herd as fully formed adults. It's no coincidence that many of the marauding elephants witnessed the murders of relatives by poachers and were then separated from their families, interrupting the critical phase of mentoring by older bulls.

"Male mammal brain development occurs at a significantly slower rate than females, and orphaned males lacked the second developmental phase of all-male socialization," the Oregon State researchers wrote. "This all-male socialization period serves the same purpose in elephants as it does in human adolescents when they experience a second phase of major brain reorganization. . . . Conditions of trauma, chronic stress and disabled rearing—such as occurs with culls, restricted resources and herd breakdown—result in hyper-aggressive behavior."

Without older males to police the young males and teach them how to behave, younger males rebel against the matriarchs and literally run amok, lashing out at anything and everything around them.

In an article for the science magazine *Seed*, Bradshaw likens aggressive elephants to troubled teens who have been psychologically scarred by social trauma and a lack of paternal care and guidance. "Picture a psychiatrist at her desk reviewing a case file," Bradshaw writes. "The report describes a young, teenaged male who, with several others his age, killed nearly a hundred victims. The case is astounding—not only because of the intensity and magnitude of the violence, but because nothing remotely like it has ever happened in the community before. Not even a single murder. As the psychiatrist turns the pages and reads on, the pieces of the puzzle start to come together. A few years before, the young killers had witnessed the massacre of their families and been orphaned. Afterwards, although still very young, they were relocated to another community with few adults to raise them; importantly, it was the absence of older, mentoring males."

If Bradshaw is right, then the maladaptive behavior of young male elephants could apply to humans as well. As more and more men grow up without fathers or a nurturing sense of community, we are faced with the chilling specter of a generation of emotionally crippled young men who have lost their social and moral moorings, lashing out at innocent victims and each other, running amok. In a culture where physical aggression is recognized as a sign of manliness, loss of self-esteem and antisocial behavior become a self-perpetuating cycle.

This double-bind of the modern male is the insidious syndrome that dare not speak its name. Men are hurting—each other and themselves—yet what's left of their masculinity hinges on keeping it all on the down-low. Like polar bears on a melting ice floe, the modern male paces in circles on a raft of shrinking options. The beautification of the American male has increased the need to express his essential masculinity at the very time that there are fewer and fewer ways for him to do it. Professional athletes, whose celebrity and physical prowess make them icons and role models, are the gladiators of our time. But in an era where hypermasculinity is the norm, traditional spectator sports no longer deliver the requisite adrenaline jolt. Pro wrestling and NASCAR, the two sports juggernauts of our times, project exaggerated aggression and pulse-quickening danger, and have opened the door to death-defying rituals like professional bull-riding and other extreme sports. Mixed martial arts, a mix of boxing, judo, jiu-jitsu, and street fighting that once operated in the shadows of pro boxing and wrestling, has moved into the mainstream. Extreme fighting organizations like the Ultmate Fighting Championship are filling arenas and boasting more than one million pay-per-view subscribers for its top events. Top UFC fighters like Tito Ortiz, a.k.a. the "Huntington Beach Bad Boy," can earn more than $4 million a year.

Extreme fighting moved beyond the status of spectator sport after hundreds of extreme fighting schools began offering classes to laymen as a way to stay fit while honing your edge. For about $250 a month, lawyers and college students can feed their inner beast by training with a former UFC champion and sparring with other would-be barbarians. Last year, in Alpine, California, near San Diego, 175 weekend *toreros* enrolled in bullfighting classes offered by the California Academy of Tauromaquia, which puts wooden-sword- and cape-wielding students in the ring with real bulls. And for those who want the thrill and regimen of all-male military training without the risk of dodging bullets, Austin Adventure Boot Camp puts recruits through a drill sergeant's menu of sprints, jumping jacks, calisthenics, self-defense, weight training, and obstacle courses.

The fetish for extreme and aggressive behavior is echoed in the media, where competitive reality TV shows stress the theme of man proving himself against other men—or nature itself. A promotional ad for extreme cage fighting on the VS. TV network literally picks a fight with its viewers. As a buff, shirtless man punches at the screen, a voice-over intones: "I'm not doing this for the money. I'm not doing this for the fame. I'm doing it because when I step in that cage I (*beep*)-ing hate you!" VS. also features a "Five-scar Cinema Series," where the best films get "two broken thumbs up."

In *Man vs. Wild*, a hit series on the Discovery Channel, a former member of the British Special Forces named Bear Grylls is dropped in a remote location with nothing more than a knife, a water bottle, and a flint, and left—TV crew and cameras notwithstanding—to fend for himself. During the show's first season, Grylls wore a urine-soaked rag on his head to survive in the desert, stripped naked and dried himself with snow after falling through an ice pond, and drank elephant-dung juice in Africa. With 3.5 million (mostly male) viewers, the show was Discovery's fourth-highest-rated show in 2006. During the second season, Grylls keeps a stiff upper lip as he evades alligators in the Florida everglades, avoids freezing in the mountains of Scotland, escapes poisonous snakes and cyclones in

Australia, and fends off sharks while skippering a handmade raft in the South Pacific.

In 2007, the National Geographic Channel went one step further with the documentary *A Man Among Wolves*. The film's subject doesn't just pit himself against wild animals, he actually becomes one. The camera follows Shaun Ellis, a wolf-behavior expert who "immerses himself in wolf society" by playing, sleeping, and even eating with his four-legged family. Ellis's food is placed in a plastic bag inside the same animal carcass that the wolf pack feeds from as he licks, snarls, and howls in ways that he had learned from observing wolves at close range for decades. He once spent eighteen months living in captivity with a trio of orphaned wolf pups, taking the place of their wolf father as they learned how to fend for themselves. Burly and bearded, he uses his knowledge of wolf calls and physical cues to communicate with the pack and keep himself safe from attack.

Ellis's fascination with wolves has already cost him his family—his partner and four children left him because of his obsessive interest in wild canines. It may eventually cost him his humanity. Ellis is "a true wolf man," Bernard Walton, the show's producer, told ABC News. "You can't get closer to wolves than he has."

At least not while staying alive.

In Werner Herzog's 2005 documentary *Grizzly Man*, Timothy Treadwell videotaped his own amazingly intimate interactions with grizzlies in the Alaskan wilderness, which Herzog then edited into a riveting and ultimately tragic narrative. As heard on a recording found in Treadwell's camera after his death, his decision to stay longer into the autumn season than usual exposed him to bears from a different area who regarded him more as food than friend.

On the Discovery Channel show *Last One Standing*, six adventurous athletes are, according to the program's intro voice-over, "hurled into a tribal world of sport and ritual." In one episode that means facing off with African Zulu stick fighters and testing their male mettle in bloodletting ceremonies where bleeding wounds are dressed with dirt. Exclaims one contestant, "I've always wanted to be a superhero."

A superhero status of sorts is available to almost anyone in Darkon, an elaborately staged live-action role-play (LARP) game. The Darkon bouts, in which hundreds of guys dressed in medieval armor gather in remote parks and forests to wage simulated warfare, can last for days. In the heat of each attack, surrounded by phalanxes of sword-wielding knights, fantasy and reality merge. Like paintball, laser tag, and other participatory war games, the Darkon battlefield allows men, in the words of one LARPer, to enter a place "where we become more than what we really are." In the make-believe arena of fake fighting with fake weapons to the fake death, guys are allowed, at least for a few adrenaline-filled moments, to feel like real men.

CHAPTER 7

Boys Will Be Boys

K en Carson came into the world on March 13, 1961, in Los Angeles, California. Ken was the offspring of Polish immigrants, but his childhood is otherwise shrouded in mystery. Nevertheless, he was quickly recognized as a good-looking young man with excellent manners and a knack for wearing the right thing on any given occasion. One day, while working on a television commercial, he met a rising young starlet named Barbara ("Barbie") Millicent Roberts. They fell for each other instantly and became one of the world's most famous couples. They traveled the world and costarred in movies together. But Ken, despite being the kind of boy most girls dream about, was often alone; Barbie's booming career left little room for a traditional relationship. Ken stayed busy, too, doing stints as a dancer, soldier, astronaut, hunter, baseball player, doctor, ice skater, pizza delivery boy, and soda jerk. He dressed up like Superman and played prince to Barbie's princess. When he wasn't escorting Barbie to a party or black-tie event, he worked out at the gym, drove his car around town, and hung out at the beach. Over the decades, his body became more muscular and his arms and neck became more flexible. He grew a beard and changed his hair color several times, from blond to dark brown and back to sandy blond again. He also went through a number of different fashion phases—leather-clad Harley

Davidson rider, flannel-wearing outdoorsman, all-American tennis pro, tuxedoed gentleman, disco glam-boy, surfer bum.

During the seventies, he grew his hair to his shoulders and dressed like a hippie. In the eighties, he started his own band and became a rock star. Then, in 1993, a year in which Whitney Houston, Mariah Carey, and Janet Jackson ruled the charts and *Details* was the men's magazine of the moment, he emerged as "Earring Magic Ken." His outfit included a purple faux-leather vest, a mesh shirt, and black jeans. The eponymous earring was accompanied by a gold chain with a ring-shaped pendant some found suspiciously suggestive of male sexual paraphernalia. To top it off, a promotional postcard depicted Ken cavorting in a convertible with "Secret Hearts," a young Liberace look-alike who was sporting a patterned rolled-collar jacket and a corsage on his right wrist.

Ken's frisky new look was a media sensation, praised and attacked with equal relish. The doll became known by fans and detractors alike as the "Alternative Lifestyle Ken." Pundits snickered that Ken had "gone gay." But that didn't stop little girls and grown men from snapping him up. By Christmas 1993, Earring Magic Ken had sold out in most stores, leaving thousands of Earring Magic Barbies alone on the shelves without a date.

"I think this particular Ken reflects infiltration of popular culture in the time period," Jef Beck notes on his site manbehindthedoll.com. An avid collector and trader of Ken dolls, Beck defends Earring Magic Ken as a product of the metrosexual zeitgeist—and the bold brainchild of a marketing team that only had Ken's best interests in mind. Originally priced at $11, the doll now trades on the collector's market for $47. "From MTV to hip activism, he mirrors what was 'in' at the moment," Beck argues. "Ken's redesign was created from the advice of the little girls who played with him. They wanted Ken to look a 'little cooler.' He was on the brink of being discontinued and being replaced with a new boyfriend. This is what makes this doll so pivotal in Ken's history. Not only for the controversy that surrounded him, but the fact that the idea was bantered around to replace him. Controversy or not, when he flew off the shelves, he proved his appeal and marketing value in the Barbie line."

When Barbie turned forty in 2003, she was celebrated around the world as an enduring icon and role model for generations of girls.

Indeed, Barbie is the number-one doll in the U.S., generating more than $3 billion in revenue with sales in 150 countries. Once derided by feminists as superficial and sexually repressed, she has since earned their respect. Like Madonna, who shares Barbie's penchant for dazzling makeovers, she was a self-made survivor, a woman who had come to terms with her molded body and had taken control of her destiny. Suddenly, the sexually confident, thoroughly professional and independent Barbie looked a lot like the young women who had played with her as little girls. She was one of them.

Ken's fortunes, meanwhile, seemed to be headed in the opposite direction. His fortieth birthday, which came two years after Barbie's, was barely noticed. And when grown-up women did pay attention, they didn't much like what they saw—a pathetic hanger-on who lacked charisma and gravitas, not to mention that his sex organs were trapped in permanent plastic underwear.

"Poor Ken," wrote Ruth Horowitz in *Seven Days* magazine. "He's a doll. A prince. A devoted friend who wants nothing more from life than to frolic on a sunny beach or spin his beloved across a gleaming ballroom. But where does it get him? And the intransigence of his underpants is just one of his problems. While Barbie basks in her role as cultural icon, an image of ideal femininity that for the last four decades has shaped little girls' dreams, Ken is at best ignored, and at worst, dismembered."

Ken's eunuch status has even entered the lexicon. According to Wikipedia, "The *Ken* gene in the Drosophila fly was so named because the gene, when deleted, caused the flies to form without external genitalia."

"Ken has not had it easy," Denise Van Patten conceded in her column on the website About.com. "He's been referred to as a dork, a dweeb, even a doofus by many, including dedicated Barbie lovers! However, most Barbie collectors DO have a soft place in their heart for Ken, and, after all, without Ken what would Barbie do with all of those fantastic wedding dresses that the fine designers at Mattel have created for Barbie over the years?"

Poor Ken, forever the perfectly groomed groom, yet eternally doomed to leave the knot untied.

In her book *Forever Barbie*, M. G. Lord dresses down and discards Ken as excess baggage, an unnecessary appendage from an unenlightened era. "True, [Barbie] had a boyfriend, but he was a lackluster fellow, a mere accessory," writes Lord. "Mattel, in fact, never wanted to produce Ken; male figure dolls had traditionally been losers in the marketplace. But consumers so pushed for a boyfriend doll that Mattel finally released Ken in 1961. The reason for their demand was obvious. Barbie taught girls what was expected of women, and a woman in the fifties would have been a failure without a male consort, even a drip with seriously abridged genitalia who wasn't very important in her life."

Intentionally or not, for better or for worse, Ken's story is the story of the American man. At a time when some women are questioning whether men are necessary at all, Ken's deevolution from the ideal mate to an emasculated fashion-forward narcissist seems eerily prescient. While Ken was on his path to self-discovery, his real-life counterparts were grappling with their own identity issues. Like Ken, they look younger than their age. They take care of themselves. They have a good life, their girlfriend is great, and yet somehow they are still failing. Some of them have lost their jobs, lost their spouses, lost their homes and their self-respect. Or they will. They change their outfits and hairstyle frequently, yet they're not sure who they are. And, like Ken, they're still wondering what went wrong.

Is it possible that being committed to that special woman in your life is no longer enough? Haven't women been saying for decades that they want their men to be caring, considerate, courteous, well-groomed, and appropriately dressed? Did Ken make the masculine mistake by allowing himself to become emotionally and financially dependent on Barbie? Didn't she know that all those hours doing Pilates at the gym were *for her*? If the most recent chapters in the Barbie and Ken saga are any indication, the answer is no, and the troubles for Ken's real-life counterparts are just beginning.

In any case, by the start of the new millennium, Barbie was having her own problems. A gang of street-savvy girl dolls called the Bratz had been stealing her thunder—and her customer base. Created in 2001 by an Iranian immigrant named Isaac Larian, the Bratz were sexier, sassier, and noticeably more multiethnic than Barbie could ever pretend to be. Their almond-shaped eyes, bee-stung lips, petite waistlines, and caramel-colored skin were easier to relate to for the Asian, Hispanic, and African-American girls who were an increasingly large part of the doll-buying demographic. J-Lo and Beyoncé were hot, and racial ambiguity was in. For millions of multiethnic 'tweens, blond hair and blue eyes were no longer the only standard of female beauty. In just a few years, the Bratz had chewed off enough of Barbie's core clientele to put a serious dent in Mattel's bottom line. One can almost see Barbie, dressed in a no-nonsense blue suit and Manolo Blahnik pumps, hastily calling a meeting of the board, excoriating her sales team, *demanding answers*.

Then, in 2004, came the shocking news: Barbie and Ken were breaking up. True, Barbie had been spotted in promotional appearances getting cozy with GI Joe. But if Ken suspected anything, he had never let on. "After more than 43 years together," Mattel announced in a press release with the headline "The Storybook Romance Comes to an End for Barbie and Ken" that "Hollywood's quintessential 'doll of a couple,' Barbie and Ken, have decided to spend some time apart." Added Mattel vice president of marketing and the pair's self-described "business manager," Russell Arons: "Barbie and Ken have always been an extraordinary couple with so much on- and off-screen chemistry. In fact, they just finished wrapping their fourth movie together, Barbie as *The Princess and the Pauper*, which debuts this fall. And now they feel it's time to spend some quality time—apart."

But what, inquiring minds wanted to know, was the real reason behind the breakup. How could a couple that had it all call it quits? Maybe it was the stress of catfighting with the Bratz, or maybe, just maybe, Barbie didn't *need* Ken anymore, except maybe to hold her bags now and then when she went on a shopping spree. Whatever the cause, it was clear that she needed some space.

"We realized it was time to allow Barbie to have more romantic options," Arons told the *New York Times* shortly after the breakup was announced. "Ken has been a great best friend and boyfriend, but after four decades it seemed time for some change in that aspect of her life." Arons added that Barbie's website had been "overwhelmed" with concerned fans offering her romantic advice and said they would be able to vote on who should be the next man in her life. Asked if the separation was temporary or permanent, Arons coyly replied, "I am sympathetic to their needs and am respecting their privacy."

Heartbroken and alone for the first time in his career, Ken set out to find himself. He learned to cook, took up yoga, and traveled to a Buddhist monastery in Tibet. There, he undoubtedly did some soul-searching. How could his wonderful life reach such a pathetic point? Hadn't he always done the right thing, said the right thing, worn the right thing? And now he was being tossed aside like last year's Prada handbag. How could Barbie do this to him? Who was he, really? How could he find the strength inside to find his own path? And where would it take him next?

But the answers, as always, were right in front of him, deep inside his own past, in the very act of his creation. Named after the real-life son of Barbie's creators, Ken was an accident, an afterthought. From the beginning, he had been an *accessory*. From the start Ruth and Elliot Handler had resisted making a soul mate for Barbie, but her fans had demanded a boyfriend, so two years later they relented—designing him to increase the dazzle of her stardom. Contrary to Scripture, Ken had evolved from Barbie's rib.

The horrible truth was that—from a marketing perspective at least—Barbie was Ken's big sister, or, worse yet, his mom. No wonder they never had sex!

In 2006, two years after Barbie and Ken's breakup, and one year before the Bratz overtook Barbie as the best-selling doll franchise in America, Mattel called a news conference to announce that Ken was back in Barbie's life—although exactly what that meant remained murky. "Ken has revamped his life—mind, body, and soul," explained Hollywood stylist and Mattel consultant Phillip Bloch, whose clients have included Jim Carrey, John Travolta, and Salma Hayek. Then, sounding more like a therapist than a stylist, he added: "Everyone knows how difficult it is to change, especially when you've lived your life a certain way for more than four decades."

What had changed, apparently, was Ken's wardrobe. The new Ken showed up in two versions. One sported tousled blond hair, blue surfer jams, a white T-shirt, and blue shades; the other was brown-haired and was dressed in cargo pants and black leather jacket over a form-fitting vintage T-shirt. His eyes were still blue, but his jaw had a rugged, more masculine cut.

Ken, said Bloch, was going for a "worldly European thing"; he "definitely wanted to be looking hot."

The buzz in Toyland was that Barbie had opened the door to a romantic reconciliation by dumping Blaine, her interim Australian paramour. Ken "really looks great," gushed Barbie publicist Lauren Dougherty. "But we'll have to stay tuned to see whether the two will get back together."

The jury on Barbie and Ken is still out, but "Fashion Fever Ken," released in 2007, showed him looking dashingly eligible in blue jeans, a gray hoodie sweatshirt, and carrying a navy blue messenger-style shoulder bag with a metallic silver strap. Ken also moonlighted in a new *Wizard of Oz* character line. Fans could choose from a heartless "Tin Man Ken," a brainless "Scarecrow Ken," or a "Cowardly Lion Ken." Barbie, for her part, was available as Dorothy, Glinda the Good Witch, or the green-skinned Wicked Witch of the West. Burning broomsticks and water buckets sold separately.

METROS, RETROS, AND GRUPS

The modern male is not so much missing as misplaced. If he isn't hiding behind a can of beer and a baseball cap pulled down low, then he's preening for the camera, feathers fanned in full peacock display. There's a whiff of defensiveness in the masculine demeanor; like a prizefighter who's been punched a few too many times, he dodges and weaves, covering his vitals, looking for an opening, a bit wobbly on his feet, praying for the bell. He feels the earth shifting under him, senses that something important has changed, yet clings to the notion that things are essentially, fundamentally, the same. And why shouldn't he? After all, the Average Guy loves his wife and his kids and comes home every day after a hard day's work. The Average Guy is secure in his sexuality, although he's starting to have doubts about the neighbors. The Average Guy doesn't worry that his butt or his gut are getting too big, or that his truck guzzles gas. The Average Guy knows that a woman won't get elected president in his lifetime, that his wife will never leave him for her female boss, that his kids will stay off drugs and look up to him for wisdom and guidance, just like he looked up to his own dad. The Average Guy is trustworthy, honest, loyal, and unflinching. The Average Guy does not fear gays, or minorities, or women because capitalism works and the American Dream, which ties everyone together, will keep the United States on top, like it always has, and always will. The Average Guy knows that there are a few things that he can always count on: his dog, his best friend, his favorite beer, and Monday Night Football. The Average Guy is not worried about incoming asteroids or global warming because in a few more years he will own his house free and clear and his pension and Social Security will cover him just fine after that. The Average Guy is happy with his city and state, his wife, his life. He can't wait to wake up on his Posturepedic in the morning, have a bowl of Cheerios, hop into his Ford Explorer, and drive to his job at Wal-Mart, where he sells Sony cameras, Panasonic TVs, and GE appliances to nice ordinary people just like himself.

Madison Avenue loves the Average Guy.

Over the years, particularly since the end of World War II and the rise of the great consumer economy, advertisers have told him what to buy and why he needs it. More important, they have told him how he should *feel* about it. They have told him, for example, that Visa is everywhere he wants to be, that Avis tries harder, that BMW is the ultimate driving machine, that Club Med is the antidote for civilization, that KFC is finger lickin' good, and that Coke is it. They have told him that he's in good hands with Allstate, that the Yellow Pages will let his fingers do the walking, and that there's Intel inside. They have told him how dirty boys get clean.

The only problem is . . . there is no Average Guy.

In the crazy-quilt crossroads of current male identity, men are variously style-averse and fashion slaves, barefoot billionaires and cubicle drones, cavemen and sensitive guys. They are returning to their manly roots and embracing their feminine side, they are horn dogs, dream lovers, cads, and gourmet cooks. They are die-hard bachelors and doting dads, dandies, slackers, rednecks, pin-striped lawyers, Christian rockers, extreme fighters, and skater boyz.

Their behaviors and tastes fluctuate from region to region, by socioeconomic group and by age, yet the entire range of male archetypes can be found in almost any suburb or city anywhere in the country. This is partly because each man, to varying degrees and in myriad ways, is all of these things, all of these men.

Masculine style has became flexible, fungible, and negotiable, reflecting the lack of consensus in male consciousness. As women become more self-confident, men are losing their nerve. While women join together in an outpouring of mutual support and celebration, too many men are dropping out or hunkering down—sullen, resentful, alone. And when a guy does go out, he's no longer sure if it's appropriate to hold the door, to order the wine, to pick up the check. Besides, his date probably makes more money than he does. She certainly has a more impressive title. Plus, she picked the restaurant. The goodnight kiss went well enough, but it was kind of weird when she asked for *his* number and promised to call. When and how did the dance of romance get so darn complicated?

Once again, Barbie and Ken are instructive.

"In Barbie's universe, women are not the second sex," writes Lord. "Just as the goddess-based religions antedated Judeo-Christian monotheism, Barbie came before Ken. The whole idea of woman as temptress, or woman as subordinate to man, is absent from the Barbie cosmology. Ken is a gnat, a fly, a slave, an accessory of Barbie. Barbie was made perfect; her body has not evolved dramatically with time. Ken, by contrast, was a blunder: first scrawny, now pumped-up, his ever-changing body is neither eternal nor talismanic . . . Critics who ignore Barbie's mythic dimension often find fault with her lifestyle. But it is mythologically imperative that she live the way she does. Of course Barbie inhabits a prelapsarian paradise of consumer goods; she has never been exiled from the garden."

But Ken, of course, was. And he has been wandering in the consumer wilderness ever since. Although, it seems, he remembered to bring along his credit card.

The growth rate in sales of men's clothing and accessories for the past ten years has held steady at just over 5 percent annually, roughly on a par with women's. Men between the ages of twenty-five to thirty-four spend 75 percent more than the average American household on food outside the home, 50 percent more on alcoholic beverages, and 83 percent more on clothing. A study commissioned by GQ in 2006 found that 84 percent of men said they purchased their own clothes, as compared to 65 percent only four years earlier. More than half of retailers surveyed reported that male customers shopped in their stores at least once a month, up from only 10 percent in 2001. On any given day, 42 percent of all men will buy something, and spend about ninety minutes doing it.

Of course, some men, perhaps addicted to the thrill of finding that Brooks Brothers suit they wanted on sale at half price, shop more. *A lot more.* According to researchers at the Stanford University School of Medicine, a survey of more than 2,500 American adults showed that nearly as many men as women experience "compulsive buying disorder," a.k.a. "compulsive shopping disorder"—a condition marked by binge buying and subsequent financial hardship. "The widespread opinion that most compulsive buyers are women may be wrong," the researchers wrote in the *American Journal of Psychiatry*. Prior to the study, it had been estimated that compulsive shopping disorder affected between 2 and 16 percent of the U.S. population and that 90 percent of sufferers were women. Victims of compulsive shopping disorder, the study reported, "are often struck with an irresistible, intrusive, and often senseless impulse to buy. It is common for sufferers to go on frequent shopping binges and to accumulate large numbers of unnecessary, unwanted items."

The rise of the male shopaholic dates back at least to *American Gigolo*, the 1980s film that starred Richard Gere as a lady-killer who loved Giorgio Armani almost as much as he loved himself. Before long men were being spotted loitering near the Clinique counter, and face-lifts for fellas had become a fact of life. During the eighties, even as Ronald Reagan charmed the masses in John Wayne drag, photographers like Herb Ritts and Bruce Weber eroticized the male body with GQ fashion spreads and giant posters of muscular young models in Calvin Klein underwear. A decade later, the "metrosexual"—a term coined by British journalist Mark Simpson to describe the foppish habits of vain straight males—entered the vernacular. Almost from the moment the term reached America, "metrosexual" became a slur, and it begat, eventually, the equally pejorative term "retrosexual." Caught in a revolving door of polarizing prefixes, the soul of the male consumer has been up for grabs ever since. Even as female identity seemed to coalesce around career, family, and sex, Ken-like men were breaking apart into multiple personalities, plastic pieces of psyche flying off in every direction.

Men, or advertisers at least, decided that the best way to cultivate the Inner Guy was to develop the Outer Ape. Girly was out, burly was in. The phrase "Defending the Caveman," became popular outside of anthropology classes when Rob Becker's play became a Broadway hit. John Gray's book *Men Are from Mars, Women Are from Venus* assured us that the sexes weren't just different, they actually came from different planets. By 2005, the "übermale" had become the male moniker de jour, a term that connoted dominance, masculinity, and the umlaut-obsessed heavy metal bands from the eighties like Mötley Crüe. Depending on what cable channel you happen to be watching, übermale icons include Barack Obama, Bill

Clinton, Bono, Lenny Kravitz, George Clooney, and Brad Pitt. Übermales, we are told, are not soft metrosexuals, or reactionary retrosexuals. Instead, they exude an easy confidence that harks back to simpler times, yet are willing to fight for their right to have emotions and, when necessary, change a baby's diapers. Übermen, we are told, are *passionate*—about work, about women, about life. And also, it seems, about shopping. But not just any kind of shopping—it is übermanly shopping for übermanly things.

Retro-butch reached a kind of apotheosis at Freeman's Sporting Club, a New York City men's store that is part hunting lodge and part frontier fashion boutique, complete with moose-head decor and a carefully selected assortment of hunting paraphernalia, outdoorsy clothing, and other manly gear. After picking up a limited-edition black Leatherman multitool or a pair of deerskin-lined bison grizzly boots made by Quoddy, fifth-generation moccasin makers from Maine, bargain hunters can amble over to the attached barber shop for a trim and a shave in antique chairs from the 1920s and '30s.

In Charleston, South Carolina, meanwhile, the Evening Post Publishing Company announced the launch of *Garden & Gun* magazine. Billed as a regional magazine for "21st Century Southern America," the magazine aims to deliver an updated, upscale version of Southern tradition. Publisher Rebecca Darwin, a former publisher of *The New Yorker* and *Mirabella*, hopes to tap young, affluent readers who aspire to "the sporting lifestyle," and are in turn coveted by high-end advertisers. "We believe that Southerners, and Southern men in particular, are looking for a magazine that speaks to their regional roots but is current, sophisticated and smart," explains founding editor in chief John Wilson. "The modern Southern gentleman is culturally involved, physically active, environmentally aware and willing to pay a premium for the finer things in life, from knowing the best place in the South to go fishing for red drum or trout, to big boy toys like the Cirrus SR22, a single-engine personal aircraft that traces its inspiration back to the first airplanes flown by the Wright Brothers at Kitty Hawk."

It turns out that even though the metrosexual panic succeeded in pushing a lot of male shoppers back into the consumer closet, the unprecedented surge in sales of male grooming products, apparel, and other products never really abated.

"The battle is over," Trip Gabriel tells me over a cup of coffee in the cafeteria of the New York Times Building. "The so-called metro-sexuals are the norm, especially for younger men in metropolitan areas." A former *Rolling Stone* editor who has presided over the *New York Times* Style section since 1997, Gabriel has helped to chronicle the evolution in men of a looser, more malleable sense of self. "The old stereotype of hypermasculine guys like Rocky Balboa," he says, "those are just cartoons from another time. I don't think many guys or women take that seriously anymore."

One of the more tangible signs of how things have changed at the *Times*, Gabriel explains, is the introduction of "Dress Codes," a section in Style that tracks the fashion consciousness of young cosmopolitan men. He is referring specifically to articles like one published in Style earlier that fall, titled "What I Like about Dracula." "It's easy—too easy—for a working man to look good today, thanks to a sea of slim-cut suits, snappy dress shirts and an Equinox [gym] in every upscale Zip code," David Coleman wrote. "How's a guy to keep his edge?" Well, one way, apparently, is to evoke Transtylevania, dressed in Alexander McQueen purple velvet jackets and glen plaid three-piece suits with crimson linings. "The look," explained Coleman, "is meant to suggest both the gentility and ferocity of the business world." In other words, cutthroat couture for those blood-suckers at the office.

"There's no question that men today are more interested in things that were traditionally more associated with women," Gabriel says, his nonjudgmental tone suggesting that we're all in this together. "Men are more interested in design and parenting than they used to be. They spend more time with their children. Cooking used to be for sissies and now it's considered kind of macho. Being interested in fashion is okay for men, especially younger men."

As the competition for high-paying, fast-track jobs has tightened, and ambitious young professionals are moving into managerial positions, they are ditching their khakis and polo shirts for crisp dress shirts and designer duds. Between 2005 and 2006, Phillips-Van Heusen reported a 14 to 15 percent increase in revenues, mostly due to strong demand for brands like Chaps, Kenneth Cole, Geoffrey Beene, and Calvin Klein.

Shopping malls are jumping on the bandwagon, not just by making sure that male-oriented stores are stocked with the right stuff, but also by increasing the number and variety of stores that appeal to different kinds of men. Shopping malls are transforming themselves from fortresslike boxes into open-air "lifestyle" centers. Inspired by the success of projects like Virginia's Reston Town Center, developers are creating shopping and entertainment environments where kids, moms, and dads can all go their separate ways and find a store that caters specifically to them, and then meet up again for dinner and a movie. And because today's businessman is probably wearing a slim-silhouette suit, luxury hotels are decalorizing their menus and expanding their gyms. Many top chains will even have personal trainers on staff.

A cursory scan of men's magazines illustrates the degree to which they have gone the way of *Cosmo*, serving up testosterone-ized versions of women's magazine staples on beauty, health, and relationships. *Men's Health*, whose explosive growth during the 1990s was widely regarded as proof that metrosexuals had won, has actor Taylor Kitsch posing shirtless on its February 2007 cover, along with exhortations to "Get Back in Shape," "Look Better Instantly," and find "The Easy Way to Hard Abs!" "There's no question that men's magazines have become more like women's magazines,"

Gabriel agrees. "It's part of what's been called the effeminization of men."

But are modern men ready to become eunuchs? Miuccia Prada seems to think so. Asked to describe the idea behind the runway show for her 2008 winter men's collection, she only half-jokingly told Guy Trebay of the *New York Times* that it was an act of revenge on men for the sartorial restrictions that males have historically foisted on women. "Like a flipped version of the Unwomen in Margaret Atwood's feminist parable *The Handmaid's Tale*, the Prada Unman was gotten up in humiliating tutu belts, severe high-collar shirts that buttoned up the back and odd cummerbunds that disappeared in a chevron down the front of trousers conspicuously missing a fly."

Tyler Thoreson, executive editor for Men.style.com, the leading men's fashion site and the online home of *Details* and GQ, maintains that media depictions of men as either hyperfeminized sissies or testosterone-soaked brutes are for the most part caricatures in the service of hype. "Like most reasonable people, I think the whole metrosexual thing is a bit of a media construction," Thoreson observes. "It's a bit of a fake trend. I mean, sure, guys are spending more time concerned about how they look, but they're still guys. They still have the DNA of males. I think that was a bit trumped up a few years ago, partially because it made a tidy little trend piece and partially because it provided something to be outraged about. Meanwhile, most guys are going about their business, trying to look good for the same reasons men have always tried to look good—to lure women."

But while men's goals may not have changed that much, the way to achieve them has. The lines of a man's suit, or code of behavior, are no longer so clear cut. The archetypes available to men nowadays are almost endless. A single feature in the now-defunct *Cargo* magazine offered guys the fashion components to be: (a) the coolster, (b) the rebel, (c) the urban bohemian, (d) the sportster, (e) the club kid, or (f) the trendspotter. "Back in the day you knew exactly how you were supposed to dress and act," Thoreson concurs. "That's no longer true, and with freedom comes a little uncertainty. And that's natural. If there's some anxiety involved in that, it's only to be expected."

If men are really free to choose how they dress, then the very notion that men should act or look a certain way is passé. That may seem superficial, but if fashion is an expression of social and economic transformation, then the new manifestations of masculine style have profound implications for all of us.

Meanwhile, a second wave of male consumer has quietly come onto the scene. It's the side of the "new man" that's truly new, the side that's starting to make buying decisions about products that used to be the exclusive domain of females. As women climb the corporate ladder and men assume more domestic chores and child-rearing responsibilities, males are suddenly a factor in everything from bedding and cookware to pediatricians and baby bottles. These men have no qualms about weighing in on what kind of window blinds to get for the living room, or making sure that the stroller for their baby can go from zero to sixty on a crowded city sidewalk. Since its introduction in the 1990s with the male-friendly promise to "never lose suction," James Dyson's sleek high-tech DC07 series has become the best-selling vacuum cleaner in the world And the popular Bugaboo baby stroller, designed by Dutchman Max Barenbrug with the modern dad in mind, looks more like space-age sports equipment than a vehicle for pushing around infants. "I daresay I played a much bigger role in our stroller decision than my dad ever considered doing," confides one young father. "When we got the Bugaboo, all I could talk about was all the cool things it could do. It's ludicrously expensive. My wife calls it the Hummer."

Men are more likely than women to regard clothing and other products as gadgets and status symbols. Design and technical specs have a special appeal to men, who use facts and price to advertise the pedigree of their acquisitions, whether it's bragging about the super-narrow-gauge Japanese weave of their three-hundred-dollar-jeans, or forwarding the Web link for a wireless USB tank that fires missiles at coworkers from a digital command center on their office laptop.

Men in their thirties, a.k.a. Generation Xers, are less conspicuous about their purchasing proclivities than their free-spending elders. Notoriously elusive and suspicious of corporate manipulation, they toggle between irreverence and self-conscious sincerity. They have grown up fending and shopping for themselves, fearlessly picking and choosing between various looks and styles, using the things that they buy to assemble and merge identities, which are then discarded or recycled, depending on their mood. Unconventional at the core, they often pass for Regular Guys, although their addictions to Halo, Death Cab for Cutie, and eco-adventure vacations are a dead giveaway. They have learned that caring about their appearance is okay, as long as they don't make a big deal over it.

Waiting in the wings is Generation Y, the 70 million "echo-boomers" now in their teens and early twenties. Internet-savvy and unabashedly materialistic, these "maturiteens" spend upwards of $100 billion a year, although their actual clout is much greater due to their ability to influence their parents and others around them. Teen boys are even more obsessed with grooming than their dads and older brothers, and more willing to try new products. Weaned on interactive media and comfortable with consumer-generated content, these proto-influencers trade tips about their favorite brands and stores on MySpace and Facebook, where kids congregate in a digital update of the corner pizza shop.

They are also happy to be involved in the personalization and design of the things they buy. Boys and young men are prime customers for companies like Adidas, whose in-store events allow kids to decorate their own sneakers. Thredless.com, another top brand with teens, lets customers create their own T-shirts and hoodies or buy shirts made by other visitors and young designers. Visitors to the site can vote for their favorites or contact artists directly after posting comments about their designs.

The trend toward buyer-generated design, particularly among younger, Internet-savvy consumers is acknowledged by fashion experts—but only up to a point. "I can count five guys I know who have good jobs but also run successful T-shirt businesses on the side," says Thoreson. "In the same sense that blogosphere cheerleaders like to say that they're the new journalists, to some extent the consumer is becoming more of a fashion designer. There's obviously a limit to that, in the same way that you can create a blog but it's not really relevant if nobody reads it, and you still need an audience. The fragmentation gets to a point where it's totally irrelevant, and you can say the same thing about clothes."

Advertisers have long known that word of mouth can make or break a brand, and that "memes"—words on ideas that spread quickly and replicate—can influence what people buy and why. A fashion *meme*, as the zoologist and evolutionary psychologist Richard Dawkins explained in his 1976 book *The Selfish Gene*, is a style or manner of dress that mutates and survives in accordance with the concept of evolution espoused by Charles Darwin. In this sense, fashion styles live or die by their ability to fill a physical or psychological need.

In a wired world, memes can cover the globe in minutes, and often do. A fad in Seattle can show up in New Delhi and reappear, in a slightly modified form, in Beijing a day later. For those who are trying to set the styles, or cover them, cultural whiplash is an occupational hazard. Online and off, down the block or around the world, men's identities and styles merge and overlap. Communities of interest and other virtual tribes can bring disparate groups of men together around a single idea, or a single man may toggle between different networks and communities, each with a different set of social rules and fashion cues.

Sometimes trends fuse and mutate, creating new categories, which soon enough get their own name. The convergence of aging Gen Xers, young urban hippies, and "indie" culture, for instance, resulted in a social phenomenon that *New York* magazine christened as the Grup, a.k.a. the Yupster, as in "Yuppie" plus "hipster," or the Alterna-Hippie. The Grup name is derived from a *Star Trek* episode in which the crew of the Enterprise land on a planet ruled by children. The children on the planet call Captain Kirk and his crew "grups," a contraction of "grown-ups," and journalist Adam Sternbergh borrowed the term to describe fully grown men and women who still dress like college students, listen to cool new bands, and otherwise subscribe to the alternative lifestyle. It's a form of arrested development for the fully developed. It is also, according to Sternbergh, "an obituary for the generation gap."

"It's about the hedge-fund guy in Park Slope with the chunky square glasses, brown rock T-shirt, slight paunch, expensive jeans, Puma sneakers, and shoulder-sling messenger bag, with two kids squirming over his lap like itchy chimps at the Tea Lounge on Sunday morning," says Sternbergh.

Grups are just another example of how some men are refusing to acknowledge traditional boundaries, taking whatever they want or relate to, and in the process redefining themselves and their gender. Grups, it seems, have committed the terrible sin of not realizing that they are old, or, more likely, they are redefining what getting older means. On their terms. Or, as Sternbergh puts it, "They are a generation or two of affluent, urban adults who are now happily sailing through their thirties and forties, and even *fifties*, clad in beat-up sneakers and cashmere hoodies, content that they can enjoy all the good parts of being a grown-up (a real paycheck, a family, the warm touch of cashmere) with none of the bad parts (Dockers, management seminars, indentured servitude at the local Gymboree). It's about a brave new world whose citizens are radically rethinking what it means to be a grown-up and whether being a grown-up still requires, you know, actually growing up."

Grups are a by-product of several intersecting trends, combining the self-centeredness and materialism of baby boomers with the anticorporate stance of Gen Xers and the nonhierarchical tendencies of dot-com techies, for whom dressing down became the new dressing up. Grups were born for "subversive" A-list brands like Gilded Age or Barking Irons, whose T-shirts feature arcane phrases and symbols on high-quality cotton, available at Barneys in New York and Fred Segal in West Hollywood for prices only an attorney or mini-mogul could afford. Grup dads aren't just pretending to like their kids' music. With alternative rockers like TV on the Radio and Clap Your Hands Say Yeah! owing an obvious debt to eighties bands like Talking Heads and the Cure, it's hard to say who is aping whom.

"You've got a whole generation of guys who are coming up whose dads dress like a cubicle drone, as opposed to *their* dads, who dressed like the man in the gray flannel suit," Thoreson observes. "It's part of the dot-com thing. And of course the pinnacle of that was the Time Warner merger, and the famous picture of Jerry Levin in a tie and Steve Case in an open-neck shirt when they announced the worst merger in history."

Thoreson sees a trend toward less attention to social labels and more emphasis on assembling a personal sense of style from the increasingly wide spectrum of personas that men can choose from. "When I was in college in the early nineties we dressed up for semiformals in a sort of semiironic way because it was fun to dress formally and act utterly informally," he recalls. "But now I think guys in college, in that generation and age group, are throwing on a blazer to go to a party, and they're just doing it because it looks good. I'm not sure that same guy who's doing that is also sitting there plucking and tweezing before the party. And I think you'll notice that we don't have a section on our site devoted to bleaching your taint. It's just not what we do. It's not our raison d'être. If guys are doing it, great. But it's not what we're here for."

As the fashion pendulum swings back and forth, the only thing certain about men is that they are in flux, and that the process of male mutation is far from over. There is no turning back, no return to innocence, and any predictions of a retreat into the comforting definitions of the past are delusional or mere exercises in wishful thinking. The feminization and objectification of men that began with Andy Warhol's fetishistic art films, and then was fine-tuned and packaged for the masses by Calvin Klein underwear ads, has blossomed into a mainstream commercial onslaught. Using male sexuality to push product has become so commonplace that the shock value is gone. When moms and dads from all over America escort their kids into Abercrombie and Fitch stores where buff, half-naked college boys parade around in little more than flip-flops for no other purpose than to be looked at, to be seen and admired (and perhaps even to sell jeans), it's a safe bet that the transformation of men into ornamental props, into *accessories*, has become not just acceptable, but respectable.

VAGUE VOGUE

But even if the metrosexual man is mostly a media fabrication, the influence of gay culture on the American mainstream is not. Over the past few years, gay men have emerged as a consumer force in their own right. The total buying power of the U.S. gay, lesbian, bisexual, and transgender (GLBT) adult population was almost $700 billion in 2006, up from just over $600 billion in 2005. While the percentage of the U.S. population believed to be GLBT is between 6 and 7 percent, or about 15 million adults, their influence on popular culture, entertainment, travel, and, of course, fashion, far exceeds their numbers. Besides spending more on clothing, home furnishings, meals away from home, and luxury items of every stripe, GLBTs are cultural innovators who mingle and mix with heterosexual trendsetters in film, music, art, and the theater.

GLBTs are also an important component of the Creative Class, the 50 million Americans who seek out lifestyle diversity, not only where they work and live, but also in the places they go and the things that they do. The cities and towns where gays and the Creative Class congregate—"Creative Centers," as sociologist Richard Florida calls them—tend to have large populations of young, highly skilled workers, many of whom are recent graduates of nearby colleges and universities. These areas become magnets not just for other educated young professionals, but also for artists, musicians, writers, graphic designers, Internet developers, and others who develop and drive content for companies involved in the creation and distribution of entertainment media, publishing, and advertising. These creative types, some of whom are gay themselves, are on the front lines of popular culture—they are the first to sport a new hairstyle, find a new band, experiment with alternative lifestyles, with unconventional modes of speech and dress, and otherwise push the boundaries of what is normal, acceptable, and familiar.

While gender bending in the art community goes back centuries, the insatiable hunger for what's new, novel, and fresh has accelerated the absorption of the counterculture into the social mainstream. As the fashion fringe is sucked into the center and spewed out again at Target and the Gap, it is acceptable, even desirable, for straight men to pass as gay, and vice versa. Blair.com's online guessing game "Gay or Eurotrash?" makes fun of the overlapping of gay and straight dress codes even as it drives home the point.

The phenomenon was officially outed in 2005 by a *New York Times* article that bore the headline "Gay or Straight? Hard to

Tell." The article pointed out that younger gay men, whose comfort level with their own sexuality had led them to abandon the leather-and-denim homosexual-clone look of the seventies and eighties, had reached a sociocultural intersection of sorts with straight men, who felt increasingly free to venture into sartorial terrain that hither-to had been the exclusive domain of gay men. Almost overnight, it seemed, certifiably straight men were bulking up at the gym and wearing open-toed footwear, while gay men adopted the straight-man uniform of jeans, T-shirt, and sneakers.

"The result is a gray area that is rendering gaydar—that totally unscientific sixth sense that many people rely on to tell if a man is gay or straight—as outmoded as Windows 2000," David Coleman wrote. "It's not that straight men look more stereotypically gay per se, or that out-of-the-closet gay men look straight. What's happening is that many men have migrated to a middle ground where the cues traditionally used to pigeonhole sexual orientation—hair, clothing, voice, body language—are more and more ambiguous."

To help out the clueless, the *Times* included a handy chart for spotting and categorizing the elusive gay vague male. Straight men, it said, wore Tommy Hilfiger underwear, Gap relaxed-fit jeans, and extra-large-size pink polo shirts. Gay men wore Baskit underwear, Rufskin jeans, and extra-small-size pink polos. Gay Vagues wore 2xist underwear, Diesel jeans, and medium polos. And size large, apparently, was ambisexual.

These days, the boundaries are blurrier than ever. In cities and suburbs across the nation, straight guys shave their privates, crop their hair close, and grow scruffy beards, a macho-metro mix that echoes the classic gay aesthetic of the eighties. Not that most men in their twenties and thirties remember, or care. *Brokeback Mountain* was groundbreaking cinema not because it showed two cowpokes having sex, but because the guys getting it on were so utterly, unaffectedly normal.

The reaction among heterosexuals still runs the gamut from

celebration to indifference to confusion to alarm. When a gay character on MTV's *Real World* brought home his straight-looking date, a housemate on the show immediately called her boyfriend and asked him why he was spending so much time sleeping over at his buddy's house. "If *that* boy is gay," she whined, "then *anybody* can be gay."

Yet these daredevils in Dolce and Gabbana are being egged on, not by gay men sporting Polo and Banana Republic, but by straight women who find vampy men alluring. Alexis Tirado, a Gen Yer who worked at *Playgirl* and freelanced for Nerve.com before becoming an editor at *Quick and Simple* magazine in New York, finds that pansexuality can actually increase a guy's chances of getting lucky with a girl at most Manhattan scenes. "It almost seems like the more feminine a guy is, the cooler he is in terms of what's cool now," she says. "So, those guys, those Alex P. Keaton, Kirk Cameron from *Family Ties*, those Christian good guys, they're kind of not cool anymore, they're kind of the dorks now."

Many guys under thirty would agree. "I have trimmed for years," confesses a single professional living in Virginia. His regimen includes bathing once or twice a week in oatmeal, baby oil, and herbs to keep his skin hydrated and smooth. "Guy friends told me how great it feels to shave your balls, so I tried it and liked it," he says. "Girls seem to like it as well."

The backlash against the metrosexual, and the rise of the retrosexual, Tirado contends, was overhyped, if it ever even happened. "I think that men are still kind of feminine in a way," she says. "I'm thinking about guys on MTV, with eyeliner, even guys like Justin Timberlake—he's in touch with his feminine side. I think that whole metro thing that happened in the late nineties, it leaked into those emo bands. And there is that whole downtown hipster scene, guys with tight jeans and tight vintage shirts, taking their shirts off and twisting their nipples for photos. Go to lastnightsparty.com, look at those photos, that's the whole downtown scene: they're all about being bi or looking bi, getting in touch with their feminine side. So, no, I don't think men have become more masculine."

The current crop of pop and rock stars are certainly reverting to a stance that's more glam and androgynous than butch.

Grunge has been replaced with a jaded mod-goth variation that is equal parts degenerate and investment banker.

On the cover of *Rolling Stone*, Panic at the Disco! posed in rakish suits and ties and sporting "guyliner," the seemingly ubiquitous black eye shadow also favored by hot bands like My Chemical Romance, Good Charlotte, and the Killers. The spectacle of rockers in skinny ties and Armani has no doubt provided plenty of cover for hip young men who might have otherwise avoided exploring their inner dandy.

Pete Wentz, the bassist for Fall Out Boy, made waves in early 2007 when graphic nude photos apparently taken with a cell-phone camera, surfaced on the Web, to the delight of his fans. Wentz, who publicly admitted that he likes taking group showers with friends, appears on his official website wearing a sweatshirt emblazoned with the words "Just a Dirty Boy Living the American Wet Dream."

The most subversive aspect of the hit metro-makeover show *Queer Eye for the Straight Guy* is not that gay men are shown fussing over a heterosexual shlub, like fairy godfathers primping Cinderfella for the ball, it's the way that the "transformed" man is paraded before the woman in his life like a Russian e-mail bride auditioning for her sugar daddy. Just like chumps at a David Copperfield illusion, our attention is diverted from the real trick going on right before our eyes. Lulled into a false sense of sexual security by their comparative masculinity—Hey, look at me, I'm straight, style-challenged, *and* tolerant—as these guys amiably allow their wardrobes to be chucked into the trash bin by clucking *fashionistas*, they don't realize that what they have actually been stripped of is their dignity.

And anyone who thinks that the accessorized man is an exclusively urban animal is simply not paying attention. In small towns and suburbs across America, young men are succumbing to the seduction of the approving glance. No longer needed by females for economic or physical security, men are free to preen, pose, and expose themselves like chicks of yore. Increasingly feckless as protectors and providers, they've discovered that they can still wield power as objects of desire. Even macho high school athletes have no problem serving themselves up as girl bait. In shows like MTV's *Two-A-Days*, ripped midwestern jocks flex their pecs and try to act like they don't know they're hot, but it's the cheerleaders on the sidelines who are really calling the shots. What these postmodern studs don't understand is that by playing along as sex symbols they are only making themselves more dependent on female approval.

After all, even the most macho high school jock knows that the girl he's got a crush on has a picture of a guy wearing mascara pinned up inside her locker.

THE TEXAS DOUBLE-CHEESE AND OTHER WHOPPERS

Maybe empowering boys to be bimbos is progress, but even guys who spend hours working on their abs still have to be able to look at themselves in the mirror without applauding. Or laughing. As Christopher Hitchens pointed out in his *Vanity Fair* article "Why Women Aren't Funny," "Male humor prefers the laugh to be at someone's expense, and understands that life is quite possibly a joke to begin with—and often a joke in extremely poor taste. Humor is part of the armor-plate with which to resist what is already farcical enough." Hitchens made the case that men were funny because humor was a mating tool—it helped them get women to relax and loosen up. Making a woman laugh is, potentially at least, a prelude to seduction. Women don't need to be funny, Hitchens contends, because men are already interested in them. In his view, this helps explain why so many successful female comedians are either unattractive or lesbians.

Women were not amused.

Around the same time, Dustin Hoffman, promoting a new movie on *The Ellen DeGeneres Show*, asked if she would be hosting the Oscars in 2007. When DeGeneres replied that she wasn't sure, Hoffman helpfully pointed out that the male statuette for the Academy Awards "has no genitalia." The pair shared a chuckle. "Oscar can alternate between male and female each year," DeGeneres joked.

This time everybody laughed.

No wonder some marketers call the Academy Awards "The Female Super Bowl."

In addition to using humor as a mating tool, men are perfectly capable of laughing at themselves. They get the cosmic joke. Self-deprecation is the flip side of arrogance. Upon encountering each other in the wild, males can fight or run—or make a joke. Laughter, for men, can be a defense mechanism; it can defuse a dangerous situation, or help them cope with the hopeless absurdity of their lives. Scientific research has shown that humor can—*duh!*—alter a person's mood. When men look in the mirror in the morning, they may like what they see, or they may be disgusted and disheartened. Guys know that, either way, it's still funny.

The trick for advertisers, of course, is to get guys to look at themselves in the mirror and then reach for the right brand of shaver, hair gel, and deodorant. This is why people still remember the Right Guard commercial where a man opens his medicine cabinet and finds another guy staring back at him. The scenario is inherently scary, alarming, amusing.

Advertisers have learned that product endorsements and spiffy graphics only go so far. Today's man is sardonic, brash, and irreverent, and he wants his advertising to talk to him the same way—the zanier and more absurd, the better. Because that's how life *really is*, right? Yet even as the content of ads aimed at men has become more blatant and outrageous, the underlying message has become more subversive. Irony and camp, the intellectual's Laurel and Hardy, have taken the sting out of self-satire. Buffoonish caricatures of Real Men lash out at Sensitive Guys for being soft, and everybody gets to be in on the joke. The Sensitive Guys are laughing because they make more money and have better sex. The Real Guys are laughing because the Sensitive Guys don't realize that this isn't a joke—that their sophisticated, self-assured exterior is just a veneer and doesn't fool anyone.

Men are laughing a lot these days. A recent ad campaign for Bud Light centers on Zagar, a primitive tribesman who wears animal skins and carries a spear. His friend Steve, a clean-cut guy with much better grooming habits, is constantly dealing with Zagar's inappropriate behavior, such as lighting a fire in Steve's bathtub. Is Zagar a stand-in for obnoxious roommates who can't shake their Cro-Magnon ways? Or is he really a symbol of Steve's suppressed wild side? Both answers, of course, are correct.

Miller beer waded into the same psychic swamp with its "man laws" campaign. The ads show a group of latter-day knights of the "square table," which includes macho celebrities like Oscar de La Hoya and Burt Reynolds, dispensing advice from an exaggeratedly male point of view. Most of the group's retrograde proclamations are so patently outrageous that even men are supposed to shake their heads and disagree. Unless, of course, they don't.

Advertisers are more than happy to stoke the perception that old-fashioned straight white males are an endangered species, particularly during the Super Bowl, which, of course, is a kind of Academy Awards for guys. During the past two decades, 221 different advertisers have bought a total of eleven hours of ads for a total of $1.72 billion. Anheuser-Busch, maker of Budweiser and Bud Light beer, is the show's number-one advertiser, spending $250 million since 1987. In 2007, CBS reportedly charged upwards of $2.6 million for each thirty-second spot. With the stakes so high, it's no wonder that Super Bowl ads have become a programming event in themselves. Super Bowl ad buzz now begins weeks before the game, driven by previews of major brand ads and dedicated websites packed with contests, viewer polls, director interviews, outtakes, and other behind-the-scenes extras.

Men laugh at themselves and each other because it drowns out the hisses and snickers coming from the balcony. And in the aftermath of Super Bowl 2007, some of the hisses were actually directed *at* Snickers. The controversy triggered by the candy bar's Super Bowl commercial, much like Janet Jackson's "wardrobe malfunction," was predictable to everyone except the advertiser, who seemed taken aback that its ad, which showed two men inadvertently kissing as they shared a Snickers bar, and then frantically ripping out their own chest hair to reestablish their masculinity, could be offensive to anybody. After complaints by the Gay and Lesbian Alliance Against Defamation and the Human Rights Campaign, Snickers apologized and yanked the ad from its website, but the commercial had already done its job. A Snickers spokesperson pointed out, accurately, that the ad had proved popular with most Super Bowl viewers, and that it had succeeded in its mission "to capture the attention of our core Snickers consumer, primarily 18–24-year-old adult males."

The only Super Bowl ad theme more prevalent than sex was violence. In TiVo households, the second-most-watched moment of the game was a Bud Light commercial in which a rock-paper-scissors game between two teens suddenly turns violent. The spot was one of more than a dozen ads that featured violent or slapstick elements. A study by FKF Applied Research, which uses brain-wave images to track viewer responses, concluded that the aggressive nature of many Super Bowl ads stimulated parts of the brain associated with anxiety and fear, as opposed to ads that usually target the parts of the brain that respond to positive, reassuring messages. In other words, advertisers were using scare tactics to pitch their stuff, in the same way that politicians use negative campaigns to get votes.

For years, Right Guard and other deodorant products made millions off men's fear of smelling bad. Then marketers realized that, for teenage boys at least, the only thing more powerful than worrying about turning girls off was the hope of turning them on. Male body sprays like Axe and Tag convinced young men to use more deodorant in more places by producing ads that portrayed their products as aphrodisiacs. As a result, in 2004, the year Axe body spray was introduced in the United States, sales in the grooming category for men aged eighteen to twenty-four rose 38 percent to $143 million, and between 2004 and 2005 the men's body-spray category was up 62 percent.

Will the "Axe effect" stop advertisers from making pitches that scare and piss people off?

Absolutely not. Probably for the same reason that men will never stop telling women jokes. In love and in sales, the only bad reaction is no reaction at all.

Controversy is no longer a deterrent, because controversy itself has become a marketing tool. Visitors who log in to view the Rolling Rock "Beer Ape" ad on YouTube are greeted by a disclaimer from vice president of marketing Ron Stablehorn, who apologizes to anyone who has been "offended" by the ad, which features a party animal in an ape costume who revives a dull party with the help of an electric guitar and some Rolling Rock. Both the VP and the controversy are phony, but the intent to lure eyeballs to the ad is quite real. Rolling Rock took a similar tack for its "Man Thong" commercial. A young man applying for a position at a "European" firm is told that (a) all men must wear ladies' thongs to work and (b) the office fridge is always stocked full of Rolling Rock. He takes the job. Stablehorn appeared on a pre–Super Bowl promotional video to report that focus-group participants were "outraged"—

even before the commercial aired. The mockumentary disclaimer approach cleverly deflects the possibility of genuine controversy, since the company has already apologized. Or have they? "If the banner had said, 'Check out the Rolling Rock ad,' no one would bother," Robert Gilbert, a professor of marketing at the University of Pittsburgh's Katz School of Business told the *Pittsburgh Tribune-Review*. "When it says, 'If you've been offended,' almost everyone has a reason to go there. . . . It's perfect in that regard."

Some ad campaigns can miss their targets without necessarily missing the mark.

Kevin Morra, a thirty-two-year-old television producer in Los Angeles has a story he likes to tell about his real-life adventures with Axe. "Though I didn't buy a can myself, I was happy that my roommate did, so I tried it," he reports. "I was convinced by the smell of it alone that it was nothing too impressive to me, and would not have been to chicks either, although I did have a girl tell me that she wears it herself because she loved the smell so much."

One of Morra's favorite commercials is a Bud Light ad called "Mighty Wingman." The commercial is a wry interpretation of a scenario that's familiar to many men. The ad shows a guy in a bar, stuck with a woman who clearly bores him while her girlfriend dances wildly with his pal. As the loyal wingman tries not to mope, a sympathetic troubadour sings of ". . . taking one for the team, so your buddy can live the dream." The commercial works because it makes fun of a situation that, under its snarky surface, is truly about male friendship.

"I definitely pay more attention if humor is involved, but for big-money purchases, like automobiles," says Morra, "I definitely prefer factual information over some gimmicky way of tricking me into buying a car."

Even so, like many other men his age, though he is neither anti-materialist nor antiadvertising, he takes everything he sees or reads with more than a grain of salt. If anything, he is a realist who understands that marketers are locked in a fierce competition for his hard-earned dollars. And if they go a little too far sometimes, so what? He doesn't worry that men will lose track of who they are, if only because the media will always be there to remind them. Guys, in his opinion, are constantly being told how to act, where to go, what to buy. If a magazine ad or commercial strikes him as ridiculous or false, he knows he can just turn the page or switch the channel.

What does concern Morra, however, is a general feeling that men have become soft—not soft as in metrosexual, but soft as in sycophantic. While he's not opposed to women's rights, he wonders if men have sacrificed something important in the negotiated truce between the sexes. What appalls him most is the knowledge that so many swaggering he-men can be reduced to cowering lapdogs by a woman's disapproving glance. "I do feel that men are losing their backbone," he says. "Nowadays I find men so easily contained and leashed by women. They no longer just do things they want to do. They ask permission. They take no for an answer, and they cook and clean, even Steven."

There are a lot of men like Kevin in America. But there is hope, because Madison Avenue feels their pain.

It knows that guys like Kevin are fed up. More to the point, it knows that they are fed up with not getting their fill. It has also noticed that these restaurants that look like beauty parlors, with menus that read like science experiments, seem to be part of some great conspiracy between women and French chefs who take pleasure in torturing full-grown guys with minuscule potions on huge white plates. It knows that back in college, when feminists were fighting for equal rights, some men were taking notes, waiting for the moment to start their own movement. Madison Avenue knows that men are ready to take a stand. But first they need lunch, a real lunch. They know what they want, and they know just where to get it. It's called a Texas Double Cheeseburger, and it's made by a friendly little franchise called Burger King.

What if men did rebel? What if they threw off their chains and took to the streets? The commercial for Burger King's Texas Double Cheeseburger, a 1,050-calorie "mountain of flavor," gives us one vision of what that might be like. "Manthem" opens as a twenty-something fellow is being served tiny *nouvelle* portions in a trendy restaurant. Disgusted by the poor excuse for a meal before him, he snaps. The guy throws down his napkin and, leaving his attractive date alone at the table to fend for herself, marches out to the street.

"I am man, hear me roar," he sings to the tune of Helen Reddy's "I Am Woman."

His roar is heard. As the man keeps singing, he is joined by an army of other men. The marchers are of all ages, sizes, and socioeconomic types, a panorama of American manliness. As the parade of protesters grows and the music swells, they burn their underwear, push a family-style minivan off a bridge, and pump their fists under banners declaring "Eat This Meat!!"

Burger King's "Manthem" manages to be funny and blatantly antifeminist at the same time by lampooning women's lib and simultaneously portraying men as rugged, famished slobs. Sure, the goal is to get men to feel okay about pigging out on big, fat burgers, even if it means getting big and fat themselves. BK supports a man's right to be overweight. But even though obesity continues to be a national problem, what's really disturbing about the ad is the way that it makes the very idea of men organizing over anything look ridiculous. While, on the surface, the commercial is lampooning militant feminism, the blade of its humor cuts both ways. Don't those guys look silly marching and singing for something that they believe in? As a matter of fact, don't *all* protesters look silly? Heck, *protesting* is silly. What self-respecting guy would ever do such a thing? And now that you mention it, aren't those silly protesters a lot like the real-life food Nazis who eat tiny portions and are trying to stop Burger King from selling us double cheeseburgers?

This time the joke is on democracy. Because, at its deepest level, BK's "Manthem" doesn't make free speech look un-American. It makes it look unmanly.

CHAPTER 8

X-Men

I went for a walk at the mall the other day. There were plenty of other people gathered around the entrance, so I decided to conduct a random survey of sorts. Two women were conversing nearby. They were both young and very attractive. One was voluptuously built with a dark-brown ponytail and a short black dress. The other was taller and blond, in a floral tube top, tight blue bell-bottoms, and black boots. As I approached, the brunette was telling the blonde that she was twenty-eight. "No, really," she was saying, "I know I look twenty-eight, but I really am."

"I believe her," I interjected. "She looks great for her age."

They stopped talking.

"Sorry," I apologized. "I couldn't help overhearing."

"That's okay," the brunette said. "Join us. Where are you from?"

I told them I was from New York—well, California, originally. "I wonder if I could ask you something," I inquired. They both looked at me.

"Shoot," said the blonde.

"Do you think women are taking over the Internet—in a good way, I mean?"

"Sure," the blonde replied, "we already did. Wanna see me fly?" The blonde, whose name was Miss Lizzy, levitated for a few seconds, then floated gently back to earth. "Why?"

"Well, actually, I'm writing a book about men," I confessed.

"Oh, Internet porn," said the brunette, who called herself Princess Leah. She moved back a few steps.

"No. I mean, yes, that, too," I said. "But it's much more about how economic and social changes are upending sex roles and, as a result, men are failing and losing their way. And nobody's sure what happens next."

Just then, Joey Baloney walked by. "JESUS, I'M NAKED!" he exclaimed, and kept going. It was impossible not to notice that he actually was.

"Sorry," Princess Leah said. "Are you really from California?"

I was starting to worry that Princess and Lizzy didn't believe me, that they thought I was just another jerk trying to chat them up at the mall, so I said, "I'm going to interview some people at Electronic Arts who work on The Sims."

"I *love* The Sims," Miss Lizzy said.

"Cool. Did you ever play? What did you like about it?"

Before Miss Lizzy could answer, Princess Leah interrupted. "I think there's a bunch of naked people at the nude beach," she said. "Let's go."

"C'mon, guy," Miss Lizzy said to me. "Follow us."

I followed. They were both much better at flying than I was, so by the time I managed to get to the beach I was alone. Off in the distance were some flesh-colored lumps that might or might not have been nude bathers. Much closer to me were a couple of men—one in board shorts, the other in jeans, shirtless.

They were both staring at me.

"Hi, guys," I said. "Can I ask you a question?"

They just kept staring, so I continued: "Do you think women are taking over the Internet?"

"Nice suit," the shirtless guy said to me. "Did you get it at the mall?"

Before I could respond, everything froze. I couldn't talk or move.

The beach boys were standing in the same place, their handsome heads still turned in my direction, their glazed expressions as static as the monochrome sea behind them.

My Second Life program had crashed, and it was shutting me down. A few seconds later, the virtual nude beach disappeared. My virtual friends disappeared. I disappeared. I was back in my first life, the actual world, what John Perry Barlow calls "meat space." It was like waking up from a dream, a dream that a lot of other people were dreaming at the same time in the same dreamy, nonexistent place. It was a very vivid dream.

But Second Life, for all its cyberspace strangeness, is also a vast ecosystem that is self-sustaining and ever-evolving. It is a parallel universe, a mirror world much like the one envisioned by scientist and writer David Gelernter, in which the real world is re-created in digital form to the point that the experience takes on its own "second" life. What makes Second Life remarkable is not just its size and diversity, but the extent to which it has been built by the people who use it. Like a real city, it has grown organically, molded and shaped by the imaginations, wants, and needs of its citizens. It is a democracy with rules, but rules that are not very different from those of Mardi Gras—anything goes as long as nobody gets hurt. And if you piss too many people off, you will be evicted, exiled to Cyberia.

Second Life has experienced a kind of corporate construction boom as more than thirty major companies have moved in to build virtual stories, showrooms, or other promotional environments. Sony BMG Music, Sun Microsystems, Reebok, and Starwood Hotels are among the major brands that have spent up to $1,250 and pay $195 per month to buy and maintain an "island," which they can then develop as they see fit. Nissan Motors built a giant vending machine that dispenses vehicles that Second Lifers can take for a spin. There is also a flourishing economy of entrepreneurs and microbusinesses that ply their trade, offering services and one-of-a-kind avatar products in exchange for Second Life cash, which can be bought with actual dollars. Individual players can use Second Life currency to buy virtual clothing, custom body parts, props, and special powers.

A few days later, I went back to Second Life to do some window shopping at the virtual mall. I logged in and took the "transporter" to the "Cozy Cove Shopping Mall," a clean and sunny cluster of boutiques that reminded me of the shops in Beverly Hills or West Palm Beach. I didn't see anyone else at Cozy Cove during my visit, but I was free to browse upscale shops like MC Designers, where I could buy a diamond ring for eighty-five Second Life dollars, or a "Tribal Yellow Flowers" back tattoo for seventy-five. Wondering where everybody else was, I checked the "most popular" menu on my Second Life dashboard. Sex clubs and nude beaches dominated the list, so I took the transporter to a "mature" hot spot called "Laguna Bay." There were about forty other people there, some dancing around a huge bonfire blazing on the beach. Others were chatting amiably as they floated on doughnut-shaped rafts in the calm water. Most were semiclothed, some completely naked. Down the beach, there was a man lying down naked, sporting what appeared to be an erection, but I didn't get close enough to be sure. A girl invited me to dance, so, in an effort to be a good sport, I clicked on my personal "inventory," which had a submenu for "male gestures." They included Stick Out Tongue, Shrug, Bored, Blow Kiss, and Get Lost, but no Dancing. I wondered if there was a place in Second Life where I could buy the ability to dance.

Meanwhile, the couple next to me seemed to be hitting it off. I could tell by their conversation, which was starting to get steamy. Chillin' Alejandro had a muscular build, close-cropped beard, long sideburns, and a bare chest. His partner, Lana Piranha, had long brown limbs, short brown hair, and was wearing tight shorts and a bra.

"I like the way you move," Alejandro said.

"Thanks—dancing keeps me in shape," Lana replied.

A thong-wearing demon with horns and a long tail glided by and disappeared in a puff of smoke. Nobody reacted.

"I can see that," Alejandro was saying. "Why don't we go back to my place?"

"Yeah, right—so you can rape me."

"I wouldn't do that, but I might jump on you."

". . . with that big thing of yours."

"I can make it smaller, if you want."

"Gee, that's sweet."

I decided to move on. The perpetual sunset was glowing at the far end of the beach. The water, complete with gently lapping waves, looked inviting. I waded in. Seconds later, I was completely immersed, wandering around on the sandy bottom. There was nothing there to see, so I headed back toward the party. When I emerged from the surf, a pink Fairy Princess with a halo floated overhead, her wand emitting a glittering cloud of stars that trailed across the sky and fell to the beach in a shimmering rain. A few people waved and bowed to show their appreciation.

Somebody I hadn't met invited me to join their group. I accepted, then logged off.

I could understand why more than 4 million people had ventured into Second Life since its launch in 1999. I could understand why they would pay real money for a piece of virtual real estate, for the chance to meet strangers, to go shopping, to run around naked, to fly.

And, most definitely, to stare, to watch, to ogle. Virtual worlds like Second Life are both immersive and voyeuristic. We know that the avatars around us aren't real, and that they may have very little in common with the people controlling them, but we look anyway. Maybe because the urge to watch others is deeply ingrained in the human species, an impulse that is rooted in our evolutionary past as social animals whose ability to "read" other individuals in the group was critical for reproduction and survival. Is our fascination with other people a genetic imperative?

Researchers at Duke University Medical Center discovered that rhesus macaque monkeys would "pay" to see pictures of female monkey bottoms and high-status monkey males, which at least one researcher has likened to humans paying for the chance to look at pictures in *Playboy* and *Fortune*.

In a series of studies conducted at Duke between 2005 and 2007, a team of scientists led by Dr. Michael Platt found that if given a choice between a neutral image and pictures of high-ranking male monkeys and female monkey bottoms, the subjects would forgo a juice reward for a chance to view other monkeys.

The experiments, sponsored by the National Institute of Mental Health and the Cure Autism Now Foundation, were designed to help understand how the "social machinery" of people goes awry in autistic patients, who are predominantly male. One of the symptoms of autism is a lack of motivation to look at other people or to accurately decipher the expressions and motives of others. One theory of autism blames it on a "hypermasculinization" of the brain that happens when a human fetus receives an overdose of testosterone in the womb.

It's still unclear, though, whether male monkeys are more willing than females to pay to see other monkeys, although the research so far suggests that the compulsive behaviors shared by male humans are also factors in male monkey behavior. Will female monkeys "pay" just as much as males to see other monkeys? And what is the monkey equivalent of *In Style*?

Dr. Platt is just beginning to measure how the behavioral effects of such contextual circumstances are affected by gender, but alpha-male monkeys also showed interest in lower-status males, probably because the ability to form alliances with others is a factor in establishing status. "Our low-ranking males show a lot of physical features that overlap with females, and they respond to social cues in ways that are more similar to the ways females respond," Dr. Platt reports. "That doesn't mean there isn't a difference between males and females—just that there is a range of variation in the dimensions along which they differ, and that where any individual sits within this range of variation reflects the combination of genes and environmental context they have experienced."

In essence, male monkeys of lower status don't stop being males, but the lower their position on the social ladder, the more likely they are to adopt female behaviors. And all it would take is a few minutes with a female CEO to make the case that the opposite is true for women; they don't stop being female, but their behavior begins to ape that of the businessmen who are now their social peers, or subordinates.

Recent data indicate that female monkeys may be even more aware of social status than males. Still, the *Fortune/Playboy* analogy may be apt, particularly if further research shows that monkeys who are willing to "gamble" and take risks for a higher reward show a similarly male skew.

After all, it is not a very big evolutionary leap from male monkeys who like to gamble and look at pictures of alpha males and female bottoms to men who like to do the same. Gambling and courting are both activities that contain various degrees of risk, with the possibility of short- and long-terms gains. Male monkeys and humans, it seems, share not just a taste for gambling and porn, but also an inborn imperative to lower risk and increase rewards whenever possible. And if digital media, with its impressive ability to send pixels over the Internet quickly and anonymously, can deliver photos—and videos—further, faster, and cheaper than ever before, then is it any surprise that online pornography generates an estimated $12 billion annually, equal to the combined annual revenue of ABC, NBC, and

CBS? The Third Way Culture Project, an antipornography activist organization, says there are 400 million Internet porn pages on the Net, or one-eighth of the total.

So, has the Internet, with its ability to let men stare at female bottoms, and a whole lot else, unleashed men's primordial libidos, allowing them to run amok without any of the social inhibitors that rule other aspects of human society? Is online porn a scourge that corrupts men's ability to sustain or even want normal, nurturing relationships with women—that is, with women who don't necessarily perform like prostitutes, or their online equivalents? Does online porn make men into panting sex addicts who spend hours of each day hunting down ever more perverted sex acts and pictures in search of the next taboo turn-on? And are the men who succumb to the Web's siren song mostly miserable and lonely, and damaged by all this uninhibited ogling?

That is certainly the alarming conclusion reached by Pamela Paul in her book *Pornified: How Pornography Is Damaging Our Lives, Our Relationships, and Our Families.* For Paul, the Web is a digital jungle where man's inner animal is unleashed, free to roam and watch with an impunity and inhumanity that would make even Hugh Hefner blush. In the real world, Paul argues, men can glance but not stare, show interest but not pursue, think lewd thoughts but never say them. In a bar, women can shoot down a salivating male with a withering glance. The "pornified world" we live in, argues Paul, has become infected by an obsession with sex that borders on dementia. Pornography, in her view, is a malady that is destroying relationships and marriages, and endangering the emotional safety and psychological well-being of our children. Paul laments the lack of a "widespread public outcry" and almost pines for a more innocent time when porn meant "gauzy centerfolds, outré sexuality, women's liberation, and the Hugh Hefner lifestyle." Back then, she writes, "the lines between softcore and hardcore pornography were clear and distinguishable."

Those were the days, all right.

But what really seems to irk Paul is the fact that, online at least, men can express their sexuality *any way they want*. Exempt from social restraint and supervision, men immediately revert to their true nature as compulsive, shameless perverts who will pounce on women with no other motive than to satisfy their monstrous libidos.

"In so many ways, a man's ability to observe is restricted by social norms that demand men not treat women as sexual objects, no matter how provocatively tight her jeans," writes Paul. "But in the porn world none of those restrictions apply. Men can look at whatever women they want in whatever way they choose for as long as they desire to do so . . . Walking down the street, a woman has the ability to look the other way or to sneer at the man who passes by her. In the office, she can write a more effective business plan than her male coworker or outperform him in a board meeting. In a bar she can refuse to give a guy her phone number or brush off attempts at conversation. But in the porn world, she has none of these options. She may retain the power to reject a man by the very nature of her femininity, but in pornography she chooses not to reject. In porn, she treats a man the way he wants to be treated, relieving him of the fears that plague everyday male-female interaction. In the porn world, men retain the power and the control."

But do they? In the world of online porn, men are certainly free to look at what they want for as long as they want. But that's not what differentiates the Internet from traditional media such as magazines, books, and movies, which have been around in triple-X versions for decades. What makes the Web unique is its capacity for interactivity. Online sex gets its gravity from the fact that behind those pictures and words flashing on the screen is—potentially, at least—a real person, who can interact in real time, if they wish. Internet porn is uniquely compelling because of the possibility of communicating with others, whether via e-mail, Instant Message, chat, live or recorded video, or in a personals community or virtual environment that combines some or all of the above.

But this doesn't necessarily mean that men get an unfair advantage. If anything, women have more power and safety online than they do in the real world. On the Web, a woman can disguise herself, lie about her age, and reveal only the details and parts of herself that she wants to disclose. On the Web, a woman can shut down a creep with the touch of a button, or a "Dear Jerk" Instant Message. And on the Web, a woman is safe from physical harm, free to flirt, prod, and explore without the specter of date rape or sexually transmitted diseases.

For at least one young, educated woman, online sex is a two-way street where girls find the going anything but rough.

"I think sex on the Internet is for both men *and* women," says Donna.* "We live in a sex society. I know friends that have sex IM, they say dirty things to guys, dirty text messages. There's a lot of porn sites out there, soft-core porn sites for women. Nerve.com has these beautiful nude photographs of people. I think it's not just a man thing to go online and jerk off to some photo. Women go online, they go on MySpace, they send messages. Granted, I'm sure more men do than women, but they're in there, too. They're on Match.com, they're on Nerve.com, trying to pick up someone. They're posting on Craig's List in the casual encounters section, like saying that they want to give a blowjob, or looking for someone to 'eat me out.' They do the same graphic things as men do, they definitely engage in the same things."

Sites like Nerve.com are equal parts dating service and online arts community. Nerve users tend to be young, educated, into art and music, and relaxed about their sexuality. Blogs and video essays of straights, lesbians, and gays are listed side by side, and nobody seems too stressed about who is doing what with whom. The journal *Nerve*, in both its online and print editions, cultivates an aura of brainy eroticism, as much a product of its New York base as its savvy, "alt-cult" clientele.

Sites like SuicideGirls.com go further. An "alt-porn" online community for goth, punk, emo, and independent-minded women, SuicideGirls was launched in Portland, Oregon, in 2001, according to cofounders Sean Suhl and Selena Mooney, with the goal of giving young women control over how their sexuality is depicted. Indeed, members volunteer their services for free and art-direct the photo shoots. Models, who often sport piercings, tattoos, spiky hair, or all of the above, are encouraged to "Redefine Beauty." SuicideGirl models, who are selected from applicants from all over the world, get free membership and a stipend. They are expected to maintain their personal site and write a blog. The company even promises a lifetime membership to anyone who gets a tattoo of the Suicide Girls logo.

The site's name was inspired by a phrase that appeared in a novel by *Fight Club* author and fellow Portland resident Chuck Palahniuk, but while some have objected to the nihilistic moniker, Mooney adds her own spin, explaining that SuicideGirls "is a term my friends and I had been using to describe the girls we saw in Portland's Pioneer Square with skateboards in one hand, wearing a Minor Threat hoodie, listening to Ice Cube on their iPods, while reading a book of Nick Cave's poetry. They are girls who didn't fit into any conventional subculture and didn't define themselves based on musical taste, like punk, metal, goth, et cetera. I think the only classification right now people identify with are 'mainstream' and 'outside of mainstream.'"

As of May 2008, there were 1,653 SuicideGirl models, searchable by chronology, geography, eye and hair color, body type, tattoos, stockings, and curves. Nudity is encouraged, but the exhibitionism is no raunchier than what might appear in *Playboy* or *Penthouse*. Members, estimated to number in the hundreds of thousands, pay four dollars a month to browse the site. The SuicideGirls brand has been expanded to include clothing and accessories, and even a traveling burlesque show. The SuicideGirls Burlesque Troupe toured as an opening act for Guns N' Roses during their 2006 North American tour.

Steve*, a single professional writer in his thirties living in St. Cloud, Minnesota, first heard about SuicideGirls a few years ago through a friend who was surfing the site at the office. "I had never heard of the SuicideGirls," he recalls, "but my friend was looking at the site, and I peeked over his shoulder to see what he was looking at, and I was, like, 'Hey, what *are* you looking at?' And of course a naked woman will always grab your attention, if you're a man. But, of course, it wasn't just the naked bodies, I also noticed that there were all these tattoos on them. And it wasn't just a cute little butterfly or a little rainbow above their ass—they were covered by large pieces on their chests and their backs, everywhere. I had looked at plenty of porn sites, but it was unusual to see women with so many tattoos, especially women that looked like that."

Steve admits that he might have been put off by the name if he hadn't seen the site first. "Most people, if they only heard about it, might just think of it as another porno site," he says. "But what's interesting about it is that it's really about the evolution of the pinup girl in the modern age. There isn't any penetration, there isn't any real sex. It's just beautiful young women posing. I think it's very empowering for these women. They have control, they've chosen to do this, to show the tattoo artwork on their bodies. It's pinups for the twenty-first century."

Once a bastion of geeky guys with engineering degrees, the Web has become female-friendly at a cultural moment when social interaction has moved online. A 2007 study by Pew Research reports that 35 percent of girls aged twelve to seventeen create their own blogs, compared with 20 percent of boys. Girls also significantly outperform their male peers when it comes to posting profiles on social networking sites and building personal websites. Pew also found that virtually all the growth in teen blogging between 2004 and 2006 came from girls. It's not surprising that girls have overtaken boys in almost every kind of social interaction on the Internet that doesn't require advanced technical skills. "I think it's about women coming into the society that we live in," Alexis Tirado says. "That's another thing—yeah, people do go online to play games and masturbate because it's easier than going into a video store and getting porn, but it's also our society, it's what's going on right now, it's what people know. I mean, people meet in bars, but it's rare, most people meet online or through a MySpace friend. It's what people are doing right now."

This alternative picture of the Web as a much more egalitarian and nonsexist environment than most people would expect is supported by David Loftus in his book *Watching Sex: How Men Really Respond to Pornography.* "Contrary to notions of male power, domination, and force," Loftus writes, "pornography that shows men and women together often depicts them as equal participants, even men as passive recipients of sexual action."

In fact, a study by psychologists at the University of Louisville and Texas Tech University found that porn users actually had a slightly higher regard for women and women's rights than other men did. "If you spend your time looking at pictures of naked women," James Beggan, a sociologist who coauthored the study, told *Psychology Today*, "that's not really consistent with not liking women, it's consistent with liking them."

Women, meanwhile, can peruse photos of guys, and vice versa, as well as same sex variations, fast-forwarding past those who are unattractive or uninteresting. Dating sites offer a variety of ways for members to signal interest, as well as filters to keep unwanted suitors at bay. And if a man crosses the line, there are a slew of ways that women can defend themselves or retaliate.

One way is to post a finger-wagging exposé on DontDate-HimGirl.com. Launched in 2006 by Tasha Joseph to give women a way to keep tabs on cheaters, liars, and creeps, the site had signed up half a million registered users in its first five months. Joseph reports that she gets e-mails daily from women who have seen guys mentioned on DontDateHimGirl.com and subsequently refused to date them. In addition to the scoop on subpar suitors, the site offers forums on Abusive Relationships, Cheating, Dating, Self-Empowerment, and Love, Marriage, and Sex. It also has a feature called "The Love Panel," where questions posted by members are answered by various experts—Alison James, Queer Eye for the Straight Girl!, Tasha Cunningham, and The Average Guy—who respond from their own point of view. "I've been dating a guy for a little over six months, but he is still seeing his ex-girlfriend," lamented "Concerned and Cautious." "He claims they're not having sex, so it's no big deal. I'm upset and worried about this. What can I do?" In this case, the panel was unanimous: Dump him!

Tirado is familiar with the site, a visit to which has become almost de rigueur for women who date online. "Yeah, they would talk about this guy, he has a small dick, he has herpes, etc.—just embarrass them," she recalls. "I think one guy threatened to file a lawsuit against the women who started the website. It's like, man hater, man cheater, loser man, one of those things. You can rake out who's lame and who's not."

Men, for their part, are much less inclined to publicize information about women they have dated. Even though DontDateHim-Girl.com offers men the chance to tell their side, few do. "Most guys just don't do that," explains a divorced man from California. "When a relationship ends, the last thing a guy wants to do is think about it, or rehash her faults with his male friends, or anyone else. Or defend himself, which only makes him look more guilty. It's bad manners to trash a woman in public, even in self-defense. For a woman, though, any guy that's not still with her is automatically a loser—I've never heard a girl talk about how great her ex is. They think, 'If he was so great, he'd still be with me.' So, for women, ex-boyfriends are losers by definition. And if a relationship ends badly, they will fester and plot and do everything they can to give you pain. They will go online to these bad-boyfriend sites and put a hex on you—the male scarlet letter. And most guys know this. Unless they are totally clueless, they are perfectly aware that their behavior on- and offline can come back to haunt them on the Web. Girls have that power, and they use it. Guys don't."

What if the dirty little secret about online porn is not that men have used it as a plugged-in platform to degrade, exploit, and dominate, but that women have quietly taken the reins—just as they have in so many other segments of American society—and are calling the shots as much as men, and in some ways possibly more. What if the gender that has been liberated by online sex is not men but women? What if it was actually men who were smarting, who felt degraded by their dildo-like utility in the service of giving women pleasure? Could it be that men are defensively trying to hold their own in an environment where the verbal and networking skills of females—and, by extension, their ability to seek out, evaluate, and seduce their sexual prey—often exceeds their own?

David Loftus reports that the majority of the men he spoke to wanted to see more plot and romance in porn, did not particularly enjoy close-ups of genitals, did not like the way that men are portrayed in porn, were turned off by violence against women, and did not find that online porn drove them toward ever more perverted and kinky variations of sexual conduct. If anything, cyberspace has liberated the female libido even more than it has men's, since online media play to feminine strengths and downplay or eliminate physical vulnerabilities.

"It's almost like women can take control of their destiny online, they have the upper hand because they can pick who they want, they can IM who they want, they can e-mail who they want," Tirado explains. "And at a bar, even now, I think, women still wait for a guy to go up to them. How often does a women go up to a guy at a bar, even now? But online, it's a little bit different, a woman has an upper hand." While some men may have caught on to this, Tirado believes that most are in for a rude awakening. "It's kinda like when a guy wakes up from a crazy night out and there's a weird girl in his bed, and he's, like, 'What the fuck happened?' And that's basically what's going to happen to men in ten years, they're going to wake up and they're going to see that women are everywhere, overrunning them, and they're going to say, 'What the fuck happened?' It wasn't a one-night stand, it was a thirty-year stand in the making. Men were raised to be these good old boys, and now the good old girls are taking over."

WONDER WOMEN

Riley Harlow is a twenty-eight-year-old woman who just moved to an affluent, medium-sized town called Four Corners. She has a best friend named Fiona, and a blond, bearded ex-boyfriend named Dylan. Agora, a girl she just met, is nice, but Riley's not sure she can trust her. Then there's this guy she's been seeing: Mickey Smith. Mickey is handsome, smart, and affectionate—he's got it all. He's made it clear that he really likes her, so why does Riley keep holding back? Could it have anything to do with that tingle she still feels when she thinks about Dylan?

Sometimes Riley feels like a basket case. She's always wanted a great job, great friends, a great boyfriend, a great life. Now she has all those things—sort of. Mickey has a reputation as a bit of a player, it's true. But so far he hasn't given her a single reason to doubt him. Plus, he's ticklish, which is soooo cute! Vince is another story—he's got this sweet tech job, plenty of money, and sex appeal, too. Word is he just got dumped by Samantha, who's supposed to be a total whack job. Vince can have just about any woman he wants, but will he crawl back to Samantha, play the field, or find true love somewhere else?

Riley keeps a diary. Here's what it says:

Tuesday A.M.
I'm finally starting to feel at home in Four Corners. Bonus—there's a place with great coffee. Couldn't live without my caffeine fix. And my new friend Fiona's just as much of a latte freak as I am.

I also met a guy. His name is Mickey and there's DEFINITELY something there. I wonder if he felt it too?

Thursday evening
I can't even believe who moved to town: Dylan! Just when I think I'm totally over him, he's back—with those big brown eyes. I have to stay strong. I like Mickey now. Don't I? Anyway I wonder if Dylan is over his little "problem."

I'm definitely not in Sim City anymore!

Sim City, of course, is the hometown of The Sims, the most popular computer game ever made. And Riley is the starring character in a new spin-off of The Sims called The Sim Stories, part of a new line of Sims games that includes *Pet Stories* and *Castaway Stories*. The Sims is a life-simulation game created by Will Wright for Electronic Arts. Since its release in 2000, 6.3 million copies of the original game have been sold, and the total franchise has sold more than 70 million.

The inspiration for The Sims, according to Wright, came from the 1991 Oakland fire, in which his home and many of his possessions were destroyed. In the wake of the fire, he imagined a kind of virtual "dollhouse" in which players could build a home from a set of domestic props and premade characters, or design their own characters, from their body type and clothing to their personalities and motives. Wright had already created Sim City, a so-called God game, in which players manage the components of a modern city.

In The Sims, players can give characters commands, or, alternatively, characters can be programmed to have a certain amount of free will. Diamond-shaped "plumbars" over the characters' heads change colors to indicate their moods. If a Sims character is not having enough fun, he or she becomes depressed. Without proper instruction and care, Sims can become nasty and violent. While Sims cannot commit suicide, they must maintain a certain level of hygiene—bathing, sleeping, eating—or they will sicken and die. Sims can also be killed by drowning, fire, electrocution, and a virus contracted from the cages of dirty pet guinea pigs.

There is no way to "win" at The Sims. The goal of the game is to guide your character and help him or her to form and maintain relationships with other Sims—to have children, to be healthy, and so on. Sims speak Simlish, a fictional language created by improv comedians, and live in a neighborhood based on architecture-simulation programs and 2- and 3-D graphics generators. Sims adults go to work, and Sims children go to school. Failure to do so can result, respectively, in getting fired or getting sent to military school. Sims can socialize, date, relax, and play games.

The Sims' focus on real-life domestic situations and characters with emotional states has attracted record numbers of female players.

An estimated 60 percent of all Sims players are women.

The success of The Sims has inspired a slew of new games that emphasize cooperation, communication, and community. The Sims 2, released in 2004, is set twenty-five years after the original game.

The sequel version takes place in a full 3-D environment and allows Sims characters to grow from infancy to adulthood, then age and die. Each Sims character has an "aspiration meter," which rises and falls, based on how well the character fulfills his or her wishes and desires. The Sims 3 is expected to take psychological and community features even further.

The Sims phenomenon proved that women are perfectly able and willing to play computer games that appeal to them. Since then, even as relationship-based games have proliferated, a new breed of girls' game has emerged, one that closely resembles the action-hero format that boys love, but with female characters in charge.

Some of those female heroes are new, while others, like the fictional girl detective Nancy Drew, have been around a long time. Since the 1930s, when the first Nancy Drew mystery novel was penned, by the pseudonymous Carolyn Keene, the series has sold 200 million copies worldwide. Though her image has been updated and revamped from time to time, Drew has remained an independent-minded, inquisitive teenager who more than holds her own with adults and her boyfriend, Ned.

Secrets Can Kill, the first computer game based on a Nancy Drew book, was released in 1998 by Her Interactive, Inc., a Bellevue, Washington-based company with a mission "to design, develop and market intelligent interactive games for girls." Since then, Her Interactive has sold 2.5 million Nancy Drew games, making it the number-one PC adventure franchise, ahead of Myst, Harry Potter, and Lord of the Rings.

"The market penetration for male-targeted games is near the saturation point," CEO Megan Gaiser told *Adventure Classic Gaming*. "But there's still a wide-open market opportunity to target the female half of the population." If girls aren't buying games in large numbers, she maintains, "it's not because they don't like to play games, it's because few developers are designing games that appeal to them." Gaiser points to studies that suggest that many girls are turned off by the repetitive and violent nature of most male-targeted games. And of those games that do cater to females, too many rely on obvious content like pink packaging, boy talk, and fashion. "To assume that those are the only things girls are interested in is absurd," she says. "Our games don't use gender stereotypes to appeal to girls. Instead, they rely on the intrigue of a good mystery, and a smart, gutsy heroine. We believe that there should be as many types of games as there are types of girls."

Including, apparently, the type who are dismissive of men.

During a podcast interview with Scott Rubin from All Games Interactive for the release of Nancy Drew: Danger by Design, Jessica Chang, a marketing producer for Her Interactive was asked about Nancy's love life. When Rubin asked Chang if Nancy would ever get married, she replied, "Well, you know, actually, Nancy has a boyfriend named Ned. But she doesn't need him. She can solve these mysteries all by herself."

At the end of the interview, Chang took questions from the Internet audience, several of whom wanted to know more about Ned. "Well, Ned is actually the useless boyfriend," she explained. "She's been with him for quite a while but he just provides hints and tips most of the time and ends up getting himself kidnapped and getting in the way anyway."

Nancy's "useless boyfriend"? After eight decades of loyal devotion, even helping to solve crimes from time to time, this is all the thanks Ned gets? What are the odds that Ned and Ken know each other? They certainly have a lot in common. Both owe their existence to stronger, wealthier, more famous women. Both know what it's like to be underappreciated, overshadowed, year after year, decade after decade, with no end in sight. They are nothing without Barbie and Nancy, but they are nearly nothing with them. So maybe, once in a while, between bespoke suit fittings, they meet at a bar to play some pool and have a beer, to gripe, to vent and drink and share a toast to the women in their lives, until they start to notice the adoring glances of the plastic hotties in the bar. Or maybe they just go home, log on to *DollsGoneWild.com*, and pretend that they did.

What if mirror worlds like The Sims and Second Life are not just a reflection of a reality but a lens that transforms it? What if the actual world is in the process of becoming more and more like the virtual world, instead of the other way around? Will people transport themselves from one place to another? Will we be able to transform our appearance into any shape or visage that we want? Will men go shopping while women fly?

THE DEATH OF SUPERMAN

During a pivotal card game in the 2006 film *Casino Royale*, James Bond, the British Secret Service agent and central character in the most profitable action-movie series in history, is bankrolled by an American CIA operative, but only after the American has proven too inept and clumsy to win the game himself. Movie critics agree that *Casino Royale* is not only one of the best Bond films ever made, but also possibly the one most faithful to the original novel by Ian Fleming, the ex-British intelligence officer who authored the Bond series. Fleming wrote the Bond books in the Commonwealth outpost of Jamaica during the 1950s and 1960s, as the American Century was hitting its stride and the sun was setting on the British Empire. Bond was suave and self-confident, quick-witted enough to outfox his enemies and too smart to get caught up in the politics of the Home Office. He had a license to kill, but his real weapon was his casual, natural virility, which never failed to evoke swoons from a long line of bimbos and femme fatales who came to be christened, collectively, "the Bond girls." In his book *The Man Who Saved Britain: A Personal Journey into the Disturbing World of James Bond*, Simon Winder makes the case that Bond's popularity in Britain, and to a lesser extent the rest of the world, was due to his ability to compensate, psychologically at least, for the growing sense of powerlessness and impotence that the British were feeling as a nation.

"When in *Goldfinger* Connery says that drinking unchilled champagne is like listening to the Beatles with earmuffs the entire swinging sixties collapses into pieces," Winder writes. "These are films for all those executives about to be fired from their manufacturing companies, for the millions of ex-servicemen, still only in their forties, for whom the economic and social changes were personally deeply threatening and who found themselves stranded, like the government, on a planet that didn't have much to say about them. The Bond films provided a profound, wistful reassurance that for at least one British male, things were still going well."

But for an entire generation of men, Bond was not just a symbolic panacea for hard socioeconomic times but an action icon who embodied and defined unfettered masculinity.

Bond was—and for many still is—the vessel into which men of all ages, classes, and nationalities can project themselves, transferring and superimposing 007's romantic, exciting antics onto their own mundane lives. Winder recalls how, in preparation for his first real job as a bookseller's agent, he went out of his way to add a Bond-like veneer to his wardrobe and attitude. Thus transformed, he "felt great and hardly noticed the gap between Bond's own sex-and-murder-themed foreign travels and my own mission to sell disturbingly out-of-date computer textbooks to Cameroon schools."

If James Bond was a stalwart stand-in for Britain's sagging confidence, his transatlantic counterpart was a muscle-bound innocent who symbolized America's rising superpower status. Both routinely saved the world from evil, scheming maniacs, but otherwise they could hardly have been more different. Whereas Bond was jaded, ruthless, and world-weary, Superman was idealistic, compassionate, and virtuous. Whereas Bond was a reaction to the fading fortunes of his nation, Superman embodied the boundless aspirations of his. Like Europe itself, Bond was cynical, cultured, and fixated on the past; Superman was a naive farm boy who owned the future.

Conceived by cartoonists Jerry Siegel and Joe Shuster in 1933, the Man of Steel first appeared in Action Comics #1 in 1938, four years after Adolf Hitler came to power and a year before Germany's invasion of Poland sparked World War II. Born Kal-El on the planet Krypton, Superman was rocketed to safety by his scientist father moments before Krypton exploded. Discovered in the wreckage of his spaceship by a Kansas farmer and his wife, he grew up learning to hide his superpowers from the humans he had vowed to protect. His everyday alter ego was Clark Kent, a mild-mannered journalist who worked at a newspaper called the *Daily Planet*. Superman soon became a national symbol of America's strength and its commitment to "truth, justice, and the American way." Superman is the ultimate American patriot—even his costume evokes the colors of the flag—but his name and power have also inspired comparisons to Nietzsche's *Übermensch*, Moses, Jesus, and the Golem, a mythical being created to protect the Jews from persecution in sixteenth-century Prague.

Over the years, Superman has appeared in countless magazines, books, radio and television shows, and movies, including a 2006 version, *Superman Returns*, starring Kevin Spacey as Superman's archenemy Lex Luther. Owing to his alien origins, Superman has extraordinary powers. He is, in a phrase first used in the early radio serials, "faster than a speeding bullet, more powerful than a locomotive, and able to leap tall buildings in a single bound." He also has X-ray, infrared, and long-range vision, as well as super hearing, fantastic strength, super breath, and the ability to fly. He was also invincible (except, significantly in the presence of kryptonite, fragments of which, from his home planet, can weaken or kill him on Earth).

But when Superman did die, it was capitalism, not kryptonite that rubbed him out.

Superman's demise was concocted in the marketing department of DC Comics in the early 1990s. The company, looking for a way to boost sagging sales, decided that the demise of Superman would prove an event with reverberations beyond its usual comic-book consumer base. But loyal Superman fans and comic-book aficionados who got wind of the idea were appalled. Chuck Rozanski, a pop culture historian and founder of Mile High Comics in Boulder, Colorado, has called the promotional stunt "the greatest catastrophe to strike the world of comics since the Kefauver hearings," referring to a 1955 Senate subcommittee report that linked violence and sex in comic books to juvenile delinquency and prompted the Comic Book Publishers Association to adopt the self-regulating Comics Code.

"What made the 'Death of Superman' promotion so much different than all the rest of the specious comics marketing schemes cooked up during the early 1990s was that it was aimed at the general public," Rozanski wrote in an essay originally published in the *Comics Buyer's Guide* and archived on the Mile High Comics website. "When I first heard about DC's plans to 'kill' Superman I immediately called DC President Paul Levitz to beg him to cancel the idea. I forcefully made the argument that since Superman was such a recognized icon within America's overall popular culture, that DC had no more right to 'kill' him than Disney had the right to 'kill' Mickey Mouse. I went so far as to state that DC didn't actually 'own' Superman, but rather was a trustee of a sacred national image."

But Rozanski's appeals landed on deaf ears. Levitz and Superman Group editor Mike Carlin were convinced that their plan would be a promotional coup with little or no long-term consequences.

The Death of Superman was a comic book story line that continued over a number of issues, and extended across several DC Comics titles, before culminating in January 1993, in Superman #75, which became an instant collector's item. In a climactic battle with the unstoppable monster known as Doomsday, the two antagonists obliterate each other with one final shattering punch. Fatally wounded, Superman dies in Lois Lane's arms on the rubble outside the *Daily Planet* building. The magazine's cover shows Superman's tattered cape flying from a stick planted over a makeshift grave.

Superman's funeral, and the various stories that immediately followed, dealt with the grief of the public and Superman's fellow DC Comics heroes. One scene even featured Bill and Hillary Clinton as attendees at Superman's funeral. The entire sequence was collected in a trade paperback edition titled *The Death of Superman*. Meanwhile, all the Superman comics took a three-month break from publication.

As a promotional gambit, the Death of Superman was wildly successful. Superman's demise attracted international media attention and introduced millions of new readers to the DC Comics roster. Imitating mourning comic-book characters, real life Superman fans, including Jay Leno, wore black armbands with the unmistakable "S" to commemorate the death of their comic-book hero. In the United States, Superman's death was front-page news and the subject of op-ed pieces and sociological commentaries. People who had never shown any interest in comics raced to stores to buy their own copy of Superman #75, standing in line for hours in some cases. Comic-book collecting, for kids and adults alike, became the new rage.

"For a little while, the wonderful earnings we all generated from this huge new flow of customers seemed to make all my arguments against the 'death' of Superman seem like a big mistake," Rozanski recalled.

Then something unexpected happened: Superman returned. But

the Man of Steel wasn't exactly resurrected; he was replaced with four new superheroes, each with their own personality and powers. To make things even more confusing, all four bore some resemblance to Superman and claimed to be him or in some way possess his spirit. In a story line billed by DC as the "Reign of the Supermen!" all four of Superman's alter egos—an armor-wearing weapons designer called the Man of Steel; a Superman Cyborg known as the Man of Tomorrow; a teenage chip off the super block nicknamed the Metropolis Kid; and a visored alien named the Last Son of Krypton— appeared in Metropolis claiming to be the dead hero.

At first, the various Supermen competed, each seeking to prove himself the true inheritor of Superman's mantle by protecting Metropolis and its citizens. But before long the contest turned into a slugfest and Superman's various personas faced off against each other. It was eventually revealed that the Last Son of Krypton stole Superman's body and put it onto a regeneration matrix in the Fortress of Solitude at the North Pole. The real Superman returned to Metropolis only to discover that Cyborg had destroyed Coast City and turned it onto a gigantic machine, where he had imprisoned Super Boy. The three other clones and the original Superman joined forces against Cyborg in a battle in which Cyborg and the Last Son of Krypton both were killed. The two surviving Superman clones, Super Boy, and the Man of Steel were, at least for a while, given starring roles in their own magazines.

The spectacle of Superman slugging it out with various versions of himself, mired in a self-defeating standoff with his own alter egos, was, in a way, more traumatic than his death.

With the true Man of Steel's persona fractured and broken into separate pieces, his identity blurred beyond recognition, it was hard to tell who he was, let alone where he was going. It didn't help that thirty-four years earlier, George Reeves, the star of a popular Superman TV series, had committed suicide by shooting himself in the head in the bedroom of his Los Angeles home. "It was a pretty big deal at the time," recalls one San Francisco man. "Superman committed fucking suicide, and everybody took note." The official story is that Reeves, whose tragic trajectory was depicted in the 2006 film *Hollywoodland*, took his own life because of depression brought on by what he perceived as a failed career. But for years afterward, fans clung to a more fanciful explanation: Reeves, believing that he really had superpowers, had killed himself by jumping out of a window and trying to fly.

If superpower is a metaphor for social clout, then Superman's disintegration into conflicting and contradictory personas is a telling twist. As the identity of men breaks down and morphs into multiple, sometimes contradictory personas, men might benefit from learning the lesson of Clark Kent, who knew that ingenuity and compassion were the real sources of Superman's strength.

In *Y: The Last Man*, it's not Superman but the Everyman who meets his doom and the hero's only special power is his dogged determination to exist. Brian K. Vaughn's award-winning comic-book series begins as a plague of unknown origin has wiped out every Y chromosome and male mammal on Earth. The only male survivors on the planet are Yorick Brown, an amateur escape artist, and his pet monkey, Ampersand. Launched in 2002 and scheduled to conclude in 2008, this apocalyptic tale traces the adventures of Yorick and Ampersand as they try to save themselves, and what's left of mankind, in a world that has been turned upside down by the sudden disappearance of men. "This 'gendercide' instantaneously exterminates 48% of the global population," explains the introduction to the bound collection, *Y: The Last Man—Cycles*. "495 of the *Fortune* 500 CEO's are now dead, as are 99% of the world's landowners. . . . Worldwide, 85% of all government representatives are now dead . . . as are 100% percent of Catholic Priests, Muslim Imams, and Orthodox Jewish Rabbis." In the United States, more than 95 percent of all commercial pilots, truck drivers, and ship captains have died, as well as 92 percent of all violent felons.

In Vaughn's surreal post-male world, the Washington Monument has been turned into a phallic memorial for the fallen gender, and a fanatical ultrafeminist group called the Daughters of the Amazon celebrate the revenge of Mother Nature against her male defilers. *Y: The Last Man*, which is being developed into a movie by New Line Cinema, frames fantastic events with familiar social issues. When Yorick expresses amazement at the high level of public services being provided by a group of former female convicts in the town of Marrisville, Ohio, an elderly woman tells him: "Hard to believe that helpless little women can get by without your kind, eh? We've all had plenty of experience making do without any men around. Back in '42, the only fellas left in this country were the goddamn 4F-ers, tryin' to get into our overalls. Girls weren't part of the workforce, we *were* the workforce." A few pages later, a member of the Daughters of the Amazon who intends to execute Yorick, declares, "The battle of the sexes enters endgame."

Vaughn, who has written for such comics as *Batman*, *X-Men*, and *Spiderman*, as well as TV's *Lost*, believes that the best fiction is anchored in fact. "The stories I like best are those that engage us in the real world," he told *Bookslut* magazine. "In a lot of the last-man-on-Earth scenarios, as soon as all the men die, women go down to the United Nations and hold hands, which just seemed incredibly patronizing. So before I started work on *Y*, I read as many feminist writers as possible. Because if you put Andrea Dworkin and Naomi Wolf in a room together, they'd fight to the death."

CHAPTER 9

Samson Unbound

They are known to millions as Bill and Bob. The story of how they met has become a kind of modern fable, the life-altering account of how two men decided to help each other out with a problem and ended up changing themselves and the rest of the world. In 1935, Bill Wilson, a Wall Street stock speculator who was on a business trip to Akron, Ohio, was introduced to Dr. Bob Smith, a local surgeon who had begun holding group sessions to help people deal with their drinking problems. Wilson and Smith, both alcoholics, shared an interest in new theories of addiction recently formulated by William James, a Harvard University psychologist, and William Silkworth, a pioneer in the study of alcoholism who happened to be Wilson's doctor. Wilson and Smith had noticed that their ability to fight off the urge to drink was bolstered by sharing their personal experiences with other alcoholics. Their book, *Alcoholics Anonymous*, a.k.a. "The Big Book," was first published in 1939, and it has never been out of print. In *Alcoholics Anonymous Comes of Age: A Brief History of A.A.*, Wilson says that Silkworth "reminded me of Professor William James's observations that truly transforming spiritual experiences are almost always founded on calamity and collapse." The organization they founded is described on the AA website as a nondenominational "fellowship of men and women who share their experience, strength and hope with each other that they may solve their common problem and help others to recover from alcoholism."

Today there are more than 100,000 AA chapters serving some 2 million participants in 150 countries. It is considered to be the most successful self-help organization ever created. The house in Bedford Hills, New Jersey, where Bill Wilson lived for thirty years before he died, in 1971, has been turned into a museum of sorts. Visitors to the house wander the rooms in awe and pose for pictures in front of the desk where Wilson wrote the "Big Book," the gospel of Alcoholics Anonymous, in which he recounts his struggle with alcohol and details the twelve-step recovery method he developed along with Dr. Bob. The core of the AA is the Twelve Steps and the AA meeting, during which participants, who identify themselves only by their first names, share their experiences with other alcoholics in an atmosphere of mutual support.

What made AA unique and extraordinarily effective was the way it gave alcoholics a safe, anonymous place to express their deepest fears and emotions without being scolded or judged. Bill and Dr. Bob also grasped that the act of helping others was in itself therapeutic. They knew that most alcoholics were in denial of their problem, so the first guiding principle of AA was to get the alcoholic to (1) admit he has a problem and (2) acknowledge that his addiction is too strong for him to battle alone. Only by acknowledging a greater power"—religious, spiritual, social, or emotional—could alcoholics find the strength they needed to overcome their addiction.

The Guiding Principles of Alcoholics Anonymous

- Admitting that alcoholics have a serious, uncontrollable problem.
- Recognizing that an outside power could help.
- Conscious reliance on that power.
- Inventorying and admitting character defects.
- Seeking deliverance from these defects.

- Making amends for those one has harmed.
- Helping others with the same problem.

What if men had a problem, a problem that was bigger than them individually? What if they were in denial about this problem and the first step was to get them to admit that there even was a problem? What if you took the example and techniques of one of the most powerful and successful self-help programs ever created and applied them to the decline of men? It might look something like this:

A Twelve-Step Program for Men

1. Admit that we've got a problem.
2. Make a fearless inventory of ourselves.
3. Apologize to those we have hurt.
4. Admit our mistakes.
5. Break the trap of male silence.
6. Make peace with Mr. Hyde.
7. Seek strength in brotherhood.
8. Embrace change.
9. Never blame women.
10. Remember that respect comes in many forms.
11. Share our experience.
12. Don't follow The Rules.

The idea of men coming together to help themselves and each other is hardly new. Men's societies have existed at least since medieval times, when the Priory of Sion and the Freemasons were like invisible webs threaded into the fabric of church and state. In America in the twentieth century, the cohesive effects of World Wars I and II created a golden era of men's clubs and civic societies. In his book *Bowling Alone*, sociologist Robert Putnam describes how postwar spikes in national unity ignited a "boom" of civic groups and associations dedicated to the common good, including the Boy Scouts, the Knights of Pythias, the Sierra Club, the Salvation Army, the YMCA, the ACLU, the American Legion, the Knights of Columbus, the Shriners, the Rotary Club, the Loyal Order of Moose, and the Optimists.

More recently, men have come together, however briefly, to bolster political and spiritual values under the banner of universal brotherhood. In 1995, the Million Man March, a rally organized by Nation of Islam leader Louis Farrakhan to increase awareness of unemployment among African-Americans and promote black voter registration, attracted throngs of men to the National Mall in Washington, D.C. Two years later, a similar number gathered in the same place for Stand in the Gap: A Sacred Assembly of Men. This event was organized by the Promise Keepers, an international organization of Christian men whose goals include "pursuing vital relationships with a few other men," who can help a man "keep promises."

Are men ready to march again, or is the whole idea of large public gatherings passé? Do men want to see themselves on CNN asking for a hand because they can't compete with girls? Not likely. In an age when avatars go shopping at the virtual mall and bloggers sitting in their bedrooms can reach a mass audience faster than the *New York Times*, why would anyone bother to join an actual, physical demonstration? When—and if—men do rouse themselves and rally, it won't be in the streets. For that matter, how do we know that the movement to reverse the decline of men hasn't already begun? Would we even know what to look for?

AN INCONVENIENT TRUTH

Change, as Bill and Dr. Bob knew, does not come easily. As the decline of men continues, males will try to hang on to the stereotype of the dominant, aggressive gender; women will cling to their position as victimized underdog. Both sides have a stake in preserving the status quo. But if the downward slide continues, both sides have even more to lose.

The sexes have not yet reached parity—misogyny is still alive and thriving in America; men as a group still earn more than women; and males still occupy the uppermost rungs of social and political power. But like a pot of water that increases in temperature for a long time before it actually boils, the empirical evidence that men are losing ground is reaching a critical threshold. And contrary to the flippant reaction that the news evokes in many women and men—*how ridiculous, how impossible, how well-deserved*—the implications are serious and far-reaching.

Ronald Mincy has been measuring the impact of shifting gender roles on society for twenty years. In his papers and lectures at Columbia University he has been sounding the alarm that a large percentage of men of all ages and races are veering into a dysfunctional economic and psychological drift, but the message has been slow to get through. Because the trend is so wide, so deep, and so counterintuitive, he says, it has been hard for the public to "grasp the larger significance."

Part of the disconnect, Mincy says, is that most people assume that only minority men are having problems. "Often when there are conversations about challenges that men are facing, people are pigeonholing those conversations into 'black men' or 'blacks and Latinos,'" Mincy says. "What they fail to recognize is that while the orders of magnitude and the dimension of the challenges that blacks and Latinos face are of a much higher order of magnitude, it is also the case that in a lot of the ways in which this society measures success, men are lagging behind quite generally, and people don't get it."

In order to better understand what's happening now, Mincy points to the work of Talcott Parsons, the great American sociologist. Parsons, who helped to define American sociology from the 1930s through the 1970s with his theory of "structural functionalism," believed that society tended naturally toward a state of equilibrium. According to Parsons, when change occurs in one part of society, there must be corresponding adjustments in the rest of society to maintain that equilibrium. The failure of a given change to be absorbed by the rest of society can cause stress and instability.

Compared to the period during the 1930s and '40s, when Parsons was developing structural functionalism, there has lately been a "sea change" in gender roles, Mincy says. "In the late thirties, the United States was unique in that it did not segregate girls and boys in education. But at the point approaching high school graduation there was a significant gender separation that occurred, and Parsons's analysis was that there were clearly defined roles for boys, for males. Their identity would be attached to their work, and as a consequence they would have this work identity, and that identity would have really substantial implications for the wife's income. Everything—the family's income, where they lived, their socioeconomic status, etc., etc.—was derived from the man's occupation. By contrast, women had this "sequential" social status that derived from the fact that at the time she was a childbearer, she was a mom; but once being a mom was over, she kind of got confused, because it wasn't clear what her role was going to be moving forward. And reading that now, it's fascinating."

The pop media spin on evolving gender roles, which tends to focus on dating and marriage, has obfuscated structural changes that are less visible but just as transformative. "The simple way I like to put it," says Mincy, "is that we've had a sexual revolution which has implications for men's and women's roles in the economy and men's and women's roles in the family. Women have latched on to this in a whole variety of ways, but I think men are in a great state of disequilibrium about what it all means."

In effect, men have become co-conspirators in keeping the lid on a phenomenon that does nothing to enhance their self-esteem.

Why call attention to something that they don't want to admit even to themselves? To top it off, men are also understandably reluctant to be seen as antifeminist. "Men have become unmoored, which has an implication for a whole variety of things," says Mincy. "Do men individually recognize this uncertainty about their status? And, secondly, does the society recognize that this is happening? I think we are seriously in a state of nonrecognition or denial about it, because once you acknowledge it, to make such a claim is automatically inferred as some statement against the progress that women have made. One of the reasons that we as a society have failed to recognize the signs of this that are all around us, is that people are reluctant— women aren't completely liberated yet, they think, so let's not get distracted. And so even those who are aware of the problem, and don't have a stake in the women's movement, are afraid of articulating it because it will be received at the outset as some kind of statement against the progress that women have made."

The decline in men's wages, Mincy believes, will only be exacerbated in coming years by the glaring education gap. He sees trouble, for instance, in the fact that 70 percent of the students at the City University of New York (CUNY) are women. "If you think of the role of the city university in terms of the production of the future labor force, sure, men will still have manual jobs, but going into the coming decade with only 30 percent of male students availing themselves of the educational system, it's just extraordinary," he says. This statistic alone "has extraordinary implications for how we're going to manage ourselves as a society. It's worrisome."

Thanks to this discrimination that nobody sees, Mincy says, society reaches out to help women in need but punishes men. If a woman can't earn enough to pay her rent, society has failed her, but if a man can't earn a decent living, society blames him for his own failure. "It is the case that men have been the quintessential undeserving poor," says Mincy. "So when men are poor, we say that's tough. But when women are poor we find our way to resolve, to identity the problem, to move on it in some way. But men are supposed to get along on their own. And we are behaving as if working poverty is a new phenomenon. We've always had working poverty in the United States, when men have earned too little for basic sustenance, but we've never really addressed it as a social problem."

The discrepancy is evident in the dilemma of divorced dads who are economically unable to pay child support; but the men who are gradually slipping behind are even more neglected. "Over the last fifteen years it's become really clear that a healthy portion of the men in the child-support-enforcement system are poor," Mincy points out. "And yet it's really an oxymoron to devise a child-support-enforcement system that acknowledges that many of the men who owe, and should be paying for their child support, don't have the capacity to do so. And we have been stuck for a period of ten years for failing to acknowledge that and act on it. And that's the low-end manifestation. At the upper end, if you're talking about males who are lagging behind in performance, who are not destitute but are still losing ground, well, no one wants to put their hands on that thing."

To understand what's happening and what might happen next, Mincy uses the example of other important social issues that had to go through a series of stages—ignorance, denial, grudging acknowledgment, discussion, and consensus—before action was taken. "You can talk about a whole array of problems—homeland security, AIDS, domestic violence—and, historically, in each case, what happens is that people begin to talk and write about these things," he observes. "And they're not just talking to policy wonks, they're talking to the general public. And there's a clarion call that goes out, announcing that there's a problem. And at first the clarion call is ignored. But if the challenge you're representing is real, then some people begin to sound a clarion call again. In the beginning there's a debate about whether or not this problem even exists at all, and then it moves to the point where we have a conversation about it, and people say, okay, there appears to be something here, and then there's another discussion for people to understand inescapably that, yes, there is a problem, but what is the nature of it? And then we go through a dialogue over a period of years to reach the point, to say, do we have a common conception of what that problem is before we decide what to do about it?"

The recognition that something is amiss with men is cropping up among college women who have noticed a lack of competitive spirit in their siblings and male counterparts. "I have female students here at Columbia, and they're saying the same thing about their brothers," Mincy reports. "They have grown up in families where the mothers have come from a generation that was in the early round of successful women, and they have been focused on showing their daughters how to replicate and surpass their own success, whereas the message to boys has been not that aggressive. 'As girls, we were oriented by our mothers to get things done,' they tell me. 'Our moms told us we've got to fight to win, and I'm going to help you get this done.' The boys weren't fired up that way, perhaps because of the presumption that they were going to be okay, and so what's emerged then is this sort of very lackadaisical attitude on the part of young males, and they're not very focused, while the girls are tearing it up, they're getting it done. And for boys it's creating an inequity, not just in graduation [rates] but in other parts of their life."

By Mincy's estimate, the realization of the plight of men is still early in the process, but it's following the same trajectory as other movements that became defining social issues. "I think we're in a place in our society where the clarion calls are being sounded," he says. "Over the last fifteen years or so, this clarion call has been made mainly in respect to disadvantaged men. And now the conversation has become more generic, and the thing that's going to crack it open is when the issue is framed in such a way that women can grasp it. And I think the way to do that is to talk about the performance of their sons, to make them understand that their sons might be more vulnerable than their daughters. They need to understand that there well may be a set of issues that make your sons vulnerable in terms of their participation in society. They need to somehow be made to understand that this is not about their five-year-old daughter, it's about their three-year-old son."

How far will men have to fall before women realize that reversing the trend is ultimately in their own interests? How bad will things have to get before the crisis in masculinity is rightly perceived as a threat to the well-being and future of all Americans?

In *The Labyrinth of Solitude*, a collection of essays by the Mexican writer and Nobel laureate Octavio Paz, he says, "Women are imprisoned in the image masculine society has imposed on them; therefore, if they attempt a free choice it must be a kind of jail break. Lovers says that 'love has transformed her, it has made her a different person.' And they are right. Love changes a woman completely. If she dares to love, if she dares to be herself, she has to destroy the image in which the world has imprisoned her."

In the decades since Paz wrote those words, the sexes have switched places. Men are the ones who are imprisoned in the masculine image that society has imposed on them. Ultimately, men may be impelled to escape from their masculine jail, but women are the ones who hold the key.

Are men, as one anonymous poster on the street in New York City proclaims, "the new women"? Are women the new men?

Women must come to grips with the undeniable reality that they are poised to become the dominant gender in America, and in many ways already are. Their highest value—to the world, to themselves, and to men—is not to become better versions of men, but to become better versions of women. As their social, political, and economic progress becomes undeniable, they must avoid the age-old trap of quietly morphing from revolutionaries into reactionaries. Men are not responsible for every single ill in the world. They are not contemptible, disposable, or unnecessary. The man-bashing and passive-aggressive rhetoric of the gender wars, which increasingly sounds like the worn-out polemics of a bygone era, no longer defines the real struggle that females now face: how to lead America and the rest of the world to a revival of cooperation, responsibility, and hope.

"When a generation of Americans early in the twentieth century reflected on both the horrors of war and the civic virtues it inculcated," Robert Putnam writes, "they framed their task as the search for the moral equivalent of war." Hence the War on Poverty, the War on Drugs, the War on Terrorism. Has the time come for the War on the Decline of Men? Will Americans answer the clarion call? Will men and women perceive the danger and join together? Or have we already lost that war, too?

BRINKSMANSHIP

Part of the answer may lie in the increasingly interdependent nature of the twenty-first-century global economy. As nations compete for markets and influence around the world, the ability to communicate and cooperate across oceans and borders is a distinct advantage. Just as women in the United States are better positioned to take advantage of long-term domestic business trends, countries with more "feminine" cultures may have an advantage in global commerce, trade, and diplomacy. The world, it turns out, may be curved after all.

Do countries have a gender? According to Christopher Liechty, the answer is a qualified yes. Liechty, the president and creative director of a global design and marketing firm based in Salt Lake City, demonstrates by opening an interactive map of the world on his laptop. As he moves the cursor across the globe, the bars on a graph of Hofstede's Cultural Dimensions Index rise and fall. Geert Hofstede, a Dutch psychologist who worked at IBM, has profiled national cultures according to four key values: Power Distance; Individualism; Uncertainty Avoidance; and Masculinity. On the Masculinity index, the United States scores relatively high at 62, as compared to countries like Sweden (5) and Norway (8), but lower than Japan, which has the highest Masculinity index in the world at 95.

"The masculine-feminine dimension is competitive," Liechty explains. "Hofstede uses 'aggressive,' but I think 'competitive' is a good term that's more measurable, and also prestige-oriented. So, Masculinity kind of is like unquestioning loyalty in exchange for protection. Although there are going to be some different degrees of this, and they manifest themselves differently in different cultures." When it comes to the feminine-masculine balance between genders, it turns out that men vary much more than women. "Women don't change as much from culture to culture as men do in the way that they perceive these things. And so, in feminine cultures, the men are closer to a traditionally female way of approaching things. Which is basically more egalitarian. Women are more consensus-building."

Liechty notes that when gender traits are projected onto corporate cultures, an interesting picture emerges. "If we look at global corporations from masculine and feminine countries, can we say that one sort of country or the other is increasing in dominance in a global situation or doing better, or are they both equal? Let's take Scandinavian companies versus Japanese companies. So in Scandinavia you have Nokia, Ikea, Lego, Volvo, Shell (oil), Phillips (electronics). If you were to assume that these companies are governed by feminine traits—these are a fair number of strong global companies. And if I notice an approach that they have—well, I notice that they are more global than the masculine countries. Take Lego, for example. They are brilliant in regard to not putting a language forward and having to translate. They've figured out how to present their toys, both in packaging and instructions. Of course, when it comes to advertising they have to deal with language more. But when it comes to their core product, the instructions for Lego are completely neutral in terms of culture. Ikea has done that. Shell is very good at feeling like it's a local brand."

Liechty believes that, as genders move toward parity in this country, America will inevitably benefit, both economically and politically.

"I feel like I take a feminine approach to a lot of things," says Liechty. "I feel that I align myself with . . . that the feminine approach is a better way. I don't know that it's a confusion of the genders; it's just more of a dominance thing, or it's that the old patriarchal systems have broken down and women have gained more influence and the feminine way is making more sense to more men. It makes more sense to think about the consequences than just to say, 'This is the way I want to do things.' So, as opposed to saying that things have gotten all confused, you might say that the traditional feminine values have gained respect among both women and men. While in the past, masculine values have had more sway with both women and men. And the women have said, 'Yes, we need to take this masculine approach.' Now, that doesn't seem to make that much sense to everybody. There's been this whole shift to a more feminine way of looking at the world."

Meanwhile, there are signs that some of the same cultural and economic shifts that have unmoored American men are taking hold in other countries. In South Korea, the industrial revolution of the past thirty years—and the corresponding economic empowerment and independence it has given Korean women—has reversed a long-held preference for baby boys and displaced the male as the undisputed head of the household. A 2007 study by the Korea Institute for Health and Social Affairs found that only 10 percent of Korean women under forty-five feel any pressure to have a son, down from 40 percent in 1991. Is it only a matter of time before Korean women start asking if men are necessary? Will Asian societies find a way to harmoniously reconcile traditional definitions of masculinity with modern realities? Or will Asian men, like nearly 50 percent of males in Italy, continue living with their parents into their late twenties and thirties, delaying the responsibilities of manhood and marriage that they no longer crave and can no longer afford?

Kenneth Willardt, a Danish-born photographer who has lived in the United States for twenty years, travels the world shooting spreads for corporate clients and magazines like *Vogue* and *In Style*. When he's not on location, he and his Brazilian-born wife oversee a New York–based staff that can grow from six to a couple dozen, depending on the job at hand. His observations confirm Liechty's hunch, and underscore the advantages of gender parity in the global workforce.

"A lot of my clients are women," Willardt says. "I'm just lucky that I'm a guy that likes to work with women. I get along with them. But a lot of American men don't like working with women, they don't know how to talk to them. They don't know how to deal with not being the one who's always in charge. American society has been very male dominated, and it's always been aggressive toward the rest of the world, though now it's more obvious to everybody."

Willardt has noticed that among the couples he knows, the women are the principal breadwinners. "Men are the new women," he says. "Just in my area of friends, most of the women are the ones with the powerful jobs. The men are one step down—and they're fine with it, it's not a problem for them. And it shouldn't be a problem. I would hire a woman any day over a guy, but you have to have some yin and yang, you can't have all women in a company. It has to be guys and girls. But on any given day, the woman is going to be doing a better job, and she's going to be more loyal and trustworthy and she'll work harder. It's just a fact."

Willardt has noticed a striking difference in the role that women play in Scandinavia compared to the United States. "Women in Europe have advanced much faster," he says. "In Denmark, the royal firstborn—if it's a girl she's the queen, if it's a boy he's the king. And so for hundreds and hundreds of years, the people have seen that both can have power and that it's okay. In Denmark, I noticed a long time ago that when I go home, I turn the TV on and all the experts are women. The ministers, the professors, the scientist, being asked, "How can we solve this problem of too many poor people on Earth, or whatever. While over here, in the U.S., the men are still hanging on. Larry King is still in charge."

Willardt, who became a U.S. citizen in 2001, has little sympathy for the apparent decline of his fellow males. His biggest concern is that by the time men in America wake up it will be too late. "Men aren't giving up—they're being run over," he says. "Because they're lazy. They're giving up because they can't multitask. You see it in many of the businesses that I'm involved in: the men are still at the top, sure, but the women, they're the ones that talk, they're making it happen, they're the ones who get things done. And let's not forget, this also applies to China, to India. It's much bigger than this. What's going on with American men, if we're not careful, that decline will happen to American society in general. Because the Indians and Chinese and the Brazilians—and whoever else, wherever they are—they still have so much to gain."

Men need to find the courage to let go of the past and find their real future, Willardt asserts. "We can't be afraid anymore. And that's the real downfall of the American male. They're afraid of everybody. They're afraid of foreigners; they're afraid of women; they're afraid of losing; they're afraid that they can't fall asleep at night; they're afraid that they can't get it up. That's the downfall, that's the underlying cause of the decline: fear. When we let go of that fear, things will change. The fear is what stops us from being men. Because men should not be afraid. Aggression is a symptom of fear. Men don't need to be so aggressive. They're supposed to be heroes and fathers and do great things. And this is not what men are doing anymore—they're playing video games and getting fat on hot dogs. The women are moving ahead. And if they can't do it with men, they'll do it on their own. We need to make this world better. Men want to be heroes and if we don't make men heroes, we're only hurting ourselves."

In *The Power of Myth*, Joseph Campbell talks to Bill Moyers about the significance of challenges and trials in the mythic hero's journey. "The trials are designed to see to it that the intending hero should be really a hero," Campbell says. "Is he really a match for this task? Does he have the courage, the knowledge, the capacity, to enable him to serve? . . . When we quit thinking about ourselves and our own self-preservation we undergo a truly heroic transformation of consciousness."

As men ponder whether to become heroes or zeroes, they might want to consider the ultimate meaning of their epic journey. Is there a lesson to be learned from Samson that does not involve self-destruction? Will males yank at their chains and pull the entire temple down with them, or will they rise to the challenge and persevere? Will they be buried in the debris of their own sense of failure, or look inside to summon a new definition of strength? If men stop struggling to prove themselves, they might find that their bonds have disappeared, because the only thing holding them back is their fear of being themselves.

HERSTORY

She goes by many names and has many faces. She is the Great Mother, the nubile daughter, the giver of birth and source of rebirth. She is beautiful and fierce, generous and fickle, seductive and serene. Her powers are infinite, because she dwells in a realm beyond time and space. She is the ruler of all life but not apart from it, because her power is not over nature but derived from it. She is the Great Goddess, Mother Earth, the Eternal Source—and after aeons in exile, her time may have come again.

"The question *Does the Goddess exist?* cannot be asked as it can of God or argued about metaphysically, or answered yes or no," Geoffrey Ashe writes in *Dawn Behind the Dawn: A Search for the Earthly Paradise.* "The Goddess is *there* in experience, and she transcends, and takes endless forms, as the goddess figures of myth and religion and as living women."

As men lose power and women gain strength, will the spiritual plane regain its sexual alignment and help to heal the real world?

Can men return to a time when males and females ruled together and not over each other?

Is the revival of the feminine "other" the key to a rejuvenated form of masculinity? The history of mankind, it turns out, is rooted in womankind, and the most ancient cults may provide a hint of what lies in our collective future.

From the beginning of human existence until the introduction of agriculture, about 10,000 years ago, the Goddess presided over a cosmos that existed in perfect balance, nurturing the sublime spirit in all living things. In the hunter-gatherer societies that worshipped her, men and women lived and governed side by side, with equal power and rights, in harmony and mutual respect. In this female-friendly Eden, family lineage was traced through the mother. Farming, which allowed the creation of cities and specialized labor, also planted the seeds of class divisions and a new social order. "Farming may have encouraged inequality between the sexes," observes the historian-anthropologist Jared Diamond in his essay "The Worst Mistake in the History of the Human Race." "Women in agricultural societies were sometimes made beasts of burden." Then, around 4000 B.C., nomadic peoples from the north and east arrived. Armed with horses and weapons, the invaders were patriarchal and androcentric, male-dominated tribes that worshipped the reductive and exclusionary Sky Father. With her influence waning, the Goddess retreated into the shadows. For thousands of years, the world was ruled by men. Cities and nations rose and fell.

Mystics and tribal societies have long predicted that the twenty-first century would witness a shift in the *axis mundi*, ushering in a period of wrenching change, followed by an era of peace and prosperity. Amid the chaos and confusion of the crumbling status quo, they see signs of an emerging new order: the world of men is ending, and the return of the Goddess has begun. That scenario may be a mix of mythology, documented fact, science fiction, and wishful thinking, but there's no question that the idea of an ascendant feminine divinity is gaining cultural traction. In the media and in the minds and hearts of millions, from politics and economics to ecology and astrology, the conviction that women are ready—and uniquely able—to take charge of the planet has assumed an aura of inevitability.

The return of the Goddess is equal parts metaphor and polemic, weaving social and political discontent with a mystical yearning for transcendence and redemption. It is grounded in the widespread belief that something important and precious has been lost, and that civilization's Faustian bargain with material progress has become too costly and too corrupt to sustain. Dan Brown's 2003 novel *The Da Vinci Code* traces the quest by a Harvard professor of symbology to unravel the secret of the Holy Grail, which, according to the story, is not a physical chalice but in fact Mary Magdalene, who carried on the bloodline of Jesus by bearing his child. The book, which sold more than 60 million copies and was an international sensation, presents the possibility that the Roman Catholic Church has suppressed the role of Mary in Jesus' life for two thousand years because it feared that the power of the sacred feminine would threaten the ecclesiastic authority of the apostle Peter. The plot incorporates the theory that Leonardo da Vinci's painting *The Last Supper* contains clues that point to the real identity of the apostle John, and that the Priory of Sion, a secret society of Christian knights, had stashed the remains of Mary Magdalene's body, and other proof, possibly under England's Rosselyn Chapel and would stop at nothing, not even murder, to keep them hidden. As the novel's protagonist, Robert Langdon, explains: "Legends of chivalric quests for the lost Grail were in fact stories of forbidden quests to find the lost sacred feminine."

The modern cult of the Goddess has also found support and inspiration in the work and writings of Marija Gimbutas, a Lithuanian-American archaeologist who claims to have found evidence of cultures in what she calls "Old Europe," where women were the queens and high priests in egalitarian, nonpatriarchal societies. While a professor of archaeology at UCLA from 1963 to 1989, Gimbutas directed major excavations at Neolithic sites in southeastern Europe and the Mediterranean. By studying the mythology, linguistics, and art associated with the artifacts she uncovered, Gimbutas developed the portrait of a society that lasted 25,000 years and which practiced equal rights between men and women on a social, political, and spiritual level.

In books like *The Goddesses and Gods of Old Europe*, *The Language of the Goddess*, and *The Civilization of the Goddess*, Gimbutas extrapolated a model that she believed holds great lessons for modern societies. "Through an understanding of what the Goddess was, we can better understand nature and we can build our ideologies so that it will be easier to live," Gimbutas told David Jay Brown and Rebecca McClen Novick in their book, *Mavericks of the Mind: Conversations for the New Millennium*. "Women were equal beings, that is very clear, and perhaps more honored because they had more in-fluence in the religious life. The temple was run by women."

The political structure of Goddess cultures were what Gimbu-tas termed "avuncular"—the queen, who was also the high priest-ess, ruled with her brother, or sometimes an uncle. The mixed-gender government was reflected in the balance of sexes in that ancient pantheon of deities, as well as the society itself. Gimbutas rejected the term "matriarchal" for the Goddess-led societies because it im-plies a system dominated by females, rather than a structure that is balanced and cooperative, with both sexes contributing equally to society and sharing power. The modern-day solution, Gimbutas believed, was not for women to replace men, or imitate them, but rather to lead both genders to an entirely new social reality.

"It is wrong to say that this is just a woman's culture, that there was just a Goddess and there were no Gods," she said. "In art the male is less represented, that's true, but that the male Gods existed, there is no question. In all mythologies, for instance in Europe, Ger-manic or Celtic or Baltic, you will find the Earth Mother or Earth Goddess and her male companion or counterpart next to her."

For theologians and mystics, the return of the Goddess carries more than a whiff of apocalypse. According to the Maya, the Long Count calendar, which began in August of 3114 B.C., will end on December 21, 2012. This "end of time" also marks the completion and destruction of the Fifth Sun and the beginning of a new era for mankind. While some have interpreted this to mean that the world is doomed, others emphasize that in Mesoamerican religions the end or death also signals transformation and rebirth. Astrologers note that in 2012, Venus will be uniquely aligned on the horizon, and that this cosmic event, known as the "Birth of Venus," repre-sents a long-due return to the primacy of the Earth Mother.

John Major Jenkins, author of *Maya Cosmogenesis: The True Meaning of the Maya Calendar End Date*, also notes that the period around 2012 coincides with a "galactic alignment" of the winter solstice sun and the axis of the Milky Way, or galactic equator, ushering in a moment of cosmic rebirth and the "transcending of opposites."

The struggle between fertile, female chaos and the hierarchical, linear definitions of androcentric technology—and their potential reconciliation—is a recurring theme in human civilization. The masculine impulse to rein in the female, to symbolically and physically dominate Mother Nature, is also a recognition of her unpredictable power. Kali, the awesome Indian goddess, is the giver and taker of life, the creator and the destroyer. She brought the world into being but can also wipe it out without warning. "The femaleness of fertility religions is always double-edged," writes Camille Paglia in *Sexual Personae*. "We cannot grasp nature's bare blade without shedding our own blood." Paglia defends the primordial male impulse to separate himself from nature and bend her to his will, and the Judeo-Christian elevation of a Sky/Father-god who presides over creation, defining a cosmic order that exists above nature, and thus able to harness its untamed potential. Both sexes, she reminds us, have benefited from the fruits of technology and progress, a development that could not have taken place without the philosophical foundation of an orderly, coherent, predictable universe.

"The book of Genesis is a male declaration of independence from the ancient mother-cults," Paglia writes. "Its challenge to nature, so sexist to modern ears, marks one of the crucial moments in Western history: Mind can never be free of matter. Yet only by mind *imagining* itself free can culture advance. The mother-cults, by reconciling man to nature, entrapped him in matter. Everything great in Western civilization has come from struggle against our origins. Genesis is rigid and unjust but it gave man hope as a man. It remade the world by male dynasty, canceling the power of mothers."

But in the first decade of the twenty-first century, as Western civilization creaks under the weight of its own success, the sky god seems to have abandoned men. It has become alarmingly clear that technology and progress also cut both ways, and that the next stage of human evolution may require the pendulum to swing back in the other direction. In *Gods of Love and Ecstasy: The Traditions of Shiva and Dionysus*, Alain Daniélou argues that ever since humans began to settle in organized communities, the spiritual order of mankind has been divided between gods that represent nature and those that represent the organization and discipline of communal life. The time is ripe, Daniélou says, for the human race to reconcile the artificial division of body, soul, and spirit and reconnect with an "erotic-mystical renewal" that reflects the divine balance of nature.

"The cult of Dionysus, like the god himself, is always reborn from its own ashes," he asserts. "Many times through the ages, the eternal tradition linked with the cult of Shiva-Dionysus has been vanquished by new religions deriving from the ambitions and delusions of men. Nevertheless, it has always reappeared, as it is bound to do once more in the modern age." In effect, the failure of man to respect and protect the Earth is directly related to his failure to relate to the "other" in himself, the feminine side that was vanquished by the selfish demands of the sky god.

In his book *The Flight from Woman*, the psychoanalyst-theologian Karl Stern points out that the words for "mother" and "matter" (*mater* and *materia* in Latin) are linked etymologically in more than one language.

"Stern shows that in Western culture there has been an almost pathological flight from the feminine, from woman, which means a flight from communion, a flight from the other," Father Thomas Hopko observed in an interview with the Catholic journal *Living in Communion*. "The individualistic, radical, fallen, male values become the values for the culture as a whole, and that's the cause of the Western neurosis."

But even for many theologians and religious writers, the spiritual severing of the masculine and feminine has dire ramifications for both sexes. "Having for so many generations undervalued the feminine, men are in general now increasingly cut off from their masculinity and are trapped in the sickly passive—that which is the feminine state when it is unhealthy and cut off from the masculine," Leanne Payne writes in *Crisis in Masculinity*. "We cannot lose the feminine principle without weakening and eventually losing the masculine; we cannot retain the good of the masculine discursive reason apart from the feminine intuitive mind and heart. All the precious and colorful strands of reality are wonderfully interconnected. To discard one strand is to loosen and therefore endanger the whole framework of life."

In Alfonso Cuarón's acclaimed 2006 thriller *Children of Men* (loosely based on P. D. James's novel *The Children of Men*), the framework of life as we know it has become undone. Two decades of ecological disaster and human infertility—specifically, the looming extinction of the human race—have led to the collapse of the social order. Terrorists and totalitarian powers vie for control as millions of refugees swarm toward the cities in search of food and shelter. Theo, a former political activist turned bureaucrat, is recruited by his estranged wife to transport a young African refugee called Kee. When Theo discovers that Kee is pregnant, he risks his life to save her and her infant. The film, which was released on Christmas Day, ends as Theo, who has been mortally wounded, guides Kee and the newborn hope of the human race to a rescue boat named *Tomorrow*. In this updated echo of the Christ-child savior, Kee's baby is a girl.

When Descartes divided the world into the material and invisible—and thereby established the basis for empirical scientific thought—man was in effect driven from Paradise. Man was empowered by his sense of being ("I think, therefore I am"), but his self-consciousness also made him ashamed and impure. The scientist must separate himself from the world in order to observe it, and in that action he suddenly finds himself alone and naked. The fig leaf might have grown in the Garden of Eden, but it was rational thought that severed it—and mankind—from its source.

DRIFTERS AND BURNERS

Every year just before Christmas, in dozens of cities across America, Santa puts on his trademark red suit, checks his fluffy white beard, and heads out for a night on the town. His destination can be a street corner, a bar, a shopping mall, or just about anywhere a cellphone call, e-mail, or text message tell him to go. There he will join up with other Santas, unsaintly Nicks who would rather be naughty than nice, drinking, carousing, and generally raising hell as they raise their glasses and sing

> Oh, you better break out
> The bourbon and rye
> Tequila and gin
> I'm telling you why
> Santa is invading your town!

Alec*, a thirty-five-year-old new-media entrepreneur from the San Francisco Bay Area, is a Bad Santa veteran. He has seen the phenomenon evolve from a subversive political statement into a national media event. "It's part of a whole shift that's part of this culture-jamming, cacophony society," he explains. "It's about doing things that turn the everyday upside down for a little while to confuse people, stimulate people, and make them think, and sometimes it has political or economic motivations behind it, and sometimes it's just for fun."

In 1994, when the first "Santa-con" rampage was held in San Francisco, the prime objective was to confront and generally upend the eggnog-induced complacency of the Christmas-shopping masses. The original Santa-cons were guerrilla theater artists armed with flash-mob tactics and a sociological agenda. "A group called Cacophony Society started it as a protest against the commercialization, the crass commercialization of Christmas and religion, and such an obvious twisting of religion for economic purposes and all the BS around this thing called Christmas," Alec explains. "It started about ten years ago with a handful of people who one year decided to dress up as Santa. It began as a social statement."

As Bad Santa parties have grown and evolved, the unisex red suit, boots, and beard have branched out with gender-bending variations. "With so many different people participating, the gender thing has split apart again," he says. "So you have plenty of girls that go dressed as Santa, and then there are girls dressed up as Mrs. Santa, or Naughty Santa, or Slutty Santa. It's definitely become more of a bar crawl."

For Alec, the main attraction of Bad Santa is neither alcohol nor hookups—although he's happy to indulge in both—rather, it's about being part of a community of people who have chosen to live their life creatively, free from the hang-ups of traditional relationships or gender roles. This loose network of unconventional convocations ranges from solstice raves on the beach in Santa Barbara to the desert "playa" of the Burning Man festival, where guys amble in combat boots and sarongs next to a sign that says REAL MEN WEAR SKIRTS.

If it all sounds a bit pagan and topsy-turvy, it's supposed to. The invocation of ancient ecstatic rites, updated and supercharged by the Internet and state-of-the-art technology, is an intentional effort to shake consciousness free of its moorings and open the mind and spirit to unfettered possibilities. It's no coincidence that the theme of the 2007 Burning Man was "The Green Man." What better way to welcome the resplendent return of the Goddess than with the symbolic immolation of the male? For the "Burner" tribes of Black Rock City, getting back to the Garden, in the words of Joni Mitchell, is still the ultimate goal, but having a last Dionysian dance before the world self-destructs has become a welcome detour on the journey.

There is also, in the extended family of lovers and friends who join together for a night or week or month before dispersing again into the ether, a feeling that the existing social order is breaking down even though nothing yet has come along to replace it. With the present behind them and the future not quite in sight, the alternative tribes of the new millennium make up their own rules as they go along, searching, looking, waiting.

"I don't think of it so much as a search," Alec avers. "I kind of go back to the wandering as opposed to searching. Without being shoehorned into traditional roles, this generation is out wandering—wandering and searching are two sides of the same coin. Some people are searching and they know that they want something and that's what they're looking for. And other people are wandering, cast adrift, and just not knowing what to do and who to be."

Meanwhile, the "alt" tribes are a refuge and refueling station, a place where men and women can drop their guard, shed their old skins, and experiment. "It's a great place for people that are searching for something," Alec says. "Because you can find all kinds of different things. You can make your own reality. And if you're directed, if you're a person who has some direction and motivation, it's tremendous because you can really find all kinds of different things. Similarly, if you're just adrift, wandering, it's a great place for maybe something to knock you into a direction, because you'll see all kinds of different things and maybe something is going to strike a chord for you, and make you say, hey, this is what I want to be, the kind of life I want to live, or the kinds of things I want to do with my life, or the kind of meaning that I want to put into my life."

The alt tribe is also an incubator for nonrestrictive definitions of gender, a place where nontraditional expression of the masculine and feminine are not just tolerated but encouraged. "It's definitely a lab, a place for experimentation," Alec says. He agrees that men overall are struggling with identity issues, but for Alec that just means that men have caught up to women, who have so many options to choose from that they can get paralyzed into doing nothing.

"There is not one clear path to follow to be a man these days," says Alec. "There's lots of choice, you can follow a lot of different paths. But it's the same, though, for women. There's not one clear path to being a woman these days. You can get married at twenty and start having kids at twenty-two—there's lots of different paths that women can choose. I think that both sexes now have all kinds of choices."

While Alec's peers may have delayed marriage and raising families, or opted out of that path altogether, he sees alternative social networks as more of a holding pattern than a new direction. "I don't think that there's anything accepted yet as a new variation per se, accepted in terms of any sort of real critical mass," he observes. "I know, coming from the Burning Man perspective—and a lot of people have written about tribes, you know, there's that book, *Urban Tribes*—I know that we are seeing group families of friends. Strong bonds of friends who hang out and party together, differently than just like the old groups of buddies. There's something more familial about it."

Still, the detachment from traditional social roles does increase the latitude allowed to both genders. Because the alt tribes, like the pagan, shamanistic societies that inspire them, have always held the feminine in higher esteem, there is less of a stigma when men take on feminine characteristics, particularly in the context of creative or artistic play. The satyr is celebrated, and men are given more leeway to indulge in social theater, which includes dressing in flamboyant costumes that have no bearing on the wearer's sexual orientation. In fact, in the alt-tribe social scene, men who ignore macho codes of behavior are considered especially attractive by women.

"Men do not need to be masculine all the time," Alec says. "There are feminine attires, and makeup and costumes, there's more dancing, more art, things that have not been seen as traditionally masculine in Western society. Dancing is very masculine in other cultures, not so much in American culture. And now . . . there are a lot of younger men that are more comfortable with that."

Is this where all men are inevitably heading? For Alec, the question is moot because the ability of both sexes to transcend their genetic blueprint has already become the norm. Change is the only constant, he maintains, and as traditional social structures break down, human beings will naturally push boundaries and test their options. "At some point human beings hit a point where our brains have evolved enough cognitive power to begin to override our instincts," Alec says.

"I think that to some degree, all that we are doing now, changing gender roles is just a continual evolution of our cognitive ability to override our programming. Because my mind is smarter than that, and I know that I don't have to be that way. And so, as men and women, we are just reaching that evolutional point in our society where that's the next thing we are questioning about our human nature."

BEING DREAMED

The quest for an altered state of consciousness, whether induced by plants, prayer, drugs, or some other technique, has always been a tool in the search for male identity. In tribal societies of the American plains Indians and Mesoamerican cultures, the shaman, or healer, derives his power by fusing the feminine and the masculine into a singularity that bridges night and day, good and evil, past and future. For thousands of years, hallucinogenic plants and herbs have been ingested—in ceremonial rites of passage, as an aid in communicating with ancestors, or when praying for good luck in hunting or farming. They have also been used by men to illuminate their deepest selves—to see not just who they are, but also what they might become.

In the remote highlands of southeast Mexico, in the state of Oaxaca, American pilgrims, risking encounters with bandits, trek through rugged, cacti-covered terrain to find someone who will sell them some leaves from the plant *Salvia divinorum*, or "diviner's sage," a form of sage, or "magic mint," that is used by the Mazatec Indians in sacred ceremonies and a healing medicine. The Mazatec *curanderas*, or "women who cure," use the drug to summon the Pastora, the Shepherdess, or "lady of the leaf," who watches over the lives of people and every living creature in the natural world. The drug, which has become popular in the United States for its LSD-like properties, has been known to make people believe they were plants or animals—or sometimes characters in a video game.

Alberto Villoldo, a psychologist at San Francisco State University and an expert on mystical healing traditions, chronicled the process of his own shamanic initiation in his book *The Four Winds*. "Shamans say there are only two kinds of people," he told *Magical Blend* magazine. "People that dream and people who are being dreamt. The dreamers are those who can consciously guide their dreams."

Villoldo believes that mankind is on the brink of an evolutionary leap forward and that inside the cerebral cortex "a new brain is awakening in humanity at large today," a brain that is "not bound by ordinary definitions of time and space." The shaman provides the teachings and tools to deal with this new power. "Shamanism is not a religion," he says. "There is no Christ, no Buddha, nobody who says, 'Follow my footsteps.' Shamanism demands that you take your own steps with courage, compassion, and vision. It requires that you learn how to learn from nature. It teaches you to meet power directly, embrace it, and claim it." One way to do that is by swallowing ayahuasca, a.k.a. "The Rope of the Dead," a jungle-plant extract that triggers powerful life-altering visions that are said to induce cathartic states of terrifying self-awareness followed by an aura of inner peace.

"It takes you beyond death to face every fear that you ever had," Villoldo says. "It's not an easy experience." The lesson, however, goes to the core of the male dilemma. "One of the key teachings of the shamanic traditions is that you cannot free yourself from the grip of fear until you exorcise violence from yourself," he explains. "The fear that lives within us is basically the fear of death, but we don't die all at once. We die a little bit at a time. So, by exorcising fear you are exorcising death. You will die, but you won't be claimed by death if you've already been claimed by life. In shamanism, fear and violence are denials of life. They are two harsh sides of the same coin."

Mitch Schultz, an Austin-based filmmaker making a documentary on DMT, the active ingredient in ayahuasca, has noticed that it is predominantly men who take the drug, and that they all experience a similar state of rapture that brings them together with a luminous being, or "creator."

"They were definitely looking for their own conception of God—and even a new and better definition of mankind," Schultz reports. "They're looking for that contact, that feeling. But I don't think anything in their wildest dreams prepared [them] for what happens. It's not about getting high—it's a fifteen-minute journey to meet God. This is not a recreational drug. It takes away your humanity and in a sense you die—and that's a very painful thing to go through. But then you come back, there's a rebirth, and that's what makes it worth it. You go past the first few minutes of pain and fear into a place of pure joy. And afterwards the world looks different."

Schultz believes that men would never go to such extremes unless they were driven to reconcile conflicting feelings about their own life and their place in the world. "There's no question that men are in a state of search and redefinition—we have to be," he says.

"When you look around, it's obvious that not just this country but the whole world is in a state of dire need. There's going to be a huge rebalance of what's happening now and what will happen in the future. This idea of female-male, black and white, night and day, the spiritual world and the earthly world—it's about pushing back toward the middle, back toward the feminine side, but also recognizing that these opposites are all united, they are one and the same. We've tipped too far to one side, and now men need to shift back some, not to become more like women, but as part of the evolution of humanity."

Can a man journey to a place that alters his definition of masculinity without the help of psychotropic drugs?

Is there such a thing as the evolutionary equivalent of ayahuasca or Burning Man's flaming effigy in everyday life? According to Gerald Levin, the answer is yes. For the former chairman of Time Warner Inc. the moment of catharsis came during the aftermath of the disastrous 2000 merger with America Online, an ill-fated marriage of new and old media that he masterminded and that is still sending shock waves through the business world.

It was in 2002, two years after having been banished from the firm he had helped turn into the world's largest media company, that Levin had an epiphany that changed his life. "I had the arrogance of power," Levin told *New York* magazine. It wasn't until that power was wrenched away that Levin realized that his whole self-identity had been built on a false foundation.

Today, he is the presiding director of Moonview Sanctuary, a holistic healing institute that offers high-end customers a spectrum of New Age wellness therapies and spiritual centering sessions. In a sun-splashed Santa Monica "temple of transformation" decorated with Buddhas and lavish antiques, Levin and his wife, Laurie, offer their clients eye-movement desensitization and reprocessing (EMDR), neurofeedback "brain painting," "holotropic breathwork," yoga, acupuncture, and men's drumming circles that Levin attends himself. He claims to be revamped, recharged, and reborn.

"It's using a ritual, archetypal setting to get at the most funda-mental questions of life," Levin said to *New York*. "Instead of a male hierarchy, it becomes almost feminine in its openness. Normally, you're defended, calculating with an agenda. Here, it melts away. Each session is particular to the individual and to the group, de-pending on what's needed. Does somebody need a rite of passage? Does somebody need an understanding of love? Ultimately, we're trying to break down male culture."

The Levin lesson is clear. For men to rediscover a better, more balanced, more enlightened version of themselves, they don't have to join pagan parades in the desert or ingest brain-warping drugs. All they have to do is fail. And through this failure and destruction they just might gain the freedom to re-create themselves as the men they know they can be.

Acknowledgments

The Decline of Men is above all a chronicle of change and hope. The evidence of change and the reasons for hope were provided by a large number of women and men, named and unnamed, who had a hand in the making of this book. (An asterisk indicates where a person's actual identity has been withheld.)

First in line to help and first to be thanked are the members of the "Y Chrome Braintrust," an ad hoc council of patient, intrepid brethren whose collective experience and feedback laid the conceptual foundation and initiated the ongoing dialogue that this book was intended to provoke: Carter Adamson, Michael Andrews Jr., Derek Beres, Colin Bill, Rob Bragin, Tarquin Cardona, Michael Carmody, Jon Cropper, Gordon Ebanks, Nathan Folkman, Will Garcia, Craig Hagen, Darrin Hong, Matt Lambaise, Kevin Morra, Steve Pena, Ed Rivera, Robert Rosenthal, Mitch Schultz, Brian Siberell, Richard Stoney, Philip Swain, T.K., Mark Uttecht, Ted Werth, and John Wilson. Gentlemen, take a bow.

I would also like to extend special thanks to those who have so generously contributed their expertise, time, and support, including, but certainly not limited to: Michael Andrews Sr., Mahzarin Banaji, John Perry Barlow, David Blankenhorn, Geoffrey Canada, Carson Christus, Rachel Cooper, Carlos Fuentes, Trip Gabriel, Briana Garcia, Warrington Hudlin, Christopher Liechty, Joe Loya,

Ronald Mincy, Joni Mitchell, Richard D. Parsons, Pedro Nogera, Michael Platt, Demetrius Porche, Glenn Sacks, Tyler Thoreson, Alexis Tirado, Sheryl Hilliard Tucker, Jean Twenge, Jerry Vukas, and Kenneth Willardt.

Finally, a heartfelt tip of the hat to Andrea Montejo, for going far beyond an agent's call of duty; to Rene Alegria, for sharpening the message and tempering the blade; and to Lisa Quiroz, whose powers of divination and devotion were instrumental in transforming my ravings, ruminations, and rants into something tangible, resonant, and real.

Index

ABC (network), 34–36, 231–32
abortion, 34, 35, 120
Abu Ghraib scandal, 7, 109, 177
Academy Awards, 217, 218
Adidas, 207
Adonis Complex, The (Pope, Olivardia, and Phillips), 164–69
adrenaline, 7
adultery, 87
advertising, 38, 50–51, 60, 64, 100, 114–15, 131–32, 162–63, 168–69, 216–24
Afghanistan War, 177
African Americans, 11, 12, 19–20, 25, 54, 69, 102–3, 119, 136–43, 194, 257
agrarian societies, 3, 269–70
agriculture, 3, 20, 21, 52, 53, 269–70
Aguilera, Christina, 113
AIDS, 25, 159, 260
alcohol, 23, 28, 65–66, 156, 253–55
Alcoholics Anonymous (AA), 253–55
Aldrin, Buzz and Joan, 118
"Alec," 276–80
alleles, 171
Allen, Craig, 34

all-male clubs and schools, 14, 15, 17–18
Allmendinger, Blake, 93
"alt" tribes, 278–80
"Amanda," 89
Ambady, Nalini, 107–8
ambisexuality, 9, 213
Ambuhl, Megan, 109
American Express, 48
American Gangster, 138
American Gigolo, 201
American Journal of Men's Health, 25–26
American Journal of Psychiatry, 200–201
American Society of Plastic Surgeons, 167
America Online (AOL), 40, 82, 283
Amsden, David, 114
amygdala, 7
Anabolic Steroid Control Act (2004), 158
anabolic steroids, 157–58, 159, 160, 167
Andrews, Michael A., 177–83
Androgel, 162
"andropause," 162
anorexia, 109–10, 164
Anthony, Susan B., 119

Archer Daniels Midland Company (ADM), 54, 55
Are Men Necessary? (Dowd), 9–10
Armstrong, Neil, 116, 118
Arnold Worldwide, 132
Arons, Russell, 195
Art of Principled Networking, The (Hubbel), 55
Ashe, Geoffrey, 269
Asian Americans, 104, 106, 194
assisted reproductive technologies, 84
Associated Press, xii, 13, 31
Atlantic Monthly, 103
Atwood, Margaret, 205
Austin Adventure Boot Camp, 187
autism, 27, 35, 230
Average Guy, 197–99
Axe, 220, 221
ayahuasca, 281–82, 283

baby boomers, 73, 210
Backlash (Faludi), 124
BaGua Juice, 53
Bakker, Amanda, 144
Bakker, Jay, 143–45
Bakker, Jim, 143–45
Bakker, Tammy Faye, 143
Banaji, Mahzarin, 101–9
Barbie dolls, 29–30, 66, 190–97, 199–200, 244–45
Bar Cross Ranch, 94, 95, 96–98
Barenbrug, Max, 206
Barlow, John Perry, 94–99, 101, 111, 113, 115, 227
Barlow, Norman, 94
Barnett, Rosalind Chait, 15
Beck, Jef, 191
Becker, Rob, 201
"Beer Ape" ad, 220
Beggan, James, 237
Benoit, Chris, 157
Bessette-Kennedy, Carolyn, 97
Bhasin, Shalender, 9
Biden, Joe, 158
Big Ugly Review, 153

bio-merging, 8–9
birth control, xvi, 35, 120–21
birthrate, 27, 46, 265–66
Black Rock City, Nev., xi, 277–78
Blair.com, 212
Blankenhorn, David, 83–85
Bloch, Phillip, 196
blue-collar jobs, 12, 22, 65, 70
Boehmer, John A., 55–56
Bordo, Susan, 163
boredom, 88–89
Bowling Alone (Putnam), 255–56
"Boy Code," 14, 169–70
boys:
    academic performance of, 10–16
    birthrate of, 265–66
    brain development of, 5–6
    fathers as important to, 127–53
    masculinization of, 14, 76, 94–99, 169–70
    mothers as important to, 261–62
    motivation of, 11–12
    physical abuse of, 145–46, 150, 161
    in sports, 13, 16–17
Boy Scouts, 142, 255
Bradshaw, Gay, 184–86
Bragin, Rob, 38–39
brain development, 3, 4–9, 28, 41, 80, 86, 88, 185, 219–20, 281
Brain Sex (Moir and Jessel), 6
Bratz dolls, 29–30, 194, 195, 196
breast cancer, 24, 26–27, 33, 159
Brizendine, Louann, 86
Brokeback Mountain, xv, 213
Brown, Dan, 270–71
Brown, David Jay, 271–72
Budweiser, 64, 114–15, 218–19, 221
Bugaboo baby strollers, 206
bullfighting, 187
bullfrogs, 172
Burger King, 222–24
Burgundy, Ron, 35
Burning Man Festival, xi, 277–78, 283

Bush, George W., 57
business careers, xi–xii, xiv, 1–2,
    17–23, 32–33, 35, 41–55, 62,
    65–71, 74, 75, 77–78, 119–20,
    121, 206, 257, 258, 259–60
"Buying Power of Women, The"
    (McPhaden), 44

Cacophony Society, 277
California Academy of
    Tauromaquia, 187
Campbell, Joseph, 268
Canada, 81–82
Canada, Geoffrey, 136–43
"Candace," 66–67
Canseco, Jose, 158
capitalism, 52–53, 90, 119–20,
    198
Carell, Steve, 39
Cargo, 205–6
Carlin, Mike, 248–49
Case, Steve, 210
Casino Royale, 245–46
cassowaries, 171
Cavemen, 38
CBS (network), 35, 218–19, 231–32
"celebrations assistants," 71
celebrities, 36, 62, 111–19
Census Bureau, U.S., xi–xii, xiv–xv,
    20, 68, 77
Center for Adolescence, 130
Centers for Disease Control and
    Prevention (CDC), 129–30
cerebral cortex, 281
Chang, Jessica, 244
Charlie's Angels, 38
Children of Men (Cuarón), 275
Child Trends Databank, 12
Chisholm, Shirley, 56
Chodorow, Nancy J., 76
Cho Seung-Hui, 157
Christianity, 87, 143–45, 256, 271,
    273
Christus, Carson, 110
chromosomes, 1–3, 4, 5, 80

Cialis, 162
Cipriani Wall Street, 1
Citicorp, 47–48
Clemens, Roger, 159
Clinton, Bill, 56, 58–59, 202, 249
Clinton, Hillary, 56–59, 249
Coca-Cola Co., 55
cohabitation, 69, 70
Cole, Paula, 98
Coleman, David, 203, 213
college degrees, xii, xv, 11–13, 19,
    65, 67–68, 74, 79
comic books, 246–52
commitment, 69, 77, 123
compulsive shopping disorder,
    200–201
Constitution, U.S., 94, 119
construction industry, 20, 21
consumers, xiv, 42–48, 100, 119,
    200–209
Coolidge, Calvin, 134
Cooper, Gary, 96, 115
*Cooperation and Competition Among
    Primitive Peoples* (Mead), 180
Corningstone, Veronica, 35
corporations, 1–2, 54–55, 264–65
corpus callosum, 5
cortisol, 7
Cosmopolitan, 165–66, 204
Coughlin, Paul and Sandy, 87
Couric, Katie, 33
Cowboy, The (Allmendinger), 93
cowboys, 92–99, 115
"coyotes," 20
Craig's List, 234
"crave parties," 43
creationism, 79–80
Creative Class, 63, 212
crime, 17, 19–20, 28, 70, 93, 129,
    132, 145–53, 155–56, 175
Crow, Sheryl, 33
Cuarón, Alfonso, 275
Cure Autism Now Foundation,
    230
custody arrangements, 132–33

Daly, Mary, 121
Dangerous Book for Boys, The,
 134–35
Daniélou, Alain, 274
Darkon, 189
Dark Side of Man, The (Ghiglieri),
 171, 172–73
Darwin, Charles, 171, 208
Darwin, Rebecca, 202
dating, 61–64, 68–70, 237–40
Dauman, Philippe P., 54
Da Vinci Code, The (Brown),
 270–71
Dawkins, Richard, 208
Dawn Behind the Dawn (Ashe), 269
Dean, James, 96
DeBeers, 50–51
DeGeneres, Ellen, 217
Delilah, xvi–xvii
De Maria, Rita, 82
Democratic Party, 56–59, 96
Demography, 67
Descartes, René, 275–76
Details, 114, 191, 205
Diamond, Jared, 269–70
diamonds, 50–51
"Diamonds Are a Girl's Best
 Friend," 50
diet, 24, 88, 161–62, 222–24
Dionysus, 274
Discovery Channel, 187–89
disidentification, 101–7
display culture, 71–79
"diviner's sage," 281
divorce, 19, 48, 69, 70, 79–91,
 128–29, 131, 132–34, 135,
 260
DMT, 282
DNA, 86, 205
Dodd, Sonora, 134
domestic chores, 88–89
domestic violence, 87, 132–33, 260
dominance fights, 172
"Donna," 234
DontDateHimGirl.com, 238–39

dopamine, 88
dot-com boom, 22, 70, 210
Dougherty, Lauren, 197
Dowd, Maureen, xv, 9–10, 59
drop-outs, school, 12–13, 129, 132
drug abuse, 129, 132
"dual market" approach, 163
Dublon, Dina, 1
"dumb blondes," 39
Dunbar, Robin, 36–38
dysmorphia, 161, 164, 168–69
Dyson, James, 206

eating disorders, 109–10, 163–64,
 167
eBay, 54, 55
Edin, Kathryn, 23
education, xii, xv, 10–16, 65,
 66–68, 70, 101–2, 110, 128,
 258, 259
Edwards, John, 57
Egan, Vince, 175
Eggleston Hall, 175
Einstein, Albert, 117
Electronic Frontier Foundation, 94
Elephant Breakdown (Bradshaw),
 184
elephants, xvi, 183, 184
Ellis, Shaun, 188
emotions, 7–8, 86, 130, 169–70
Emperor penguins, 172
Engels, Friedrich, 119
England, Lynndie, 109
environmentalism, 88, 90
ephedra, 162
estrogen, 7, 88
evolution, 7–8, 28, 36–38, 40–41,
 79–80, 85–86, 208, 230–31,
 281–82
Extenze, 162
extreme fighting, 154–57, 170,
 186–87
eye-movement desensitization
 and reprocessing (EMDR)
 neurofeedback, 283–84

Faludi, Susan, 116–19, 124
families, xiv, xv, 22, 23, 35, 60, 69, 70, 74–91, 128–29, 258
Farhi, Paul, 34, 35
Farrakhan, Louis, 256
Farrell, Warren, 121–23
fashion, 135, 163, 164, 200–201, 204–11
Father's Day, 134
Federman, Daniel, 27
Female Brain, The (Brizendine), 86
Feminine Mistake, The, 62
"feminine" nations, 263–64
Femininities, Masculinities, Sexualities (Chodorow), 76
feminism, 7, 13, 14–15, 16, 57, 60, 90, 98–99, 101, 119–26, 130, 133–34, 135, 192, 222, 223, 259
"fence-plowing," 112
Ferraro, Geraldine, 56
Fetman, Corri, 82–83
fetuses, 4, 27, 80
Fidelity Investments, 132
Field and Stream, 174
Fifteenth Amendment, 119
Fight Club, 155, 235
fight clubs, 154–57, 170
Fincher, David, 155
FKF Applied Research, 219–20
flight attendants, 78–79
Flight from Woman, The (Stern), 274
Florida, Richard, 212
Food and Drug Administration (FDA), 24, 162
football, 16, 103, 218–21
Forever Barbie (Lord), 193
Fortune, 30, 54–55, 230, 231
foster fathers, 78, 151
Fourteenth Amendment, 119
Four Winds, The (Villoldo), 281–84
Freeman's Sporting Club, 202
Freston, Tom, 54
Freud, Sigmund, 76, 125

Frey, William, 61
frontal cortex, 5
Frye, Marilyn, 121

Gabriel, Trip, 29, 30, 203–5
Gaiser, Megan, 243–44
Gap, 60
Garden & Gun, 202–3
Gay and Lesbian Alliance Against Defamation, 219
gays, xiv, xv, 22, 47, 80–81, 141, 144, 162–63, 164, 167, 191, 211–16, 219, 234–35
Geico, 38
Gelernter, David, 227
Gender and History (Smalley), 174
"gender wars," 121–26, 263
Generation Me, 73–79
Generation Me (Twenge), 74–75
Generation X, 73, 207, 209, 210
Generation Y, 73, 207
Genesis, Book of, 273
Genetic Legacy of the Mongols, The, 176
genetics, 2–3, 4, 28, 80, 171, 205, 208
Genghis Khan, 176
Gentlemen Prefer Blondes, 50
Gere, Richard, 201
Ghiglieri, Michael P., 171, 172–73, 176
Gibson, Charles, 35
GI Joe dolls, 166, 182, 194
Gilbert, Robert, 221
Gimbutas, Marija, 271–72
girls:
    academic performance of, 10–16, 109–10
    brain development of, 5–6
    mother figures for, 137
Giuliani, Rudolph, 56
Glamour, 165–66
Glenn, John, 116
Gods of Love and Ecstasy (Daniélou), 274

Goldfinger, 246
Goldman Sachs, 1
Gore, Al, 57
gossip, 37–38
GQ, 135, 200, 201, 205
Grameen Bank, 52–53
Graves, Jenny, 2, 3
Gray, John, 201
Great Britain, 102, 111, 175
Great Mother, xv, 268–76, 277
Greenwald, Anthony, 105–6
Grizzly Man, 188
grooming, 36–38
*Grooming, Gossip and the Evolution
    of Language* (Dunbar), 36–38
"Grups," 209–10
Grylls, Bear, 187–88
Gulf War, 177

hallucinogens, 280–82, 283, 284
Handler, Ruth and Elliot, 196
Handmaid's Tale, The (Atwood),
    205
Harlem Children's Zone (HCZ),
    136–43
Harman, Sabrina, 109
Harvard University, 44, 97, 102,
    106–7, 108
Hefner, Hugh, 232
Henley-Jensen, Rita, 29
Heritage USA, 143, 144
Herzog, Werner, 188
heterophobia, 88
heterosexuality, 83–85, 88
Hilton, Paris, 39
hip-hop music, 138, 148–49
Hispanics, 10, 12, 26, 47, 54, 69,
    194, 257
His Side, 131
Hitchens, Christopher, 216–17
Hoffman, Dustin, 217
Hofstede, Geert, 264
Hofstede's Cultural Dimensions
    Index, 264
Hollywoodland, 251

Holzer, Harry, 12
"Homework" ad, 131–32
homophobia, xiv, 141
Homo sapiens, 37–38, 79–80
Hopko, Thomas, 274
hormones, 4, 5, 6, 7, 24, 80, 86–87,
    172
Horowitz, Ruth, 192
"How Schools Shortchange Girls,"
    13
Hubbel, Julia, 55
Huffington, Arianna, 35
Human Rights Campaign, 219
humor, 216–24
hunter-gatherer societies, 269
hunting, 8, 37, 173–74, 176, 180, 269
Hurt, Byron, 139
Hymowitz, Kay, 69
hypermasculinity, xiii–xiv, 16–17,
    63, 146, 148–51, 157–69, 173,
    186–87, 203, 230

I Am a Man, 139
"I Am Woman," 223
Icahn, Carl, 41
Ikea, 265
immigrants, 12, 20, 101–2, 109
Implicit Association Test (IAT),
    105–6, 108
India, 101–3, 183–84, 267
Industrial Revolution, 16, 98,
    119–20
industrial societies, 3, 16, 93–94,
    98, 119–20
Information Age, 21, 22, 63, 70
Internet, 22, 70, 72, 94–95,
    99–100, 112, 117, 156–57,
    207–8, 225–27, 231–45. *See
    also names of specific web sites*
Ipsos Insight Web, 99–100
Iraq War, 7, 29, 34–35, 58, 59, 66,
    109, 177
Israel, Steve, 10
Italy, 46, 266
iVillage, 45

Jackass, 111–12
James, William, 253
Jencks, Christopher, 69
Jenkins, John Major, 272–73
Jenner, Brody, 113–14
Jenner, Bruce, 114
Jessel, David, 6
Johnson, Ben, 158
Joseph, Tasha, 238
Journal of Clinical Endocrinology and Metabolism, 9

Kali, 273
Kandel, Eric R., 8
Ken dolls, 190–97, 199–200, 201, 244–45
Kennedy, John F., Jr., 96–98
Kerry, John, 57
"Kid's Toy" ad, 132
Kindlon, Dan, 128
King, Larry, 267
Kitsch, Taylor, 204
Klein, Calvin, 163, 164, 201, 204, 211
Kleinfield, Judith, 14
Knoxville, Johnny, 111
Korean Institute for Health and Social Affairs, 266
Kraft Foods, 54, 55
Kruger, Daniel, 17
Kuhn, Peter, 19

Labyrinth of Solitude, The (Paz), 262
Ladette to Lady, 175
"lads," 111
Landes, Ruth, 180
Larian, Isaac, 194
lastnightsparty.com, 214–15
Last One Standing, 188–89
Last Supper, The (Leonardo), 271
Lee Senior High School, 157
left brain hemisphere, 5–6
Legato, Marianne, 7–9
LEGO, 6, 264–65

Lennox, Annie, 51
Leno, Jay, 249
Leonardo da Vinci, 271
leopards, 42
Letterman, David, 72
Levin, Jerry, 210, 283–84
Levin, Laurie, 283–84
Levitra, 162
Levitz, Paul, 248–49
Liberated Man, The (Farrell), 122
Liechty, Christopher, 263–65
Light, Audrey, 67
Lin, Maya, 33
lions, 40–41, 42, 126
Lithwick, Dahlia, 35
live-action role-play (LARP) games, 189
Live Science, 169
Loftus, David, 126, 237, 239
Long, A. Alexander, 179
Lord, M. G., 193, 199–200
Loya, Joe, 145–53
Lozano, Fernando, 19
Lucas, Geralyn, 29–30
Luhrmann, Tanya, 102

McCain, John, 56, 59
McCarthy, Cormac, 127
McEwan, Ian, 31
McGovern, George, 56
McGrath, Judy, 54
McGwire, Mark, 158–59
"macho male strategy," 171, 172–73
McKinley, Janet, 52–53
McPhaden, Wanda, 44
Maguera, Bam, 111
Male Body, The (Bordo), 163
Man Among Wolves, A, 188
"man laws" ad, 218
Mannion, Lance, 16
Mansfield, Nick, 113
"Manthem" ad, 223–24
"Man Thong" ad, 220–21
manufacturing sector, 12, 20, 21
Man vs. Wild, 187–88

Man Who Outgrew His Prison Cell,
　The (Loya), 147, 150, 152
Man Who Saved Britain, The
　(Winder), 245–46
March of the Penguins, 172
marriage, xiv, 19, 22, 46, 48, 61–70,
　79–91, 120, 128–29, 131,
　132–34, 135, 232, 260
Marriage and Caste in America
　(Hymowitz), 69
Marriage in Men's Lives (Nock),
　84–85
Married but Not Engaged (Coughlin
　and Coughlin), 87
Marx, Karl, 119
masochism, xiv, 111–14
Masochism: The Art of Power
　(Mansfield), 113
MassMutual, 47, 48
matriarchy, xvi, 26, 139, 184
Mattel, 193, 194, 195, 196
Mavericks of the Mind (Brown and
　Novick), 271–72
Maya Cosmogenesis (Jenkins), 272–73
Maya Long Count calendar, 272
Mazatec Indians, 281
Mead, Margaret, 180
"memes," 208
memory, 7–8, 86
men:
　aggressiveness of, xiii–xiv, 3, 6,
　　16–17, 90–91, 111–14, 154–89,
　　219–20, 268
　biological development of, xvi, 2,
　　4–10, 40–41, 80–81, 85–86,
　　88, 89–90, 171–73, 185
　black, 12, 19–20, 25, 102–3, 119,
　　136–37, 143, 257
　brain development of, 3, 4–9, 28,
　　41, 80, 86, 88, 185, 219–20
　business careers of, xi–xii, 17–23,
　　69–71, 74, 75, 206, 257, 258,
　　259–60
　commitment and, 69, 77, 123
　as consumers, 200–209

"cowboy" mythology of, 92–99, 115
dating by, 61–64, 68–70, 237–40
disenfranchisement of, 101–15,
　259–62
divorced, 70, 79–91, 128–29, 131,
　132–34, 135, 260
as dominant sex, 27–28, 40–41,
　51–52, 60, 65–66, 101–15,
　121–22, 237, 261–62, 265–66
education of, xii, xv, 10–16, 65,
　66–68, 70, 101–2, 110, 128,
　258, 259
emotions of, 7–8, 86, 130,
　169–70
fashion for, 135, 163, 164, 201,
　204–11
as fathers, 16, 19, 74, 75, 78–79,
　83–85, 127–53, 172
"feminization" of, 9–10, 16, 17,
　75–76, 107–8, 174, 204–5,
　206, 211–16, 282–83
future trends for, 253–84
genetics of, 2–3, 4, 28, 80, 171,
　205, 208
health care for, xv, 23–28
as hunters, 8, 37, 269
"ideal," 74–76
life expectancy of, xv, 25, 28
married, 62–70, 76–77, 79–91,
　128–29, 131, 132, 134, 260
masculine identity of, xiii–xiv,
　3–4, 14, 15–18, 63, 64, 75–76,
　79, 88, 90–91, 94–99, 101–15,
　117–19, 124–26, 136–43, 146,
　148–51, 157–73, 186–87,
　193–94, 198–99, 203, 230,
　258, 265–66, 280–84
media image of, xii–xiii, 15, 60,
　63, 71–73, 76, 93, 111–14,
　117–18, 131–32, 138, 148–49,
　162–69, 197–99, 211, 216–24,
　258
muscularity of, 157–69
physical strength of, 3, 40–41,
　125–26, 154–89

risks taken by, 28, 40–41

role models for, xiii, 16, 19, 74, 75, 78–79, 83–85, 127–53, 172

salary levels of, xi–xii, 18–19, 22–23, 69–71, 74, 257, 258, 259–60

self-esteem of, xvi, 18, 19, 64, 65–67, 71–79, 112, 113, 168–69, 258

sexist attitudes against, 88–91

sexual desire of, 80–82, 120–21

single, xv, 22, 62–64, 67

social role of, xiii–xiv, 6, 107–8, 257–58

stereotypes of, 6–7, 14, 60, 100–104, 135, 168

testosterone levels of, 6, 9, 17, 27, 86, 156, 157–58, 159, 162, 172, 205

See also boys

Men Are from Mars, Women Are from Venus (Gray), 201

menopause, 27, 86–87

Men's Health, 204

Men's Health Network, 24, 28

menstruation, 124–25, 160

Men.style.com, 205

Merrill Lynch, 48

metrosexuals, 121, 152, 191, 201, 202, 203, 204, 211, 214–15, 222

"Mighty Wingman" ad, 221

Military Review, 178

Million Man March, 142, 256

Mincy, Ronald, 18–19, 257, 258, 259–62

minorities, 102, 103, 104–6. *See also* African Americans; Hispanics

misogyny, xiv, 121, 257

Moir, Anne, 6, 87–91

Moir, Bill, 87–91

Mondale, Walter F., 56

Money, 32

monkeys, 108, 230–31

Monroe, Marilyn, 39, 50

Montana State Prison, 93

Mooney, Selena, 235

Moonview Sanctuary, 283–84

Moore, Ann, 30

Morra, Kevin, 221–22

Mortensen, Tom, xii

Moyers, Bill, 268

MTV (network), 54, 72, 111–12, 114, 214

Mulcahy, Anne, 55

music, 138, 148–49, 207, 210

MySpace.com, xiv, 117, 156, 207, 234, 237

Myth of Male Power, The (Farrell), 122

"Myth of 'The Boy Crisis, The'" (Rivers and Barnett), 15

"Myth That Schools Shortchange Girls, The" (Kleinfield), 14

Nancy Drew, 243–45

NASCAR, 115, 186

National Institute on Drug Abuse (NIDA), 160, 161

National Marriage Project, 67–68

National Organization for Women (NOW), 122

Native Americans, 54, 180, 281

natural selection, 86, 171–73

NBC (network), xiv, 35, 231–32

Nerve.com, 234–35

neurons, 8, 81

New Age, 122, 280–84

Newsweek, 13, 27

Newton North High School, 109–10

New York, 209, 283, 284

New York, N.Y., xii, 65, 136–37

New Yorker, 53, 64, 69

New York Times, 48, 49, 61, 69, 99–100, 195, 203, 212–13, 256

"Nicole," 65–66

Nissan Motors, 227

Nock, Steven, 84–85

Nooyi, Indra, 1, 54–55
Norton, Edward, 155
Nosek, Brian, 105–6
Novick, Rebecca McClen, 271–72
nuclear families, 70, 128–29

Obama, Barack, 57–58, 201
Office, The, 39
"office spouses," 82
Ojibwa Indians, 180
Olivardia, Roberto, 164–69
Onassis, Jacqueline Kennedy, 96–97
One Punk Under God (Bakker), 144
orgasms, 81–82, 121
Ortiz, Tito, 186
Outdoor Life, 174
overachievers, 109–11
oxytocin, 7, 86

Page, David, 2–3
Paglia, Camille, 124–26, 273
Pakkenberg, Berte, 5
Palahniuk, Chuck, 155, 170, 235
Parsi, 102
Parsons, Richard D., 39–42
Parsons, Talcott, 257–58
patriarchy, 70, 123–24
Paul, Pamela, 232–33
Payne, Leanne, 275
Paz, Octavio, 262
"Pearls of Wisdom," 48
Pease, Barbara and Allan, 16–17
Pelosi, Nancy, 55–56
People, 30, 36
PepsiCo, 1, 54–55
Personal Relationships, 17
"Person of the Year" (2007), 71–72
Philistines, xvi–xvii
Phillips, Katherine A., 164–69
Phillips-Van Heusen, 204
Pine Bush High School, 10
"Ping Pong" ad, 132
Pitt, Brad, 155, 202

plastic surgery, 167
Platt, Michael, 230–31
Playboy, 152, 230, 231, 236
Playgirl, 165
podcasts, 31–32, 72
politics, 37, 55–59, 77, 119–20, 257
Pollack, William, 14, 169–70
Pontius, Chris, 112
Pope, Harrison G., 164–69
Porche, Demetrius J., 24, 25–26
Pornified (Paul), 232–33
pornography, 231–37, 239
postfeminism, 123–24
post-traumatic stress disorder (PTSD), 140, 177, 184
Pound, Richard, 158
poverty, 129, 259–60
Povich, Lynn, 29
Power of Myth, The (Campbell), 268
Power of the Purse, The (Warner), 46
Prada, Miuccia, 205
Pratt, Spencer, 114
"pretty male strategy," 171, 172–73
primates, 36–38
Princes of Malibu, 114
prisons, 19–20, 70, 93, 145–53
progesterone, 86
prolactin, 172
promarriage movement, 82–91
Promise Academy, 136
Promise Keepers, 256
prostate cancer, 26–27
Psychology Today, 164–65, 237
purchasing power, 42–50
Putnam, Robert, 255–56, 263
Pygmalion (Shaw), 175

Queer Eye for the Straight Guy, 72, 215

Radio and Television News Directors Association, 33–34
Raising Cain (Kindlon and Thompson), 128

rape, 125–26, 161
rap music, 138
Ravitch, Diane, 13
"Ray," 66–67
Reaching Up for Manhood (Canada), 143
reading rates, 30–33, 38–39
Reagan, Ronald, 201
Real Boys (Pollack), 14, 169–70
real estate, 43–44
reality shows, 72–73
Realty Times, 44
Real World, 72, 214
Redstone, Sumner M., 54
Reeves, George, 250–51
Reinemund, Steve, 1, 55
"relationship coaches," 82
religion, 87, 143–45, 180, 256, 268–76, 280–84
reporters, news, 29, 33–36
Republican Party, 58
Reston Town Center, 204
retirement, 48
retrosexuals, 201, 202, 214–15
Revolution Church, 143
rhesus macque monkeys, 230–31
Richeson, Jennifer A., 107–8
Richie, Nicole, 113–14
right brain hemisphere, 5–6
Right Guard, 217, 220
Right Stuff, The (Wolfe), 115–16
Ritts, Herb, 201
Rivers, Caryl, 15
Road, The (McCarthy), 127
"Robert," 86
Rodriguez, Richard, 147
Rolling Rock, 220–21
Rolling Stone, 215
Roman Empire, 181–82
"Rope of the Dead," 281–82, 283
Rosenfeld, Irene, 55
"Rosie the Riveter," 120
Rozanski, Chuck, 248
Rubin, Scott, 244
Ryan, Joan, 129–30

Sacks, Glenn, 130–34
same-sex marriages, 83
Samson, xvi–xvii, 268
Santa Claus, 276–77
"Sarah," 48–50
SAT scores, 104
Scarred, 112
Schleichkorn, Adam, 112
Schultz, Mitch, 282–84
sea horses, 172
Second Life, 225–29, 245
Secret Service, U.S., 96
Seed, 185
self-aggrandizement, 71–79
Selfish Gene, The (Dawkins), 208
"sequential" social status, 258
serotonin, 88
services industry, xii, 20
Seven Stages of Marriage, The (de Maria), 82
Sex, Art, and American Culture (Paglia), 124–25
Sex and the City, 62
sexism, 39, 88–91, 121–23, 131–32, 139, 273
sexual abuse, 133, 161
sexual attraction, 80–81, 120–21, 125–26
"sexual imperialism," 90–91
Sexual Personae (Paglia), 273
Sexual Revolution, xvi, 120–21, 258
shamans, 180, 280–84
Shane Homes, 44
Shaw, George Bernard, 175
Shiva, 274
shopping malls, 204
Shuster, Joe, 247
Siberian dwarf hamsters, 172
Siegel, Jerry, 247
Sildenafil, 162
Silkworth, William, 253
Simpson, Jessica, 39
Simpson, Mark, 201
Sims, xiv, 226, 240–43

single-parent families, xiv, 23, 70, 83, 84, 85, 128–29
Slate, 36
slavery, 138, 139
Small, Meredith F., 172
Smalley, Andrea L., 174
Smart, Henry Jackson, 134
Smith, Anna Nicole, 36
Smith, Bob, 253–54
Smith, Helen, 100
Smith, Michael P., 33
smoking, 23, 28, 83
Snickers, 219
soap operas, 38
Social Security, 22
software engineering, 21
Sommers, C. H., 13, 123–24
South Korea, 265–66
space program, 115–19
Spacey, Kevin, 247
sperm counts, 88
SPIKE TV, 138
sports, 13, 16–17, 30, 32, 103, 157–59, 160, 173, 186, 189, 218–21
Sports Illustrated, 30, 32
SRY hormone, 80
Stablehorn, Ron, 220–21
Standardized Narcissistic Personality Inventory, 73–74
Stand in the Gap, 256
Stanton, Elizabeth Cady, 119
Star Trek, 209
start-up businesses, 52–54
Steele, Claude, 102–3
"stereotype threat," 103–4
Stern, Karl, 274
Sternbergh, Adam, 209–10
steroids, 157–62, 166, 167
"Steve," 236
Stevenson, Robert Louis, 170
Steve-O, 112
Stiffed (Faludi), 116–17
Storm, Bob, 151

Strange Case of Dr. Jekyll and Mr. Hyde, The (Stevenson), 170
stress, 7–8, 74, 100
"structural functionalism," 257–58
Suhl, Sean, 235
suicide, 28, 129–30
SuicideGirls.com, 235–36
Sullivan County, N.Y., 10–11, 15
Super Bowl, 218–21
Superman, 246–51
Superman Returns, 247
Supreme Court, U.S., 36
Swain, Philip, 154
Sweetser, Susan W., 48
"Sylvia," 86

Tan, Robert, 27–28
taxes, 48
technology, xv–xvi, 21, 22, 46, 63, 70, 94, 100, 173, 179
television, 29–30, 33–36, 38–39, 72–73, 100, 218–21
testicular cancer, 159
tetrahydrogestrinone (THG), 158
Third Way Culture Project, 232
"Thomas," 62–64
Thompson, Michael, 128
Thoreson, Tyler, 205, 210–11
Thredless.com, 207–8
Timberlake, Justin, 17, 214
Time, 30–32, 71–72
Times (London), 37
Time Warner, 39–40, 41, 210
Tirado, Alexis, 214–15, 237, 239–40
Title IX programs, 13
TiVo, 219
Treadwell, Timothy, 188
Trebay, Guy, 205
Treby, Bruce, 112
tribal societies, 278–84
"Trouble with Boys, The" (Tyre), 13
Tucker, Sheryl Hilliard, 29, 30–32, 46–47
Twelve Step programs, 254–55

Twenge, Jean, 73–79
Two-A-Days, 216
Tylka, Tracy, 169
Tyndall, Andrew, 34, 35
Tyre, Peg, 13

übermales, xvi, 201–2
Ultimate Fighting Championship
  (UFC), 186–87
unemployment rate, 22–23, 38,
  70–71
Uttecht, Mark, 156

vacations, 45
vacuum cleaners, 206
Van Patten, Denise, 193
Vargas, Elizabeth, 34–36
Vaughn, Brian K., 251–52
vegetarianism, 88, 90
Venezuela, 165
Verizon, 131–32
Versace, Donatella, 58
Viacom, 54
Viagra, 162
Vietnam War, 177, 178
Vietnam Women's Union, 52
Villoldo, Alberto, 281–82
Virginian, The, 115
Virginia Tech shootings (2007), 157
Viva La Bam, 111
Volvo, 132

Walford, Geoffrey, 27
Wall Street Journal, 32–33
walruses, xvi
Walton, Bernard, 188
War Against Boys, The (Sommers), 13
Warhol, Andy, 72, 211
Warner, Fara, 46
Washington Post, 12, 15, 34
Watching Sex (Loftus), 126, 237
Waters, Alice, 32–33
Weber, Bruce, 201
Welch, Grace, 53
Wentz, Pete, 215

West Point Military Academy, 178
"What Women Want—Media,
  Myth, and Reality," 29–31
Whitman, Meg, 55
"Who's in Charge?" (Richeson and
  Ambady), 107–8
Who Stole Feminism? (Sommers),
  123–24
Why Men Don't Iron (Moir and
  Moir), 88–91
*Why Men Don't Listen and Women
  Can't Read Maps* (Pease and
  Pease), 16–17
*Why Men Never Remember and
  Women Never Forget* (Legato),
  7–9
"Why Women Aren't Funny"
  (Hitchens), 216–17
Wildboyz, 111–12
Willardt, Kenneth, 266–68
Williamson, Debra Aho, 100
Wilson, Bill, 253–54
Wilson, John, 202–3
Winder, Simon, 245–46
Wired, 72, 94
Woertz, Pat, 55
Wolfe, Tom, 115–16
wolves, 188
women:
  Asian, 69
  biological development of, 4–9,
    41, 80–81, 85–86
  black, 54, 69
  brain development of, 4–9, 41
  business careers of, xi–xii, xiv,
    1–2, 19, 23, 32–33, 35, 41–55,
    62, 65–67, 68, 69–70, 74,
    77–78, 119–20, 121, 257, 258,
    259–60
  communications skills of, 5, 15,
    31, 38
  competitiveness of, 109–10
  as consumers, xiv, 42–48, 100,
    119
  dating by, 62–64, 68–70

women (*continued*)
discrimination against, 13–14,
   108–9, 121–22
divorced, 61–62, 79–91, 132–34
education of, xii, 10–16, 65,
   66–68, 74, 79, 102, 109–10,
   258
feminine identity of, 58, 76,
   77–79, 117–18, 124–25, 141,
   278–80
future trends for, 253–84
as heads of households, xiv, 23,
   137
health care for, xv, 23–24
Hispanic, 54, 69
hormones of, 7, 24, 86–87, 172
as housewives, 74, 77–78, 88–91,
   121
as hunters, 173–74, 176, 180
life expectancy of, xv, 25
married, 61–70, 74–91, 120
"masculinization" of, 38–39,
   63–64, 74, 160, 175
media image of, xiv, 29–31, 60,
   71–73, 77–78, 117–18, 258
in military, 7, 109, 174–83
as mothers, 38, 41, 48, 69, 74,
   77–78, 86, 89, 120, 124, 125,
   129, 137, 172, 176, 261–62
in politics, 55–59, 119–20, 257
pregnancies of, 35–36, 66, 84,
   120, 132, 172
salary levels of, xi–xii, 23, 65,
   69–70, 74, 257, 258, 259–60
self-esteem of, 71–74, 78
sexual desire of, 80–81, 120–21,
   125–26
single, xiv, 61–70, 77, 84
social role of, 6, 107–8, 257–58
stereotypes of, 6–7, 168
   as widows, 48, 61
   See also girls
Women and Company, 47–48
"Women in Combat?" (Andrews),
   178
"Women in Media 2006: Finding
   the Leader in You," 33
women's movement, 14–15, 66–67,
   108–9, 119–26, 133–34, 141,
   168–69, 173, 222, 232, 259
"Women Travelers: A New Growth
   Market," 45
Women Who Make a Difference
   Gala, 1–2
Woodruff, Bob, 34–35
World News Tonight, 34–36
World War II, 120, 174, 255
"Worst Mistake in the History
   of the Human Race, The"
   (Diamond), 269–70
wrestling, 173, 186
Wright, Will, 241
Wyoming, 94–99

X chromosome, 2–3, 4
Xerox, 54, 55

Y chromosome, 2–3, 4, 5, 80
Yossi (elephant), 183
Young, Andrew, 139
Young, Camille, 53
Young, Cathy, 87
"young cosmopolitans," 63
yourstamps.com, 72
Youth Conservation Corps, 96
YouTube.com, 99, 112, 139, 156
Y: The Last Man (Vaughn), 251–52
Yunus, Muhammad, 52

Zoroastrians, 102